An Introduction to Human Resource Management
An Integrated Approach

Michael L. Nieto

palgrave
macmillan

First published 2006 by
PALGRAVE MACMILLAN
Houndmills, Basingstoke, Hampshire RG21 6XS and
175 Fifth Avenue, New York, N.Y. 10010
Companies and representatives throughout the world

PALGRAVE MACMILLAN is the global academic imprint of the Palgrave Macmillan division of St. Martin's Press, LLC and of Palgrave Macmillan Ltd. Macmillan® is a registered trademark in the United States, United Kingdom and other countries. Palgrave is a registered trademark in the European Union and other countries.

ISBN 13: 978–0–333–98665–3
ISBN 10: 0–333–98665–2

This book is printed on paper suitable for recycling and made from fully managed and sustained forest sources.

A catalogue record for this book is available from the British Library.

A catalog record for this book is available from the Library of Congress.

10 9 8 7 6 5 4 3 2 1
15 14 13 12 11 10 09 08 07 06

Printed and bound in China

This book is dedicated to
Jim Dent
(12 March 1926 to 6 September 2001)
who put others before himself

Contents

List of Figures

Introduction

Welcome to the changing world of human resources in organizations. The objective of this book is to provide a user-friendly, yet academically rigorous HR course for HR or management students studying HR units, whether as part of an HR specialist course, or as one element of other business or management qualifications. One of the underlying philosophies of this book is that HR is adaptive and responsive to the organizational environment. This approach encourages a situation-specific outlook to the design and delivery of HR services, so you will find learning activities based on contemporary primary and secondary research with organizations. HR is not just for large organizations, so the materials included in the chapters reflect the differing needs of private, public and not-for-profit organizations. I have also included studies and materials that reflect the diversity and global nature of the modern workplace.

Welcome Notes
for Students

If you're a student and have got this far to see if this book is worth reading, please have a look at the next few notes.

HR Student?

If you're an HR student, in this book you'll learn about the integrated approach to HR, which may change the way you see your present and future career, as well as help you to succeed in your HR programme. It will enable you to develop the knowledge and skills to understand the strategic managerial place of HR in organizations.

Management Student?

If you're a management student on a full- or part-time degree programme, this book can provide you with the kind of knowledge and skills to succeed in your course and help you to be a more successful manager. You will learn how to integrate HR knowledge and skills into your current and future workplace. If you are already in a job, you may be looking for the next step in management. Read on to learn how to be a more effective manager.

There are more SMEs (small to medium-size enterprises) than large corporations around the globe. Many SMEs or family businesses do not have or cannot afford to have an HR specialist, so managers and future managers need to be able to plan the development of their staff and understand strategic HR issues so that they can select, develop and motivate their teams.

International Student? Thinking Local and Global

In a global economy, effective HR is both locally sensitive and globally aware. In this book you will find discussion and references to HR and management from around the globe. There is also a chapter on international HR and how to plan and manage expatriate deployments. This book has activities that help you to develop the knowledge and skills to manage people in a global context.

The Voluntary Sector?

Perhaps you are studying or interested in the voluntary sector? I have helped to design and taught on a masters programme specifically for the voluntary sector (Voluntary Action Management), so I recognize that there are differences in the needs and motivations of volunteers compared to paid employees. Conversely, if commercial managers are encouraged to develop the most effective attitudes, knowledge and skills to increase profits, then it is arguably just as, if not more, applicable for people to work effectively in the voluntary sector. Be the best you can be to help others.

Not Sure What you Would Like to Do?

That's OK, although a chat with your university's careers advice team could help you to clarify the options. In this book you will find activities about a variety of organizations, including large international corporations, SMEs, public sector organizations and the voluntary and charity sector. You will read about real people in real organizations and how they have or have not managed HR effectively.

You will also learn about yourself and others by using the personal development questionnaires and activities, which can help you to get a clearer picture about who you are and what interests you most.

Online Support

The HRM in Action studies, exercises and questionnaires are also available on the publisher's (Palgrave Macmillan) website (www.palgrave.com/business/nieto – subject to the publisher's acceptance of appropriate registrations). I've also included tips on how to improve your assignments, presentations and prepare for examinations. There are references at the end of each chapter so that you can follow-up sources and do background reading.

How Do I Know the Contents Will be Interesting?

The teaching materials have been tried and reviewed by postgraduate and undergraduate students from around the world. The fact is, I don't like delivering dull lectures and seminars anymore than you want to sit through them, so I've put a lot of thought and effort into designing learning tools linked to the study programme which are interesting, even fun to do. Also, anonymous academic reviewers, colleagues from several universities and experience publishers have provided thoughtful recommendations and comments, which have improved the book's content and design.

Note from the Author to Students

You may be working your way through university for the first time or studying for a postgraduate qualification as a mature student. Learning is a lifelong journey. This book can help you to take some important steps forward in your career path.

Throughout my working life I have enjoyed being involved in new and interesting work projects. This has included both paid work in management, consultancy and lecturing as well as voluntary work. My dad once told me that 'knowledge takes up no space'. In other words, it's always worthwhile learning new transferable skills. I have never stopped been excited by learning something new.

If you would like me to come and talk to your programme, please ask your programme leader to contact me. I'll do my best to come to your university, work schedules and my student responsibilities permitting.

I wish you every success.

Michael L. Nieto

Welcome Notes
for Lecturers

If you are reading this note, then you may be considering using this book as a course text.

Designed for the Contemporary HR Environment

From the beginning this book was designed to be different. It is based on contemporary research materials, consultancy work and workplace studies. I hope you enjoy using it and find the materials helpful in delivering your course. *An Introduction to Human Resource Management: An Integrated Approach* is designed to provide you with an easy-to-use, student-friendly, yet academically rigorous book.

When Palgrave Macmillan approached me to consider writing an HR textbook, I was flattered, but not sure what more could be added that has not already been offered by other writers. Universities already have many 'encyclopedia-style' (covering every aspect) HR texts in their learning resources centres. There are also numerous specialist practitioner guides published by professional bodies such as the CIPD (Chartered Institute for Personnel Development) that summarize most aspects of operational HR.

However, this text has been specifically designed for 12–14 week courses focusing on contemporary HR, to be used by HR or management students on undergraduate and postgraduate programmes. Hence the focus is on strategic and HR managerial issues, recognizing that HR is becoming, arguably, less about traditional personnel and more about a value-adding service to organizations. Additionally, many management students can benefit from learning key HR transferable attitudes, knowledge and skills, irrespective of their core discipline or whether they plan to work in public, private or voluntary organizations.

Peer Review

Anonymous academic reviewers, colleagues from several universities and experienced publishers have provided thoughtful recommendations and comments, which have improved the book's content and design.

Online Support and PowerPoint Slides

All the exercises and questionnaires in the chapters are also available at **www.palgrave.com/business/nieto** to help lecturers in the preparation of their course materials and student learning. Additional materials, including brief guidelines on the organizational studies and suggested lecturers' PowerPoint slides, are available for each chapter.

An International Outlook

An Introduction to Human Resource Management: An Integrated Approach has been designed to provide contemporary view of HR within an international environment. Modern theories are supported with real examples from organizations on what works, as well why some HR plans can fail. The research-based studies and activities have also been piloted and developed through UK and international courses, so the book's content is relevant to business students in the UK, Europe, the USA and Southeast Asia.

Note from the Author to Course Leaders and Lecturers

I hope you enjoy using this book and if you would like me to come and talk to your students, please contact me via the publisher. I'll do my best to come to your university, work schedules and my student responsibilities permitting.

I wish you every success.

Michael L. Nieto

What This Book Offers Teaching Staff and Students

- **A flexible learning programme:** *An Introduction to Human Resource Management: An Integrated Approach* can be used to provide a week-by-week scheme of work for modular HR courses. Alternatively, individual chapters can be used as stand-alone units in business modules or units which contain an HR section or selectively used to supplement existing HR modules and units.
- **Subsections in each chapter:** Subsections are provided so that teaching staff can focus on particular aspects, if they so wish. Students can quickly find study subjects and use the sections to build projects and presentations, or prepare answers for examinations.
- **Reviewed by anonymous referees:** The book has been reviewed and revised in accordance with reviews by academic colleagues from several universities.
- **Activities have been piloted and refined:** The activities in this book have been developed and refined with students on undergraduate, postgraduate programmes, both in the UK and abroad.
- **Supporting materials in text:** *An Introduction to Human Resource Management: An Integrated Approach* provides teaching staff with a complete unit, containing activities for seminars, private study and presentations. Each chapter contains additional seminar materials such as group activities, questionnaires or case studies to support student learning.
- **HRM in Action:** These are short organizational studies and research-based materials to be used in seminars.
- **Practising HRM:** These provide students with the opportunity to practise the new attitudes, knowledge and skills they have learnt.
- **Group Activity:** These encourage interactive student work in either self-learning sets or facilitated seminar groups.
- **Exercise:** These provide independent learning and reflective materials.
- **Online support:** The learning resources contained in the chapters (Exercises, Group Activities, Practising HRM and HRM in Action) are available at **www.palgrave.com/business/nieto**. Online PowerPoint slides are avail-

able to teaching staff (subject to the publisher's acceptance of appropriate registrations).

- **Subject tracking system:** This enables tutors and students to follow inter-linked subjects throughout the chapters.
- **Chapter Summary notes:** A summary is provided at the end of each chapter to help students in revision planning.
- **Personal notes on chapters:** Space is provided at the end of each chapter so that students can make their own notes (for revision purposes and memory joggers).

About the Author

Michael L. Nieto is programme leader to the MBA at Bournemouth University. His lecturing experience includes international masters, HR and CIPD-accredited programmes at several leading university business schools, including two centres of CIPD excellence as well as AMBA-accredited MBA programmes. He has taught at Kingston University, University of Roehampton, South Bank University, Surrey University and University of Westminster. Additionally, Michael has taught international business for Marymount University USA, the ACI Paris and management strategy at Valencia University, Spain.

Michael has also been part of academic groups within several universities developing postgraduate and undergraduate programmes including MBA, HR undergraduate programmes, business ethics, CSR, Masters in Voluntary Action Management and a pre-masters programme for international students.

His research interests focus on strategic HR and business ethics. He is a member of Bournemouth University's centre for corporate social responsibility. He was also a founding member of the Surrey University's centre for applied business ethics and has published academic journal papers on HR and related research areas. Prior to entering higher education, he worked in management and consultancy. His consultancy experience includes working with international companies, SMEs, distributor networks and not-for-profit organizations.

Preface

● THE INTEGRATED APPROACH

This textbook has been designed for students who want to understand the place of human resources in contemporary management settings. You may be working or planning to work in a for-profit or not-for-profit organization. In fact, modern managers are more likely than at anytime before to move jobs and change career directions. The days of one job for life have long gone. This means that your ability to integrate into new situations and work with a variety of organizational environments will give you more choices about where you work and what you do. This book will equip you to make more informed decisions about issues such as whether to retain internally based HR functions or, conversely, the implications of out-sourcing some or all of the operational elements of HR. Either way, it places more responsibility on managers to develop HR knowledge and skills and plan HR initiatives, whether delivered internally or by external professionals.

The case for the value-adding benefits of HR is persuasive, if it is seen as an integral part of whatever the organization is planning to achieve. There is significant research evidence, ranging from motivation to human relations, indicating that how people are managed influences organizational performance. However, during the course of researching this book, I still found ample practitioner evidence, from a wide range of sectors, indicating that their experiences varied regarding the level of acceptance or value placed on HR within their organizations. Even if there is a persuasive case supporting the value of HR, it still has to be effectively presented and each organization will need to be convinced of what an investment in HR can do in its specific situation. Hence, if it is a for-profit organization, then the HR people should set themselves the task of serving to improve the delivery of agreed performance targets with their operational colleagues. In the public and not-for-profit sectors, the objectives are likely to be focused on improvements in service delivery whether this be education, healthcare or the delivery of charitable aid.

USING THE BOOK CHAPTERS, SUBJECT TRACKING SYSTEM AND CASE STUDIES

Each chapter begins with a set of learning outcomes and follows through with discussion points, activities and learning activities to support and facilitate successful student progress. Additionally, readers can study broad subject areas across the chapters through the use of the highlighted tracking system in the text whenever the same or a related subject is significantly discussed in other parts of the book.

The interlinked system suits the integrated approach to HR. It is also easier for students to conduct projects and work studies by following up related subjects in different chapters. For example, if you are following a theme such as **attitudes**, **knowledge** and **skills**, the tracking system enables you to quickly find related information. Hence, *attitudes*, such as sensitivity to diversity, may be found in *Chapter 9*, attitudes in recruitment in *Chapter 6*, while examples of HR **knowledge**, such as models of analysis, can be found in *HR models of analysis, Chapter 11*. HR **skills** are developed throughout the book in case studies, activities, discussion questions and questionnaires followed by self or group evaluations.

Designed, Refined and Piloted

The sequence of the chapters has been designed in conjunction with academic readers to provide a complete course on HR. The learning materials and exercises have also been piloted with groups of students on both undergraduate and post-graduate courses. I was also aware that many modern business courses include team projects and seminar activities as part of the assessment, so readers may like to dip into Chapter 3 in preparation for this kind of group project or seminar work.

EXPERIENTIAL LEARNING

Learning is an activity and to learn is to change. The process of being involved, through note taking in lectures and seminars, listening to other viewpoints and contributing to seminar activities, is an important part of learning. Moreover, interpreting and evaluating ideas helps us to assimilate new materials.

Each chapter provides a 'personal notes' space where you can write you own thoughts, either as a personal aide-memoire or a springboard for seminar discussions. You may also find it useful to make lists of valuable memory joggers for revision or future study. Learning 'as you go' is easier that 'cramming' at the end of the course. It's *your work* in progress!

How much do you remember of what you have been taught after a lecture?

Less than 20%? *or* More than 80%?

Experiential learning is not an exact science. However, if one student sits through a seminar and take notes and participates, s/he is more likely to enjoy and learn from the course than if s/he sits through the session impassively. It's your course. Be an active learner and you are more likely to enjoy the experience and get better results.

Acknowledgements

The theme of this book is integrated HR. Learning and developing the attitudes, knowledge and skills in the area of human relations can help you to be more successful, in whatever area you choose to work in. We usually achieve more by working with and learning from other people than by trying to do things alone. I am therefore grateful to all the people who have shared their time, thoughts and organizational experiences, commented and helped to make this book work more effectively.

LEARNING IS A LIFELONG JOURNEY

My first experiences of listening to people talking about their work was as a boy when my dad and his friend Paco Alcala would discuss the company they both worked for. Apparently, it was a bureaucratic, hierarchical place where positional power and status included everything from where employees could or couldn't park their cars to the colour of the ties that managers (different colours denoted managerial rank) were allowed to wear. Years later, my father-in-law Jim would tell me about his days as a lorry driver and trade unionist. Jim would usually go out of his way to help someone. Whether they needed a lift to the next town or a friend to support their case at work. Jim Dent was from Yorkshire, he said little and did a lot.

Some of the most valuable insights into organizations can be gleaned by carefully listening to the experiences people have to share. Everyone has a story and each story forms part of the complex world we share.

BY FAITH WE PREVAIL

Many thanks to my wife Trudy. I really couldn't have completed the book without your encouragement, support and faith, and it certainly took a lot of faith to move from the earliest rough drafts to a published book.

● SPECIAL THANKS TO ...

Sarah Brown, the commissioning editor who originally introduced me to Palgrave Macmillan.

Ursula Gavin, who kindly agreed to take over editorial responsibility when Sarah moved on to join the CIPD. No publisher, no book, so thank you Ursula, and the Palgrave Macmillan team for all the work you have put into bringing the manuscript to the bookshelf.

The anonymous referees, who have given their time to read, review and recommend improvements to this book.

Friends and colleagues in academia, for your insights and conversations. It's what makes being part of a university community such a privilege. Particularly colleagues and friends at: Bournemouth University, Croydon College, Kingston University, Manchester Metropolitan University, Marymount University USA, Oxford Brookes University, Oxford University, Portsmouth University, Surrey University, Roehampton University, University of Westminster, University of West of England.

Students. You are the purpose of my work. Thanks for inspiring me, for taking part in the seminar activities and listening to the lectures.

To the authors of academic journals and books both referenced in this book and many others too numerous to cite. Please accept my thanks for the opportunity to read and learn from your work.

To all the respondents and other participants who kindly gave their insights and observations into contemporary management and HR. The primary academic research depended so much upon the goodwill and cooperation of numerous people in organizations large and small, from the public, private, corporate, SMEs and voluntary sectors, who have given their time to be interviewed and/or fill in questionnaires and allowed me to observe their work. The background studies have also been greatly enriched by numerous candid, although necessarily anonymous observations of people who agreed to allow their critical evaluations to be used in the learning materials.

Thank you to many close personal friends who have supported and encouraged me, provided cheerful socials and critical commentary.

Finally, everyone remembers one special teacher. For me he was Bernard Rosewall, who believed that I could write and encouraged me to try.

Michael L. Nieto

Every effort has been made to trace all the copyright holders but if any have been inadvertently overlooked the publishers will be pleased to make the necessary arrangements at the first opportunity.

Chapter 1

An Introduction to Integrated Human Resources

Learning outcomes

After reading and completing the activities in this chapter, you should be able to:

1 Understand the context and historical background to integrated HR.

2 Evaluate the relevance of the scientific (Taylor) and human relations (Mayo) approaches to modern HR management.

3 Recognize the role and contribution of integrated HR to organizational management.

4 Critically evaluate the influence of the new management movements on HR.

5 Appreciate why HR initiatives need to be situation-specific, serving local management situations (micro) and advising on how best to enhance performance in relation to the organization's broader (macro) needs.

6 Recognize the differing HR needs of commercial, public sector and voluntary sector organizations and how to develop situation-specific HR initiatives.

7 Present a discussion paper (individual or group) on the role that HR has played in organizations during the last century and the changes in modern HR.

INTRODUCTION

What does human resources (HR) mean to you? Whatever your preconceptions of HR, modern HR has been changing. Indeed, there are contemporary organizations that have chosen to outsource (use external providers) their operational HR functions. There are also many more small-to-medium-sized enterprises (SMEs) that cannot afford to employ a full-time HR specialist. This means that contemporary non-HR managers need to have the appropriate attitudes, knowledge and skills to manage their people. HR is for every manager, not just the specialists.

IN THE BEGINNING: THE EVOLUTION OF PERSONNEL AND HUMAN RESOURCES

Actually, in the beginning there was no personnel management theory at all. The theoretical basis for much of our work has evolved from other disciplines in academia. Hence those elements of management theory, organizational behaviour, psychology, sociology, employee relations and practice that have come to be included in the management of people are relatively modern. In the eighteenth and nineteenth centuries (long before HR was formed into a professional discipline), most of the workforce was engaged in agriculture. So the relationships between landowners and serfs, and later the 'new' industrial factory owners and workers, were shaped more by tradition and local custom and practice than any notions derived from human relations planning and management theories. As industrial organizations grew in the twentieth century, many opted for a functional structure *(structure is discussed in Chapter 2)*. Essentially, the key managerial functions were separated into departments where specialists could gather together to deliver services to the organization. These large, functionally structured organizations were collectively described as 'bureaucracies' (see Eisenstadt, 1968). By the nature of their structure and culture *(see Chapter 2 for culture),* bureaucracies tended to focus on adherence to regulations, whether externally imposed or internally constituted.

Personnel management therefore evolved from the need to provide some functional centre within organizations around which those activities that were specifically oriented towards people management could be pooled together. The traditional personnel departments also provided their organizations with a centre of expertise. This departmental, specialist approach fitted neatly within the context of organizations that were structured functionally *(structure is discussed in Chapter 2),* such as sales, production, finance, personnel and so forth. Personnel departments therefore grew within twentieth-century bureaucracies, typically, although not exclusively, dispensing prescribed management policies and procedures.

By the late twentieth century, a more individually centred HR approach had begun to emerge, although the debate as to where personnel ended and HR began was a matter for much debate in the 1980s and 90s. For example, it is still quite possible for someone whose job title is 'personnel officer' to actually be working strategically (as a key member of the management decision-making process) inside his or her organization and for someone whose job title is 'HR manager' to be fulfilling a purely operational role (implementing decisions and managing procedures that originated elsewhere in the organization).

In the past, it may have been sufficient for the personnel or HR department to operate at just the operational levels of organizations, even to be marginalized rather than be at the centre of strategic planning. Within the traditional operational role, personnel/HR professionals would be required to manage policies that had already been decided, partly or even wholly without their research or professional input. In practice, this included implementing compliance documentation and dealing with day-to-day employee contractual matters such as holiday and sickness entitlements, employment contracts and disputes.

In preindustrial society, the relationship between master and serf was conditioned by tradition and custom. There were no 'personnel departments' where the worker could seek advice or redress for any 'unfair' treatment. In the industrial bureaucracies, legislation and controls, combined with strong trade unions, meant that industrial relations were negotiated collectively. Hence, trade union representatives agreed settlements with management that could be nationally as well as locally enforceable. In the later part of the twentieth century, the trade unions adapted, not always willingly, to the more individualistic trends in employee attitudes. The term 'human resources' could be argued as dehumanizing people into a resource like any other commodity. Notwithstanding the legitimate arguments of terms and their meaning, modern HR has tended to move more towards individual contracts than collective national agreements (Figure 1.1):

Preindustrial society	**Personnel**	**HR**
Custom and practice	Operational services	Strategic input
Master/servant	Collective approach	Individual employee approach

Figure 1.1 Stages in HR evolution

WHICH LEADS TO …

● THE INTEGRATED APPROACH

Within the above definitions of personnel and HR, it is understandable if some managements began to question what value-adding benefits an in-house HR department could provide over and above outsourced firms who specialize in areas such as recruitment, employee development, payroll, legal matters, standards compliance or incentive schemes. Also SMEs could not necessarily afford to employ a department of professional HR people. Therefore it made both practical and economic sense to use outsourced expertise on a need-to-have basis. This does not mean that organizations do not need HR people but rather that the HR role is changing and HR may be provided internally, externally or by a balanced combination of both.

As with any other service to an organization, HR needs to be, and be seen to be, value adding. If, in some organizations, there has been resistance to recognizing the value of HR, perhaps one of the barriers to improved trust may be that managers needed to be convinced of the real value-adding qualities of effective HR interventions. According to research by Maitland (2003), trust is an important factor in organizational performance. HR can begin by nurturing the development of employee relations *(employee relations is discussed in Chapter 4)*, gaining the respect and trust of colleagues. HR ought to be part of the organizational solution to the challenges that their operational colleagues are dealing with *(communications and presentation of HR are discussed in Chapter 12)*.

The modern HR professional should therefore be more proactively involved within his/her organization's policy making and management. In contrast to the integrated strategy, practitioners might, with some justification, argue that certain organizations have management structures and cultures *(structure and culture is discussed in Chapter 2)* which are less conducive to the development of integrated HR activities. It is, therefore, arguably a relevant part of the HR agenda to improve communications within organizations regarding the potential value of improving organizational performance through people. The case for the value-adding benefits of HR is persuasive, if it is seen as an integral part of whatever the organization is planning to achieve. Modern research has indicated that the effectiveness of HR practices can add significantly to organizational performance. Referring to the substantial weight of research evidence regarding the value of HR activities, Alberg (2002, p. 23) has observed that over thirty studies conducted in both Britain and the US during the 1990s found a positive correlation between people management and organizational performance. However, during the course of researching this book, I still found ample practitioner evidence, from a wide range of sectors, indicating that their experiences varied regarding the level of acceptance or value placed on HR within their organizations. Hence, even if there is a persuasive case supporting the value of HR, it still has to be effectively presented.

● INTEGRATED HR IS SITUATION-SPECIFIC

Each organization has to be convinced of what an investment in HR can do in its specific situation. Hence, if it is a for-profit organization, the HR people should set themselves the task of serving to improve the delivery of agreed performance targets with their operational colleagues. In the public and not-for-profit sectors, the objectives may be centred on improvements in service delivery, whether this be education, healthcare or the delivery of charitable aid.

Operational managers, team leaders and executives are often preoccupied with their core tasks and so they usually welcome productive input that may offer solutions to the issues with which they are dealing. Within such circumstances, the HR person can render significant value-adding input by providing a strategic planning overview that can lead to performance-enhancing interventions. Essentially this requires studying the local management (micro) situations and advising on how best to enhance performance in relation to the organization's broader (macro) objectives *(HR research, auditing and planning are discussed in Chapter 11)*. These kinds of micro/macro initiatives require a range of managerial attributes and the HR person should be encouraged to develop sound research and communication attitudes, knowledge and skills in order to critically evaluate situations and discuss possibilities empathetically with colleagues *(communications skills are discussed in Chapter 12)*.

The design, details and local implementation of initiatives should, ideally, be directed by operational managers who are best placed to manage local operational matters because they are close to the opportunities and problems of their area. In the modern organizational environment, the professional HR person therefore needs to be sufficiently sensitive to situation-specific requirements and design initiatives that fit into the structure and culture *(structure and culture are discussed in Chapter 2)* of the organization they are working with or for. So it is arguable that some of the old bureaucratic HR systems – the 'one-size-fits-all' approach – may meet with employee resistance, rendering them less effective than the alternative, integrated, tailor-made approach. According to research by Professor Sparrow of the Manchester Business School, the one-size-fits-all approach is not the most effective way to deliver HR because employment relationships are becoming increasingly individual and person/situation-specific (Roberts, 2003, p. 11). Furthermore, each organization has its own style of management and ethos, which in turn influences the psychological contracts (Guest and Conway, 2001) *(psychological contracts are discussed in Chapter 4)*. For example, employee expectations in the public and private sectors may be quite different. Hence, some of the governmental interventions during the 1980s and 90s, where private sector policies were imposed on public sector organizations, were not always as efficacious as their governmental designers might have anticipated (O'Neill, 2002). Although the issues surrounding such approaches may be contentious, the use of methods designed for a different organizational structure and culture are likely to encounter difficulties. It is not that the interventions, such as performance targets, competencies or compliance procedures, may have been useful elsewhere, but rather that the method of application, even the language used to communicate the intervention, needed extensive consultation and adaptation to meet the requirements of the situation-specific locations *(recognizing and working with a diversified workforce is discussed in Chapter 6)*.

Similarly, the use of terms normally associated with the for-profit sector may not always sit comfortably with the cultural norms of the not-for-profit environment. For example, a doctor whose primary interest is to care for patients may be less than motivated by terms such as 'unit cost minimization' (spend less on each patient), or an aid worker whose work is focused on helping to organize food for starving people might be forgiven for failing to respond to a 'management by objectives' drive. Thus modern, integrated HR ought to be more situation-specific, actively recognizing and responding to the needs and values of those it serves. Effective modern HR can thereby provide relevant and practical initiatives in a language and format that is locally user-friendly and, of course, designed to be effective.

The integrated approach has evolved from a long tradition of academic research and debate. Indeed, the underpinning theoretical research for the management of people ranges from a broad church of academic disciplines encompassing organizational psychology, sociology and management studies. Within the area of managing people, there are prominent differences among the various theoretical protagonists between those researchers/academics who favour the view that management is a 'science', a concept first propagated by Taylor (1947), and those who have taken the human relations approach which was initiated by the Hawthorne experiments and the work of Mayo (1933). This debate is interesting to management students in that both approaches and other related management theories have sought to observe the role that people play and interpret in organizational performance. The integrated approach recommends a 'fitness for purpose' approach and it will be argued that both the scientific and human relations schools have a role to play in modern HR.

The Scientific Approach

Initially it might appear simpler to view organizational activities as purely scientific, because this offers the potential security of predominantly quantitative study, which can produce neat statistical outcomes. In the case of Taylor's (1947) experiments, the results concluded that segmenting work activities into tightly controlled elements enabled the more efficient movement of pig iron in an early twentieth-century factory. Interestingly, the original writings of Taylor were concerned with addressing the exhausting conditions under which workers toiled and his aim was to improve both working conditions and efficiency. Therefore, although Taylor's work has become associated with managing processes, his intentions were also to improve working conditions. Indeed, during the nineteenth and twentieth centuries, workers were exposed to sometimes life-threatening dangers, even on the leading technological projects, such as the construction of the Brooklyn Bridge or the Hoover Dam (Cadbury, 2003). Part of Taylor's vision was therefore to apply scientific methodology and thereby improve working processes.

One of the first corporations to recognize the advantages of scientific management to productivity was Ford, who adopted Taylor's methods to replace craft-like working practices with the first of the modern car production lines. The scientific method of segmenting work into a series of allocated tasks enabled the company to employ a less skilled workforce because they were only required to learn how to complete their allocated task, rather than work as automotive engineers. It was therefore possible for a person with no knowledge of how to build a complete car to work successfully on a production line. The scientific approach thereby reduced the cost of manufacture by increasing efficiency and the number of cars produced per day. Ford also made precise calculations of the productivity and price needed to make the required profit level (see Pickard, 2003).

The manufacturing process was very effective at mass production, as the late

Henry Ford is reported to have said: 'You can have any colour, as long as it's black' (the original model T Fords were all painted black). Essentially the scientific approach to task management dissects work into managed elements, thereby reducing the autonomy of the human input in favour of the systematically organized process. This is why the scientific approach and its derivatives are still an integral part of the modern workplace. For example, burger restaurants can produce the same product in New York, London, Paris and Tokyo by specifying the exact ingredients, cooking method and delivery in every outlet. A similar approach can be utilized in other organizational activities such as call centres where the client is led through a series of preset questions and their answers are inputted into a computer program which can then offer a response such as a credit rating, an insurance quotation, airline ticket and so forth. The advantage of such systems is that employees can be trained to operate and deliver a standard service package. Even where interaction between the service provider and client occurs, the responses can be 'scripted' so that the organization retains uniformity and conformity to its service parameters. The scientific approach can be taken further where the client simply presses buttons on a telephone to receive services. Full automation can remove all direct human contact whereby the customer interface is the service provider's computer system, via the internet.

Scientific management therefore has a significant place in today's organizations. Fortunately for human beings, there are many tasks where human input is required or preferable. Even when a client/organization service can be fully automated, there are likely to be situations where some clients prefer to talk to a human being rather than a computer. Furthermore, sophisticated levels of service delivery are likely to require a greater depth of knowledge than just pre-prepared answers. Interestingly, the original work of F. W. Taylor also recognized the implicit contribution and necessity of human motivation in enabling the system to work. So, the scientific model and its later derivatives, apart from those completely led by computers, are at least in part dependent upon human input, thereby implicitly accepting the importance of HR for their successful operation.

The Human Relations Approach

The alternative philosophical platform to HR, commonly referred to as the 'human relations approach', began with the research work of Elton Mayo (1933) referred to as the 'Hawthorne experiments'. This approach offered a more holistic view of employees as complex human beings with beliefs, loyalties and personal motivations. In a series of experiments at the Western Electric Company, researchers found no evidence that minor changes in the working environment changed behaviour, while conversely taking an interest in employee welfare did produce productivity improvements. These experiments thereby highlighted that even in an industrial production environment, where a scientific approach might be easily employed, performance could be improved when people were more involved and consulted about the work they were doing.

The following four types of experiments were carried out:

1   *The illumination room experiments.* These studies were carried out in an

assembly area of the factory. The levels of lighting were varied to evaluate any potential correlation between the general environment and work output. No significant or conclusive correlation was established.

2 *The relay room experiments.* These experiments were conducted in an area where electrical relays were being assembled. In this experiment, a group of employees were encouraged to discuss their working conditions, such as break periods and working hours. The researchers listened and were empathetic to the needs of the employees, who were then provided with more breaks and rest periods than was the norm. Productivity increased.

3 *The interviewing experiments.* Employees were interviewed about their attitudes to work. As the experiment progressed, the interviewing techniques became less structured, allowing respondents to express their views on a wider range of issues, through which the researchers found some evidence indicating the influence of informal groups. This is arguably the genesis of modern human resources.

4 *Wiring room experiments.* The influence of peer groups was found to have an influence on workplace behaviour. Employees tended to conform to the work rates and norms of colleagues rather than those promoted by management even when additional incentives were provided to produce more work.

The research by Mayo and the Hawthorne experiments provided modern HR researchers with some useful points of reference from which to continue studying aspects of human behaviour in organizations. For example, Mayo (1945) also recognized the importance of groups *(teamwork is discussed in Chapter 3)* and how organizations could prosper when individuals were joined into teams that interacted with each other to form an environment where people attained a sense of belonging and identification with the organization's mission and objectives.

As with the scientific approach, it is possible to criticize the academic, methodological rigour of the Hawthorne experiments with regard to the extent to which their findings can be generalized across other organizations. Modern academic writers usually research a wider spectrum of sectors to underpin the validity and reliability of their studies. Conversely, the place of the experiments has been assured, in that they have provided a point for further academic debate on the place of HR in the workplace. Further critical evaluations of the Hawthorne experiments can be found in Sonnenfeld (1985) and Franke and Kaul (1978).

Both the Hawthorne experiments and Taylor's experiments on scientific management are still relevant to the ongoing discourse on how people are best managed and motivated. Indeed, most management texts usually make some reference to these two contrasting pieces of research because of the enduring influence they have had on organizational behaviour. From the specialist perspective of HR, the two models serve to inform us of the tendency for organizations to focus either on processes (getting the work done) or the human input (improving productivity by developing people). The workplace reality is that work has to be done efficiently and this involves the motivations of people. It may therefore be surmised that it is more useful to argue for the application of either the scientific or human relations approach on the basis of fitness for purpose rather than philosophical preferences for one or other theoretical methodology. However, in all cases, the motivation of workers is central to successful performance *(employee motivation is discussed in Chapter 6)*.

Exercise 1.1

THE HUMAN FACTOR?

There is a story which alleged that Henry Ford, the American car company's founder, asked a union leader what he would do when all cars were made by robots?

The reply was: 'Who'll buy your cars?'

By contrast, Pickard's (2003, p. 30) research found that Ford recognized the importance of an affluent workforce. Apparently, Ford doubled his workers' pay to $5 a day to ensure that they could afford the cars they made, recognizing that affluent workers create more customers.

Consider the following questions:

1 Evaluate what HR can learn from the scientific approach and the human relations approach.

2 Would you prefer to work in an organization where the managerial system was predominantly process-oriented (scientific) or people-oriented (HR)? Why?

3 In what ways, if any, might there be considered to be some overlap in the use of process and people-oriented approaches?

4 Humans are more than 'robots' to be directed by management. Discuss.

● **MANAGEMENT MOVEMENTS: GURUS AND NEW SCIENTISTS**

The Gurus

The integrated approach recognizes that many people in organizations are likely to be reading and or influenced by the work of the new management writers. In contrast to the research approaches of traditional social scientists *(HR research methodologies are discussed in Chapter 11)*, the later part of the twentieth century produced a different cadre of management writers, sometimes labelled 'gurus' by the popular media. This was because, in some cases, the delivery of their materials drew from a paradigm more akin to religious evangelism than the more reflective research methodologies of traditional academia. However, the movement has also been successful in promoting discussion with a larger audience by presenting ideas and arguments in a user-friendly language and style. A sample of writers from the new management movement might include: Bell (2002); Covey (1999); Drucker (1989); Handy (1997); Harvey-Jones (1995); Kotter (1990);

Morgan (1993); Moss Kanter (1990); Pascale (1990); Peters (1994); Semler (1994); Senge et al. (1994), to name just a few. For more background on gurus, it is also worth looking at Kennedy's (1993) guide to management gurus and Crainer's (1996) book on management ideas. What is interesting about these modern writers is that they have, in different and often distinct ways, opened up the debate on the changing role of organizations in society. Their work has also informed us of the changes in underlying values that are influencing modern organizations. For example, the popular gurus have highlighted the influence of issues such as organizational culture, managing change and strategic HR. More-over, they have brought, even thrust, new ideas into the contemporary psyche, stimulating debate into the complexity and uncertainties of twenty-first-century life and work *(life–work balance is discussed in Chapter 5)*.

The growth of alternative approaches to management writing has coincided with, perhaps promoted by, changes in the organizational environment towards greater diversity and a more rapid rate of change in organizational/ product/service life cycles. Therefore the new gurus provide us with critically eval-uative insights into different ways of thinking about modern workplaces and people. Critical evaluation and students with a critical intellect should be encour-aged and certainly not suppressed or made to conform to prescriptive curriculum (see Fuller, 2005, p. 4). The unconventionality is arguably one of the strengths of the modern movement, in that they tend to write outside the conventional box of academic conferences and journals, offering us different insights into organi-zational life and communicating to a wider audience management audience.

The New Scientists

In contrast to the genre of management gurus, there has also been a resurgence in new applications of scientific management systems. The late twentieth century therefore saw interventions such as: *re-engineering* (Hammer and Champy, 1993; Champy 1995), *competencies approach, monitoring and information technology solu-tions*. These are systematic approaches to management that can be found to have a heritage in the management approaches first shaped by scientific management. This can also be seen in productivity processes such as JIT (just-in-time), whereby materials are delivered just as they are required, as opposed to storing stocks of components. Wilson (1995) argues that these modern initiatives are in fact derived from the earlier work conducted in Ford's factories. According to Boje and Winsor (1993, pp. 57–70), the work of F. W. Taylor (1947) has been resurrected by the new scientific methodologies (also see Jones, 1997, pp. 13–24).

In common with the early twentieth-century scientific management system, the new scientific methods have often been associated with the pursuit of greater efficiency and performance through cost reductions and greater control of employee behaviour. The new variants also share scientific management's predis-position to control the detail of working processes. These methods might be crit-icized for overly 'micromanagement', because they usually increase management's controls on job content, working practices, monitoring and super-vision and take away autonomy from the people closest to the work, be they factory workers, teachers or doctors. Thus, where management micromanage the detail of work, employees have less autonomy in their interpretations of how to do their jobs. This may be counterproductive to employee motivation. Yet, in each situation, the issue is that of fitness for purpose. For example, if the product/service is completely uniform, there is little need for creative input, although matters of employee motivation would still need to be addressed. So, if a standard burger is the required outcome, a highly managed approach might serve the organization's objectives. Alternatively, those who favour the human relation's approach would argue that people are more likely to respond positively to being asked to participate in decision making. Handy (1985, p. 185) has observed that anyone who has spent time with a variety of organizations would recognize the differing atmospheres, ways of managing and individual freedom. Organizations are diverse in structure *(structure is discussed in Chapter 2)* and management style, so HR initiatives should be designed to be situation-specific. This places a special responsibility on management, and those HR people who advise them, to nurture and build up the competence, confidence and motivation in their teams.

NEW PROPHETS?

Perhaps organizations are seeking a perfection that is humanly unattainable? If so, it would shed light on the attractiveness of both the gurus and the new scientists, the former offering an aspiration, the latter a formula. But perhaps neither aspirations nor formulas are enough, rather, a recognition that changes in organization are likely to be frequent and that what is required is the vision (organizational prophets) to encourage people towards adjustments at appropriate times. It is also easier said than done.

HR: Public, Private and Not-for-Profit

One of the criticisms that can be levelled at generic HR models and older textbooks is that they tend to focus on old paradigms of HR/personnel as departments functioning within large for-profit organizations. Yet many organizations operate in the not-for-profit, voluntary or public sectors that have different HR requirements. For example, in the voluntary sector, many 'workers' are not 'employees' and HR approaches need to be sensitive to the differing aspirations and motivations that a volunteer might express (Cunningham, 2000, pp. 226–39). Even in the for-profit sector, the diversity of modern organizations may require different approaches to the traditional forms of HR management. For example, the term 'strategic planning', which was originally derived from the military, might be inappropriate in some sectors. It is crucially important to present HR initiatives in the right, user-friendly language because words can evoke different iconographies (mental images) in different organizational situations. A simple example of this would be terms such as 'downsizing' (reducing the number of employees) or creating a 'lean organization' (reducing the number of employees). Although it may provide a short-term profits boost to shareholders, downsizing also causes concern to employees who would be made redundant! Returning to the example of 'strategic planning', it is doubtful that the practice of reflecting on the organization's situation in its environment (strategic) and then designing appropriate initiatives (planning) would be 'inappropriate' in every organization, industry or sector. However, the language used should be situation-appropriate. Hence, within the more loose form of a cooperative environment or a voluntary aid group, people might be more comfortable with terms such as 'client-centred focus group discussion' or 'project development reviews' instead of 'strategic planning'. The exact terms used should be in harmony with the culture and values of the organization, hence the expression, 'situation-specific HR'. This provides opportunities and challenges to business management students and professionals, in that they need to recognize the importance of tailoring their HR recommendations to the situation-specific culture it is designed for *(communications and business presentation for HR are discussed in Chapter 12)*.

In the design of modern HR research and auditing *(see Chapter 11)*, it is recognized that sectors such as the public services and not-for-profits tend to prefer different approaches to HR than of the for-profit area. Indeed, there may often be significant differences between organizations in a similar environment due to the particular cultures and norms that have grown up around their specific situation *(organizational culture is discussed in Chapter 2)*. The design and implementation of any new HR initiative therefore needs to be sensitive to the local and specific variables and preferences of the people it serves.

Another area where HR professionals should take organizational attitudes into consideration is the use of jargon. Although the use of jargon is common to all professions, it is worthwhile pausing to consider that HR people are in the business of communication and so any language that interferes with that work can easily become part of the problem, rather than part of the solution *(business communications is discussed in Chapter 12)*. It is also respectful to be sensitive to the organization's culture. For example, Ilsley (1990, p. 4) recognized the resistance to managerial language and negative connotations it can have for some people in the voluntary sector. Hence the workplace metaphor of viewing volunteers as equivalents to employees is based on assumptions about what motivates volunteers, how they can be inspired and how they should be supervised. And Billis and Harris (1996, p. 194) agreed that volunteers are not the same as paid staff and therefore should not be treated in the same way. The HR professional or student consequently needs to be particularly sensitive to the prevailing organizational culture, norms and how people perceive their organization (Gordon and Tomaso, 1992, pp. 793–8). It is also worth noting that terms such as 'organizational culture' are actually part of our (business schools and management students) jargon and that other people may not understand what questions about 'their culture' means. Instead, think about asking questions that encourage people to tell you what it is like to work in the organization *(the design of research questions can be found in Chapter 11)*. The not-for-profit sector has its own distinct requirements. HR initiative should therefore to be grounded in the situation-specific requirements and values of the organization they serve.

INTEGRATED HR

Present a discussion paper (individually or with a group) on the role which personnel/HR has played in organizations during the last century and the changes in modern HR, considering the following questions:

1 What do you think the role of HR is in a modern organization?

2 Explain what you understand by the term 'integrated HR'.

3 To what extent do you think HR can contribute to organizational performance?

4 Is HR just about helping people to feel better about their work or do you think it can be a real investment in an organization's core objectives?

5 Why do you think HR approaches need to be tailored to a specific organization's requirements?

6 In what ways do you think organizing volunteers in a not-for-profit organization is different from managing paid employees?

CHAPTER SUMMARY

This chapter introduced you to integrated HR. Remember to use the *Subject Tracking System*, which can help you to follow up related subject areas and themes.

A recurring theme of the book is the modern integrated approach to HR and the importance of designing HR initiatives that are situation-specific. To set out the context into which modern, integrated HR is formed, this chapter considered the relevance of the traditional scientific (Taylor) and human relations (Mayo) approaches towards the creation of personnel management and their influence on modern HR management systems.

Modern approaches to HR needs to be sympathetic to organizational culture and, where practical, be designed as situation-specific initiatives, serving the local management (micro) situation and advising on how best to enhance performance in relation to the organization's broader (macro) needs.

Students and practitioners of HR and management therefore should be able to recognize the differing HR requirements of commercial, public sector and voluntary sector organizations to be able to design situation-specific initiatives.

REFERENCES

Alberg, R. (2002) Counting With Numbers. *People Management*, 10 January.

Bell, D. (2002) *Ethical Ambition. Living a Life of Meaning and Worth*. London: Bloomsbury.

Billis, D. and Harris, M. (1996) *Voluntary Agencies. Challenges of Organization and Management*. Basingstoke: Macmillan – now Palgrave Macmillan.

Boje, D. M. and Winsor, R. D. (1993) The Resurrection of Taylorism: Total Quality Management's Hidden Agenda. *Journal of Organizational Management Change*, **6**(4).

Cadbury, D. (2003) *Seven Wonders of the Industrial World*. London: Forth Estate.

Champy, J. (1995) *Reengineering Management: The Mandate for New Leadership*. HarperCollins: New York.

Covey, S. R. (1999) *The 7 Habits of Highly Effective People*. London: Simon & Schuster.

Crainer, S. (1996) *Key Management Ideas. Thinkers that Changed the Management World*. London Financial Times/Pitman.

Cunningham, I. (2000) Sweet Charity! Managing Employee Commitment in the Voluntary Sector. *Employee Relations*, **23**(3).

Drucker, P. F. (1989) *The Practice of Management*. London: Heinemann.

Eisenstadt, S. N (ed.) (1968) *Weber on Charisma and Institution Building*. Chicago: University of Chicago Press.

Franke, R. H. and Kaul, J. D. (1978) The Hawthorne Experiments: First Statistical Interpretation. *American Sociological Review*, October.

Fuller, S. (2005) *The Intellectual*. Icon Books: Cambridge.

Gordon, G. G. and Di Tomaso, N. (1992) Predicting Corporate Performance from Organizational Culture. *Journal of Management Studies*, November.

Guest, D. E. and Conway, N. (2001) *Public and Private Sector Perspectives on the Psychological Contract*. Results of CIPD Survey. London: CIPD.

Hammer, M. and Champy, J. (1993) *Re-engineering the Corporation: A Manifesto for Business Revolution*. HarperCollins: New York.

Handy, C. B. (1985) *Understanding Organizations* (3rd edn). London: Penguin.

Handy, C. B. (1997) *The Hungry Spirit*. London: Hutchinson.

Harvey-Jones, J. (1995) *All Together Now*. London: Manderin.

Ilsley, P. (1990) *Enhancing the Volunteer Experience*. San Francisco: Jossey-Bass.

Jones, O. (1997) Changing the Balance? Taylorism, TQM and Work Organization. *Work And Employment*, **12**(1).

Kennedy, C. (1993) *Guide to the Management Gurus. Shortcuts to the Ideas of Leading Management Thinkers*. London: Century Business Press.

Kotter, J. P. (1990) *A Force for Change. How Leadership Differs from Management*. London: Collier Macmillan.

Maitland, R. (2003) A Question of Trust. *People Management*. 6 November.

Mayo, E. (1933) *The Human Problems of an Industrial Civilization*. New York: Macmillan.

Mayo, E. (1945) *The Social Problems of an Industrial Civilization*. Cambridge: Harvard University Press.

Morgan, G. (1993) *Imaginization. The Art of Creative Management*. London: Sage.

Moss Kanter, R. (1990) *The Change Masters. Corporate Entrepreneurs at Work*. London: Unwin.

O'Neill, O. (2002) Is Trust Failing? *Reith Lecture*. BBC Radio 4. 17 April.

Pascale, R. T. (1990) *Managing on the Edge. How Successful Companies Use Conflict to Stay Ahead*. London: Viking.

Peters, T. J. (1994) *The Tom Peters Seminar. Crazy Times Calls for Crazy Organizations*. Basingstoke: Macmillan – now Palgrave Macmillan.

Pickard, J. (2003) 100 Years of Ford. *People Management*, November.

Roberts, Z. (2003) Culture Key to Global HRM. *People Management*, December.

Semler, R. (1994) *Maverick! The Success Story Behind the World's Most Unusual Workplace*. London: Arrow.

Senge, P. M., Roberts, C., Ross, R. B., Smith, B. J. and Kleiner, A. (1994) *The Fifth Discipline Field Book. Strategies and Tools for Building a Learning Organization*. London: Nicolas Brearley.

Sonnenfeld, J. A. (1985) Shedding Light on the Hawthorne Studies. *Journal of Occupational Behaviour*, April.

Taylor, F. W. (1947) *Scientific Management*. London: Harper Row.

Wilson, J. M. (1995) Henry Ford: A Just-in-time Pioneer. *Production and Inventory Management Journal*, **37**(2).

PERSONAL NOTES ON CHAPTER 1

Notes for seminars

NOTES ON CHAPTER 1 CONTINUED

Notes for revision/reminders

Chapter 2

Human Resources in an Organizational Context

Learning outcomes

After reading and completing the activities in this chapter, you should be able to:

1 Appreciate how the role of HR is changing in modern organizations.

2 Understand the use and application of integrated HR.

3 Recognize the differing HR requirements of public, private and voluntary sectors.

4 Identify organizational structures and the influence they have on HR.

5 Evaluate how and why HR is adapting to meet the needs of modern organizational management structures.

6 Study organizational context and environment – the REACT model.

7 Evaluate and discuss a range of international research on organizational structure and cultures.

8 Appreciate the relevance of modern HR approaches to not-for-profit organizations.

9 Critically evaluate the challenges and factors influencing HR in the modern workplace.

● INTRODUCTION

In the previous chapter, we reviewed the historical developments and progress of human resource management (HRM). Although many of the HR practices established in the twentieth century are still valuable and relevant today, there is also a need for HR professionals to serve modern organizations with new strategies that are appropriate to the current environment. The modern trend towards the use of matrix structures (flexible multidisciplinary teams), instead of large functional departments, has also created opportunities for different approaches to HR. Furthermore, organizational delayering (reducing the number of levels of management) has placed more responsibility on managers to implement HR rather than be dependent on the large HR/personnel departments that were more common in the twentieth century.

Modern HR is consequently in the process of being redefined to deliver the services designed to meet the evolving requirements of twenty-first-century organizations. Furthermore, there is a growing recognition that one size does not fit all. The private, public and voluntary sectors require different, tailor-made approaches. Therefore, HR needs to be locally inspired rather than universally modelled on a notion of best practice (Das and Sen, 1991; Farnham and Horton, 1996; Farnham, 1997). Hence, in recent times, there appears to have been a paradigm shift in HRM philosophy, away from employee relations, with its tendency to paternalism, towards a more empowering employee partnership (Nieto, 2003, p. 213). This has meant that the large bureaucratic personnel management departments of the past are being replaced by smaller teams of HR professionals providing strategically focused recommendations to section managers. The responsibility and authority for areas such as recruitment, appraisals and remuneration are also being devolved to managers, which means that we are all becoming responsible for HR.

Research published by the CIPD (Chartered Institute of Personnel Management) provided new evidence supporting indications of a paradigm shift in HR perceptions and roles. The survey included in excess of 1000 organizations in the UK and Ireland, across all sectors and sizes, and highlighted the following changes in the HR function over the past three years:

1 72 per cent say they have more influence with senior colleagues
2 43 per cent employ more people in the function
3 37 per cent employ more specialists
4 25 per cent employ more people with experience outside HR.

Looking to the future:

1 80 per cent agree that HR needs new skills and approaches such as the ability to influence and that HR is becoming more a source of in-house consultancy.
2 66 per cent agree that HR administration will increasingly be computerized and outsourced to realize efficiency gains, another key HR goal.

(Brown and Emmott, 2003, p. 16)

● THE STRATEGIC INTEGRATION OF HR

The change in the role of HR has created new opportunities and challenges for line managers and HR specialists alike. For example, internal HR managers have to oversee and coordinate outsourced operational elements with external service providers. This may involve working together with a number of specialist consultancies for specific assignments; so one firm might be engaged to select a sales manager, another a maintenance engineer and yet another an IT project manager. This is because specialist recruitment consultancies can build up in-depth knowledge and contacts in their chosen areas, which can therefore provide organizations with a faster, more cost-effective service. So where does this leave the HR professional? According to Hall (2000, p. 23), losing some administrative responsibilities will free up HR people to invest their time working with other departments. The key to this new role is the strategic integration of HR activity. For example, Watkins (2003, p. 7) reported that Procter & Gamble (P&G) has outsourced its HR function to IBM Business Consulting Services, in a ten-year deal worth $400 million (£247). IBM then provides HR services to 98,000 P&G employees around the globe, including payroll and expatriate relocation *(see Chapter 14 regarding training for expatriates).*

If the modern movement in HR is towards less in-house operational administration, then where is HR moving? According to research involving 1188 professionals reported by Higginbottom (2003, p. 7), 7 out of 10 HR professionals reported that chief executives recognize that HR is the key to achieving their organizations' aims and objectives. While these statistics indicate the presence of encouraging new developments, it would be incautious to be overly optimistic as to the new ascendancy of valuing people in modern organizations. The term 'people are our greatest asset' has been in management circulation for some time, and yet any review of the business pages and current journals can usually produce examples of short-term profit maximization over longer term strategic performance through employee development. What does appear to have become an established pattern is the movement away from old-style personnel towards newer, more interactive integrated HR, where HR professionals become more involved in the strategic development of the organizations they serve.

HRM IN ACTION

THE CHANGING ROLE OF HR IN ORGANIZATIONS

The extracts below come from a journal paper I published on the changing role of HR professionals. I was first invited to write the following article for *Network* (Nieto, 2001) and shortly afterwards the paper was given an international audience by HR.COM on the web.

During lectures and other situations where I have the opportunity to meet senior managers, the diversity of views expressed regarding HR is remarkable. Indeed, it can be quite amusing, and sometimes a little alarming, to ask managers what they really think about the human resources departments in their organizations. [On MBA and HR masters courses] I invite postgraduates to make a list of the 'positive' and 'negative' points about their HR departments. Sometimes, the list of negatives offered by managers is just as long as the positive one and occasionally rather longer ... Yet by contrast when I meet practitioners for my research or consultancy work it is evident that many HR people are working very hard delivering the best services they can, sometimes with limited resources in terms of both numbers of staff and finances.

It may be that the human resources team are working very hard, but are they delivering the kind of services their management colleagues' want? For example, if an HR team is going to be relevant and effective it must understand the *client* organization it serves. I use the term client because it can be helpful to visualize HR as a service, supporting organizational activities, whether these are commercial or not-for-profit.

Senior managers may like to consider the following question:

- Is the HR team in your organization designing services that you would be happy to pay for if they were an outside provider?

Another question, this time for the HR team:

- How confident are you that your HR team could be successful as a stand-alone HR service?

In a competitive services marketplace it seems prudent for internal HR functions to ensure that they are proactively involved in producing solutions or finding outside advisors, who can address their organization's requirements. This kind of approach draws HR into the core activities of their organization, yet recognizes that, realistically, they will not be able to provide a solution for every situation. Instead, the integrated approach makes use of external input as and where it is necessary. It is also sufficiently flexible to enable managers to receive advice from a variety of sources: there can be safety in seeking more than one counsellor.

AN INTEGRATED APPROACH

- The practical involvement of HR staff (or specialist external advisers, if the organization does not have a dedicated HR team) in strategic staff planning.

- A recognition of the organization's culture and, as necessary, a re-evaluation of policies where they are more a part of 'tradition' than modern practice which meets the organization's current needs.

- Training and development: Team leaders and managers should receive appropriate training so that they are in a position to make informed decisions regarding their sections' and departments' staffing requirements. This can include internal courses, and external management development via business schools or an appropriate management training company.

- [The use of] external providers such as recruitment consultancies and law firms.

- [The use of] external advisers such as business schools and professional bodies such as the CIPD.

- [The use of] experienced professionals who have decided to work part time, such as men or women electing to invest more time with their family, or those who have decided to 'retire' from full-time working, but who have many years experience to offer.

DISCUSSION QUESTIONS

1   What are the key differences between traditional personnel/HR departments and modern integrated HR?

2   If you were employed as an HR specialist within a small, integrated HR team, how do you think your duties might differ from those of someone in a traditional personnel department?

3   In what ways do the non-HR manager's roles and responsibilities change where organizations have a small HR team instead of the larger traditional personnel department?

4   Why is it arguably more helpful to have HR professionals involved in the top level of strategic management development informing strategic decision making than at a lower level reacting to established policies?

THE INFLUENCE OF ORGANIZATIONAL STRUCTURES ON HR

The way an organization is structured will influence how HR operates. In a hierarchical structure it could be difficult to get information moving inside the structure because protocols might inhibit people coming forward with new ideas. So the HR person has to begin by being able to recognize the situation they are in and what is 'doable' in such a context. The integrated approach to HR recognizes that the HR function may be less effective if it is just 'bolted on' to the organizational structure. Instead, HR should be part of every manager's primary remit.

> Management is about people so we are a person first, then an accountant or administrator, designer, engineer, salesperson, social worker, teacher, volunteer.

According to Berends et al. (2003), research found that organizational learning involves the distribution of social practices. The successful communication of these practices was found to depend on the effective and creative input of knowledgeable individuals. These HR initiatives could be encouraged or constrained by the organization's structure. What follows is a guide to the main organizational structures you are likely to encounter. Be prepared for hybrid organizations that mix elements together, as the way an organization is structured can have important implications for the effectiveness of HR.

● FUNCTIONAL STRUCTURES

The functional structure is one of the most common forms of organizational formations. It is designed to provide departments of specialist knowledge, which interact with each other (Figure 2.1). The formal lines of management control from CEO to other employees are clearly specified. In multidivisional organizations, the functional structure often includes directors for each area of operation.

Many organizations are structured by products, market sectors or regions, with a small HR presence in each division or unit (Figure 2.2). This allows the local HR people to gain in-depth knowledge of their specialized area. There may also be an HR presence at a corporate headquarters. In this situation, it would be valuable to develop some coordinated HR systems, which are sufficiently flexible to include situation-specific variations to meet local needs. One of the challenges HR people may face in this situation is actually getting all the HR people in the various divisions or sections together to discuss common policies and approaches. However, the modern technologies available make it possible to keep everyone informed. There are clearly strong advantages to presenting top management with a coherent and coordinated set of policies and strategies for the organization. Even if no central HR presence exists, a coordinated approach can be organized from the divisional sections. Such an approach can also reduce workloads in the individual units, as it should be possible to share some, although probably not all, policy guidelines throughout the organization.

This type of approach can be particularly useful to international organizations where a whole range of different practices and policies may have developed. While it is clearly important to retain local aspects that reflect regional legislative differences and practices, there is much to be gained from sharing ideas and developing some core organization-wide systems. Indeed, to be truly acting locally but operating internationally, a strategic overview of what kinds of HR interventions are helpful would enhance rather than detract from local autonomy.

Figure 2.1 Functional structure

Figure 2.2 Functional structure (regional model)

● OLD-STYLE PERSONNEL

The functional system traditionally provided a personnel department. Functionally structured organizations also tended to be bureaucratic, but this depends on the individual management team and the environment in which it operates. Old-style operational personnel management persists in some situations where internal and external regulatory constraints leave little opportunity for more flexible approaches. In some public sector institutions or organizations in highly regulated environments, the requirement is to adhere to the stipulations of regulatory bodies. In such circumstances, HR people may spend a lot of time preparing formal compliance documents. This can place limitations on the time available for any new strategic HR initiatives. One of the challenges facing HR professionals in this type of situation is how to persuade managers to re-evaluate their approaches to meet the needs of a changing organizational environment. It is worth evaluating whether internal generalist HR operators are the best people to do such work or whether some of the work could be outsourced to specialist consultancies.

Within rigid mechanistic models of organization, the worker or employee has to obey the rules and norms of the organizational system (Zijderveld, 1972, p. 1). As the metaphor 'mechanistic' describes, organizations displaying these characteristics tend to be bureaucratic and constrained by the inflexibility of their structure. Mechanistic organizations therefore favour adherence to rules and narrowly defined job roles and tasks, typified by old-style personnel management. In such circumstances, employee initiatives may be more difficult to bring to fruition or less valued than adherence to predetermined procedures and policies.

The twentieth-century German sociologist Max Weber believed that bureaucracies were characterized by the following factors:

1 *Control* (employees are required to perform standardized tasks)
2 *Hierarchy* (the managerial structure ensures compliance and subordinate accountability to the strictures of the bureaucracy)

3 *Rules* (strictly defined policies and procedures and documentary reporting systems)

4 *Equity* (employee rights and responsibilities are clearly defined for each situation).

Weber recognized that, in long-term stable conditions, employees were more likely to be compliant in accepting the dictates of the bureaucracy in return for employment security (Eisenstadt, 1968, p. 69). Hence these organizations tended to be inflexible but predictable and secure work environments. Bureaucratic structures dominated the organizational environment until the later part of the twentieth century, when the increasing rate of change in the work environment placed inflexible bureaucracies at a disadvantage to their more responsive competitors (see Blau, 1955).

The history of enterprise is, regrettably, littered with well-meaning people who mistakenly supported a 'safety first' approach to management, opposing the more ardent voices of innovation. One example is British Leyland, who closed its MG factory in the 1980s because it could see no market for open sports cars. Japanese car producers responded by manufacturing a variety of sports car, which they exported around the world. British Leyland was later sold off and two decades later, under new management, produced a new MG. Another example is the international computer manufacturer IBM that allowed other competitors to move into the 'niche segment' of desktop computers unchallenged. In a global marketplace, supported by easy access communications, consumers can be reached by a much larger range of alternative goods and service providers. Responding quickly to the market has become the new norm, whether you work for a car company, IT company, a charity or a university. Structurally imposed rigidity can stifle the innovation that modern organizations require.

● ORGANIC HR ORGANIZATION

The metaphor 'organic' describes a form of organization that can grow, change and respond to its environment. The organic structure may be more compatible with multitalented employees to work in interdisciplinary project teams. The organic organization also tends to be decentralized and encourages a high degree of employee autonomy and initiative. 'Matrix' is another term used to describe the use of multidisciplinary teams interacting, forming, disbanding and reforming to meet the needs of the organization.

In the matrix model, each person can be involved in several projects simultaneously. Instead of the organization's expertise being concentrated in departments, it is redistributed into project teams. Whilst the matrix approach may be empowering for employees, it can also suffer from multiple leadership fatigue. This is where disaffection arises from confusion regarding competing project and management priorities. Managers may also complain of having the responsibility to complete projects without the necessary authority to control the resources, as it is quite possible that people are involved in several projects simultaneously. Therefore instead of a harmonious interaction, employees may experience several project leaders requesting their input and commitment. Hence, according to Kotter (1990, p. 89) leadership emanating from several directions can produce conflicts. Unlike systems based on departments, the organic structure offers the possibility of freer deployment and redeployment of people to whatever project requires their skills. The system also demands higher levels of team-working awareness from all employees, which may highlight the need for some specific training in team-working skills. This approach can require managers to trust that their teams are getting on with their assignments even when they are not monitoring their every action (see Handy, 1995). The antithesis of trust is, arguably, the imposition of strict compliance regulations, such as a national curriculum for schools or quality standards regulations in the private and voluntary sectors (see Broadhurst, 2000). Where it works well, the flexible working approach can deliver a productive form of working. However, if the teams fail to cooperate, it may lead to confusion as to priorities and accountability.

HR services may be required to assist in the internal selection of team members for projects and to coordinate the demand for key people. In this role, the HR service providers are in a position of considerable influence regarding who is selected onto projects and this may raise issues of organizational politics, which need to be recognized and dealt with. There also needs to be a coordination between teams so that work is not unnecessarily repeated. Indeed, it is quite possible for individual project teams to become so involved in their own work that they do not share ideas which may be helpful to other parts of the organization. The extent to which HR people are invited to assist in coordinating these activities will depend on the structure and culture of the organization. This is certainly a legitimate area for HR staff to discuss with top management, as improvements in team performance and cooperation have clear performance and productivity implications.

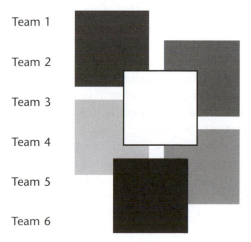

Figure 2.3 Matrix model

Instead of the linear and departmentally organized functional model (shown in Figure 2.1), within a matrix, the teams form and reform so that a person could be working in several interdisciplinary teams at any one time (Figure 2.3). The

'overlapping' commitments can have synergetic advantages; learning is transferred from one team to another.

● MECHANISTIC OR ORGANIC?

The mechanistic organization can be successful in stable, unchanging environments. While it has become less prevalent in the private sector, it still endures in
the public sector and not-for-profit environments where governmental regulations and compliance requirements abound. The burgeoning compliance requirements may render it difficult for HR professionals to change anything without
preparing a discouragingly large amount of documentary justifications.

The mechanistic structure discourages risk taking, so it can also operate usefully
in parts of the private sector, such as pharmaceuticals, where the development of
new drugs and treatments is highly controlled. It is interesting to note that
compliance, which may be required in one area, tends to spread to other parts of
organizational operation. For example, a product development manager in a
pharmaceutical company told me that even the employee expenses claim form
was exactly the same across Europe!

The organic organization provides more opportunities for interdisciplinary
cooperation. Conversely, the operation of management accountability and
multiple project monitoring can be difficult in practice, if elegant as an organizational theory.

As with other aspects of HR and management, the selection of structure ought
to be shaped by fitness for purpose. Organizational design is more likely to be
effective when it is in harmony with situational requirements (see Buelens et al.,
2002, p. 521). However, the organizational environment can change so that the
structures and cultures that were previously appropriate may even become
hindrances to future sustainability. According to Peters (1994, p. 38) smaller
organizational structures can be more flexible, observing the entrepreneur Richard
Branson, who asserts that it is important to maintain smaller, more personal work
groups of 50–60 people (also see Garrett, 1992). However, for many multinational
organizations, local and national government and larger institutions, it may not
be possible to have no more than 50 people in one building, so what can HR do
to help? It may be possible to recommend the development of some interacting
clusters of workers, each with its sets of smaller work teams so that individuals
form a sense of belonging in, what might otherwise be a large and anonymous
office. Although again, this model may incur similar advantages and disadvantages as the matrix forms discussed earlier.

In Figure 2.4, the arrows denote progressions. However, the reality of people
and management is that all these models may exist, even co-exist, in organizations and sometimes the strategies employed require a mixture of methodologies.
There are no lines in the sand. Integrated HR is inclusive, recognizing that some
strictly controlled environments will require less flexible managerial styles.

Old-style operational personnel/HRM
Compliance/control
Operational services

HR
Progressively more strategic

Integrated HR
Progressively more flexible

Figure 2.4 Progression of HR development

PRACTISING HRM

REACT MODEL

In Chapter 11 you will study how to evaluate an organization's HR requirements. The REACT model below provides a plan to begin studying an organization within its environmental context. This model can also be used to begin a team research activity in an organization's HR activities.

● **Research:** Conduct an HR audit *(see HR audits in Chapter 11)* of the organization to establish the current position and where HR investment is most likely to yield the most productivity benefits.

● **Evaluate:** Examine the results from the audit and consider what most needs doing, when and where investment would be best applied, how the HR initiatives should be delivered and who would most benefit from immediate assistance.

● **Action:** People expect: to see concrete actions and new initiatives in response to the research and evaluation; make recommendations and get the new initiatives implemented as soon as possible; consider whether initiatives can be delivered internally, or if a business school or consultant may be better able to produce the outcomes required.

● **Control:** Monitor the progress and adapt the new HR initiatives as and where necessary. Even the best-laid plans need fine-tuning. Be prepared to respond flexibly to people's needs. Remember, it is results that count, if HR is to justify its place in the organization. So focus on outcomes, not processes (what actually happens rather than paper trails or 'quality assurance').

● **Time:** Set realistic, time-bound objectives so that colleagues can be kept informed of progress. Staff morale can be boosted by recognition, so praise improvements and successes throughout the process, not just at the end.

● ORGANIZATIONAL CULTURE: HOW WE DO THINGS HERE

The term 'organizational culture' emerged from the earlier expression, 'organizational climate' which first appeared during the 1960s (Hofstede, 1994, p. 179). During the late twentieth century, the study of organizational culture had become a significant area of academic and commercial interest (see Deal and Kennedy, 1982; Payne, 1991). In the twenty-first century, the place of organizational culture in influencing HR is generally recognized, although its nature is arguably situation-specific and therefore difficult to generalize. For example, Den Hartog and Verburg (2004) researched 175 organizations from a selection of different sectors in the Netherlands. The researchers questioned senior HR managers about HR practices and the chief executives on organizational culture. However, the HR student should not overemphasize the importance of organizational culture in isolation from other interactive HR practices. Indeed, the ebb and flow of organizational performance over the long term indicates that areas such as adaptability and a capacity to change in response to the organizational environment are also important influencers in maintaining a successful organization.

Some of the late twentieth-century's popular commentators have argued for the centrality of culture in the pursuit of organizational excellence (Peters and Waterman, 1982). It is worth noting, however, that in the history of corporations, large private sector organizations do not usually remain as independent entities for more than one century. Many last much less time. This should not be confused with brands, which may long outlive their founding organizations.

Organizational structure is reasonably easy to identify because it is often available in documents such as management flow charts. Identifying organizational culture can require more research. Most employees know the managerial rankings and who is in a senior position. However, organizational culture is less self-evident because it exists in the norms, beliefs, values and unwritten practices. The interaction of structures and cultures can have an influence on how people work (see Payne, 1991). Denison (1990, p. 83) conducted quantitative research with 34 companies from a diverse range of industries, and argued that cultural and behavioural measures could predict the performance and effectiveness of an organization over the years. Conversely, it is arguably difficult to measure complex human interactions that form organizational culture. Perhaps an agreed definition of culture would be a helpful starting point, yet even here there appears to be little academic consensus of thought.

Since the 1980s, many writers have offered possible definitions of culture, each model adding some new perspective to the subject (see Deal and Kennedy, 1982). However, there appears to be no single definition, which has been universally accepted. It is hardly surprising that writers such as Brown (1995, p. 32) have asserted that there is no consensus on how culture should be defined. This may be because the subject contains such a complex mix of influences, including national cultures, individual and group motivations, professional and trade union affiliations and a variety of management styles. For Argyris (1990, p. 11), the subject is extremely complex because organizations are complex systems. Indeed, each organization therefore emits a distinct set of external impressions, which may not necessarily be shared by all its employees and other stakeholders. The actual values, as opposed to the espoused values that an organization regards as important, tend to inform how they act. For Hofstede (1994, p. 18), corporate culture is a soft, holistic concept, although the psychological assets of an organization, the people, may predict what will happen to its financial assets in the future. So what influences people, the 'psychological assets', can have an impact on the profitability of for-profit businesses and the effectiveness of not-for-profit voluntary and public sector organizations.

If culture is complex and difficult to quantify, this does not preclude its influence on HR and performance. As with other key aspect of human organizational interactions, it may become subsumed beneath more 'quantifiable' elements such as performance targets or the profit and loss accounts. Yet every institution, for-profit, public or voluntary, depends crucially on the cooperation and collective success of its people, whether highly paid executives, public servants or unpaid volunteers. The collective organizational norms, motives and motivations are reflected in the culture. For example, the research work conducted by Rashid et al. (2003), on the influence of corporate culture and organizational commitment on financial performance in Malaysian companies (over 200 managers in public listed companies participated in the study), indicated a correlation between organizational culture, commitment and financial performance of the companies studied.

The increasing awareness over several decades of academic research regarding the place of culture in organizational behaviour has led to an understandable desire by managers to categorize and harness the power of organizational culture. For additional background, see Zijderveld, 1972; Touraine, 1974; Deal and Kennedy, 1982; Peters and Waterman, 1982; Hofstede, 1984, 1994; Morgan, 1986, 1993; Handy, 1993; Shane, 1993; Semler, 1994; Watson, 1994; Brown, 1995, to name a few – the subject has engaged many excellent minds. The complexity of culture means that establishing a common framework or definition that all researchers may agree upon has been elusive. Instead, it may be more useful to the management student to consider organizational culture as a situation-specific phenomenon that may or may not share some commonality with other organizations. This complexity can be approached methodologically through the use of an HR audit *(see Chapter 11)*, or by conducting case study research similar to the example below. These research-based methodologies provide HR students with a disciplined approach to study the way an organization is managed. Furthermore, it can illuminate areas such as employee/stakeholder expectations and the ebb and flux of psychological contracts *(see Chapter 4)* as they are influenced by changes in the fortunes of the organization over time.

HRM IN ACTION

THE ADVERTISING AGENCY

This HRM in Action is based on research with a successful advertising agency. I was researching organizational culture and values during a time when the St Luke's agency was breaking new ground in the advertising industry. The agency became well known inside the advertising industry, academia and the wider world for its egalitarian management style and alternative approach to managing work in a competitive industry. St Luke's won the agency of the year award in 1997.

Sometimes HR management initiatives are bolted on to the existing organizational structure and culture. This was certainly not the case at St Luke's. The main departure from conventional office management at St Luke's was the adoption of a range of alternative management methods, including the use of cooperative ownership (employees owned the company), team working *(teamwork is discussed in Chapter 3)* and hotdesking (no one has their own desk, people use whichever desk/computer is available each day), to enable employees to focus on progressing their work, not the organizational bureaucracy.

The chairman (now former chairman) Andy Law told me that the use of technology enabled people to do their work more flexibly than conventional office practices allowed. The research I conducted indicated that the new approach was also well received by the staff (Nieto, 2002). Several interviewees, both in focus groups and individually, expressed positive attitudes towards the agency. For example, one respondent noted the importance of nurturing employees by asserting that: 'If people leave, we're losing talent and loyalty.'

Traditional methods of HR management such as strategic planning *(planning is discussed in Chapter 11)* were rejected as an outdated paradigm: 'That paradigm is out of date, it isn't useful to this situation.' Evidence I gathered from the chairman, senior staff and members of St Luke's also indicated that their adventurous experiment into a cooperative form of working was commercially successful; so much so that major organizations as diverse as BT, IKEA and HSBC were part of their client portfolio. The work of St Luke's has since been researched by other academics, management writers and journalists and has consequently received considerable journal and press interest. According to Coutu (2000, p. 148), St Luke's vision was to enable workers to relax and enjoy employment security long enough to see beyond the short term.

However, by 2003, the apparently utopian management dream was being criticized for significant HR failings. Guest (2003) reported that some major clients had left the agency as well as a number of key personnel including the chairman, who reflected that he might have been a little bit more dictatorial.

Perhaps instead of the emotive term 'dictatorial', it would be more progressive to use the word 'assertive'. Nevertheless, the difference between whether a manager is dictatorial or assertive may be more perception than reality. One of the managers who stayed with the agency noted a marked change in HR strategy, reflecting that cooperative ownership led to difficulties in leading the business. This appears to be a complete turnaround of strategy, if one is permitted to use the term strategy, in an organization that experimented in a free form of cooperative management. Yet this is completely in harmony with a proposition that argues for situation-specific HR that is sufficiently flexible to change in response to its environment.

What can the HR student learn from the St Luke's experiment? To begin with, we should recognize the need to be responsive to changing organizational requirements. Even the most innovative of HR initiatives needs to adapt to new circumstances. The case of St Luke's demonstrates how organizations require different HR approaches as they develop. For example, while communication is likely to be easier in smaller, newly established organizations where pioneering employees may enjoy the exuberance of innovation, this may become more routine as the organization matures.

The case of St Luke's' therefore raises some interesting issues for HR students and practitioners.

DISCUSSION QUESTIONS

Consider the following:

1   Nothing fails like success. Why should even successful organizations continually consider new opportunities and approaches to working practices?

2   Why is it important for HR professionals to regularly monitor staff attitudes and morale?

3   How do you think employees who have become accustomed to a cooperative management structure and culture are likely to react to the imposition of new 'rigorous systems'?

4   What are the advantages and disadvantages of an informal management style?

5   How might an HR audit or culture case study inform and assist in the development of a new management approach?

6   In sensitive areas of management change, why is employee consultation important?

HR IN NOT-FOR-PROFIT ORGANIZATIONS

In the voluntary sector, the term 'employee' may be completely inappropriate because the 'workers' are volunteers (see Butler and Wilson, 1990). The organic approach to organizing people who give their time freely is more likely to be effective than a mechanistic mode that tends to demand compliance. Thus, more consultation and inclusion can be helpful in working with volunteers. HR should respond to local organizational cultures and norms. This means designing initiatives that steer away from the notion that one size fits all or universal best practice prescriptions.

The experiences I have enjoyed, both working as a volunteer and lecturing on a postgraduate voluntary sector masters degree, have encouraged me to believe that those who manage unpaid people have to employ some of the most positive HR approaches. The voluntary sector coordinator cannot use simple carrot-and-stick management approaches (financial incentives and punitive actions or dismissal) because volunteers work for reasons other than remuneration. Conversely, this should not be taken to be an argument in favour of well-meaning, inefficient amateurism. If the for-profit sector expects professionalism in the pursuit of profit, the clients of voluntary and public sectors should be able to expect the same high standards of work. This can also include employing research and evaluation to the charity or not-for-profit's performance in their 'market sector' (see Hankinson, 2000, 2002).

The culture of public sector organizations tends, although not always, to lean towards the bureaucratic. The stability that this promulgates can be attractive to people who prefer a more stable career path. Hence, the introduction of changes in psychological contracts, working conditions and environments requires sensitive consultation. Although the public sector is a 'paid' environment, professionals often have particular pressures and constraints and HR initiatives should be empathetic to the environment in which it serves. Hence, nurses are more likely to have joined their profession to spend time with patients, not administration. Teachers or lecturers can usually do a better job if they are allowed the time for scholarly development. Public services face considerable challenges pertaining to the stakeholders they serve as well working within finite budgets and resources. Although the trend has been to require more financial accountability from the public sector, the focus on finance is not the same as a for-profit organization. So, for example, teaching less able children is not as cost-effective as selecting the most able when pursuing a better place in a performance league table.

It is helpful to study not-for-profit organizations' structure, culture and current practices before attempting to initiate any HR interventions. Modern HR specialists would usually refer to such activity as an HR 'audit' (auditing HR is discussed in Chapter 11). However, the term 'audit' also has close associations with accountancy and commercial practices, which may not always be the most appropriate language in a not-for-profit environment. 'Study' may be a more appropriate term to use in the voluntary sector. However, as with any HR assignment, study the linguistics by listening to the language that people use. The kind of language you use should also be situation-appropriate. For example, an aid worker surrounded by starving children may understandably be unimpressed by someone who plans to audit his/her managerial performance. It is therefore important to invest time studying the structure and culture of the not-for-profit organization to appreciate how customs and behaviours have developed over time. This preparatory research can then inform any subsequent recommendations, tailoring the development of initiatives to local, situation-specific needs. This approach is more likely to produce a positive outcome than any attempt to impose an external best practice model on a not-for-profit organization. HR begins by listening and studying requirements, not imposing external solutions.

HRM IN ACTION

THE VOLUNTARY SECTOR

Names and details have been altered to respect the anonymity of individuals and the voluntary organization from which the research for this case study was derived.

The 'Happy Holiday Play Scheme' was organized for children with educational learning difficulties. The ratio of children to supervisors was good and further improved by the addition of unpaid volunteers. In general it was accepted that the paid staff would contribute more to the work of the play scheme, although the scheme's coordinators valued the volunteers' work. Both paid and voluntary staff were provided with specific training sessions to meet the children's needs. The volunteers were also provided with a certificate of attendance.

The scheme was successful in recruiting students studying education and related areas. This was because the work experience helped them to develop knowledge and skills, which enhanced their CV portfolio. The ambition of most of the unpaid volunteers was eventually to find full-time paid employment in the voluntary sector. Consequently, the scheme's provision of training sessions and attendance certificates, together with the practical experience of working with the children, was particularly helpful in recruitment.

This kind of structured approach is by no means universal in the voluntary sector and some volunteers may find themselves doing routine paper work or tidying up tasks. However, that was not the case in the happy holiday play scheme. The feedback evaluations from former volunteers were mostly positive and in turn assisted the future recruitment of new volunteers. However, given that the volunteers were usually motivated by career development, they didn't tend to stay with the scheme for long. One of the concerns for the scheme's permanent workers was the need to constantly recruit and train new volunteers. Although the training was essential to the effectiveness of the scheme, it also represented a cost in terms of staff time.

Another matter for concern was that the relatively low-paid employees were acting as training managers, supervisors and mentors to volunteers who were doing aspects of their jobs for no pay. It was therefore arguable that the paid employees might have been in a better position to negotiate improved wages if there was not such a healthy flow of willing unpaid volunteers. The high volunteer turnover also created challenges in relation to continuity of individual contact with needy children. Conversely, the presence of volunteers provided the scheme with an improved staff ratio, thereby enabling more day-to-day, individual attention and support for the children.

DISCUSSION QUESTIONS

1   Do you think that the students are being provided with an opportunity to gain work experience or being exploited as unpaid workers?

2   To what extent, if at all, do you think that pay levels in the care sector are influenced negatively by the use of volunteers doing similar work to the employees, for free?

3   Many of the volunteers were students developing their professional skills for future employment in the sector. Do you think that working on the play scheme should be incorporated into their professional training programme, thus providing the scheme with a more regular stream of workers and the potential for more formal accreditation?

4   The turnover of volunteers was highlighted as a concern in the case study. What are the potential problems for continuity and stability in voluntary organizations?

5   What attitudes, knowledge and skills do you think might be developed in voluntary sector student placements that are distinct from being placed in a for-profit organization?

6   The play scheme provided training, a certificate and an opportunity to gain professional experience. How common do you think this is in the voluntary sector?

7   Consider the organizational challenges of integrating the work of full-time, paid professionals with short-stay volunteers.

⬤ CHAPTER SUMMARY

This chapter explored the integrated HR approach and the changing role of HR in modern organizations. It discussed organizational structure and cultures and the implications they have to modern HR initiatives. There are differences in the approach and form of HR in different sectors. Modern integrated HR recognizes the situation-specific requirements of the public, private and voluntary sectors. This includes an awareness of the need for differences in the design of HR for not-for-profit organizations.

The delivery of HR can be drawn from a variety of sources including internal department staff, external advisers and providers. If the right mix is selected and delivered effectively, the net result should be improved performance, whether that is translated as profit, or service delivery in the charity and not-for-profit sector.

Managers may also reflect upon the value of recognizing the role they play in HR.

In one sense, everyone is involved in HR management, because most tasks require the cooperation of other people, which means responding to individual personalities, variations in attitudes, knowledge and skills within a situation-specific context.

REFERENCES

Argyris, C. (1990) *Integrating the Individual and the Organization*. London: Transaction.

Berends, H., Boersma, K. and Weggeman, M. (2003) The Structuration of Organizational Learning. *Human Relations*, **56**(90).

Blau, P.M. (1955) *The Dynamics of Bureaucracy*. Chicago: University of Chicago Press.

Broadhurst, A. I. (2000) Corporate Ethics and the Ethics of Social Responsibility: An Emerging Regime of Expansion and Compliance. *Business Ethics: A European Review*, **9**(2).

Brown, A. (1995) *Organisational Culture*. London: Pitman.

Brown, D. and Emmott, M. (2003) Happy Days. *People Management*, 23 October.

Buelens, M., Kreitner, R. and Kinicki, A. (2002) *Organisational Behaviour* (2nd edn). Maidenhead: McGraw-Hill.

Butler, R. J. and Wilson, D. C. (1990) *Managing Voluntary and Non-Profit Organisations. Strategy and Structure*. London: Routledge.

Coutu, D. L. (2000) Creating the Most Frightening Company on Earth. *Harvard Business Review*, September/October.

Das, J. P. and Sen, J. (1991) Planning Competence and Managerial Excellence. Paper presented to the International Association of Cross Cultural Psychology. 4–7 July: Debrecan, Hungary.

Deal, T. E. and Kennedy, A. A. (1982) *Corporate Cultures. The Rites and Rituals of Corporate Life*. Wokingham: Addison Wesley.

Den Hartog, D. N. and Verburg, R. M. (2004) High Performance Work Systems, Organisational Culture and Firm Effectiveness. *Human Resource Management Journal*, **14**(1).

Denison, R. D. (1990) *Corporate Culture and Organizational Effectiveness*. Chichester: John Wiley.

Eisenstadt, S. N (ed.) (1968) *Weber on Charisma and Institution Building*. Chicago: University of Chicago Press.

Farnham, D. (ed.) (1997) Employment Flexibilities in Western European Public Services: An International Symposium. *Review of Public Personnel Administration*, **17**(3).

Farnham, D. and Horton, S. (eds) (1996) *Managing the New Public Services*. Basingstoke: Macmillan – now Palgrave Macmillan.

Garrett, E. M. (1992) Branson the Bold. *Success*, **39**(9).

Guest, K. (2003) Commercial Breakdown. *Independent*, 20 March.

Hall, P. (2000) Feel the Width. *People Management*, 6 January.

Handy, C.B. (1993) *Understanding Organizations* (4th edn). London: Penguin.

Handy, C.B. (1995) Trust and the Virtual Organisation. *Harvard Business Review*, May–June.

Hankinson, P. (2000) Brand Orientation in Charity Organisations: Qualitative Research into Key Charity Sectors. *International Journal of Nonprofit and Voluntary Sector Marketing,* **5**(3).

Hankinson, P. (2002) The Impact of Brand Orientation on Managerial Practice: A Quantitative Study of the UK's Top 500 Fundraising Managers. *International Journal of Nonprofit and Voluntary Sector. Marketing,* **7**(1).

Hofstede, G. (1984) *Culture's Consequences. International Differences in Work-Related Values.* London: Sage.

Hofstede, G. (1994) *Cultures and Organisations. Software of the Mind.* London: HarperCollins.

Higginbottom, K. (2003) HR Influence on the Increase. *People Management,* 23 October.

Kotter, J. P. (1990) *A Force for Change.* New York: McMillan.

Morgan, G. (1986) *Images of Organization.* London: Sage.

Morgan, G. (1993) *Imaginization. The Art of Creative Management.* London: Sage.

Nieto, M. L. (2001) Do Managers Need HR? *Network,* (4), and *HR.Com,* 1 October.

Nieto, M. L. (2002) *Marketing the HR Function* (2nd edn). London: Spiro Press.

Nieto, M. L. (2003) The Development of Life Work Balance Initiatives Designed for Managerial Workers. *Business Ethics: A European Review.* **12**(3).

Payne, R. (1991) Taking Stock of Corporate Culture. *Personnel Management.* July.

Peters, T. J. (1994) *The Tom Peters Seminar. Crazy Times Calls for Crazy Organisations.* Basingstoke: Macmillan – now Palgrave Macmillan.

Peters, T. J. and Waterman, R. H. (1982) In Search of Excellence. New York: Harper Row.

Rashid, M. Z. A., Sambasivan, M. and Johari, J. (2003) The Influence of Corporate Culture and Organisational Commitment On Performance. *The Journal of Management Development,* **22**(8).

Semler, R. (1994) Maverick! *The Success Story Behind the World's Most Unusual Workplace.* London: Arrow.

Shane, S. (1993) Cultural Influences on National Rates of Innovation. *Journal of Business Venturing,* **8**(1).

Touraine, A. (1974) *The Post-Industrial Society. Tomorrow's Social History: Classes, Conflicts and Culture in the Programmed Society.* London: Wildwood House.

Watkins, J. (2003) IBM Lands P&G HR Operation. *People Management,* 25 September.

Watson, T. J. (1994) *In Search of Management. Culture, Chaos and Control in Managerial Work.* London: Routledge.

Zijderveld, A. C. (1972) *The Abstract Society. A Cultural Analysis of our Time.* London: Penguin.

PERSONAL NOTES ON CHAPTER 2

Notes for seminars

_____
_____
_____
_____
_____
_____
_____
_____
_____
_____
_____
_____
_____
_____
_____
_____
_____
_____
_____
_____
_____

Notes for revision/reminders

_____
_____
_____
_____
_____
_____
_____

NOTES ON CHAPTER 2 CONTINUED

Chapter 3

Human Resources: The Team Builders

Learning outcomes

After reading and completing the activities in this chapter, you should be able to:

1 Understand the HR applications of teamwork in organizations.

2 Appreciate the benefits of teamwork in completing work projects.

3 Understand the role of HR trained people in developing team working in organizations.

4 Recognize the stages of team development.

5 Identify team roles.

6 Appreciate the value of diversity in teamwork.

7 Recognize the difficulties associated with groupthink.

8 Apply the AKS integrated approach to team building.

9 Present the case (individual or group activity) for effective team working in modern organizations.

10 Critically evaluate the role of HR in developing organizationally effective work teams.

11 Make practical use of the knowledge and skills gained from this chapter by performing teamwork activities more effectively.

INTRODUCTION

Team working is a valuable transferable skill for students to develop because it is commonly used in modern organizations. The movement towards greater efficiency and flexible working practices has also encouraged the employment of people who are able to work within multidisciplinary teams. I would like to think that people who have studied business management or followed an HR pathway have benefited from exposure to knowledge and practical skills, which are of value to their future careers. Indeed, I am often reminded of the significance of teamwork to organizations when I am asked to provide references for former students. Prospective employers frequently request specific information requiring evidence of team working on coursework assignments and the student's performance and experiences of team working. According to Newall and Scarbrough (2002, p. 40), team working is one of the most popular new forms of human resource management. Furthermore, modern integrated organizations are replacing old-style departmental delineations and encouraging multidisciplinary workers to seek solutions and manage projects through team cooperation. In the new work environment, HR professionals have to facilitate a wider range of activities. Therefore the HR professional has a valuable contribution to make in developing the team-working capacities of their co-workers and improving organizational performance.

Students who are conducting teamwork projects may find it helpful to study this chapter early on in the course so that they have the time to incorporate the attitudes, knowledge and skills of teamwork into their personal development plans. Specialist HR students also need to understand team working, so that when they enter the workforce they are able to advise colleagues on how to achieve the best from people in teams and, equally important, how to avoid potential pitfalls. Over the years I have worked with many teams of students in several universities and found that, in the majority of cases, team-based projects are successful and those involved enjoyed the experience. However, the responsibility for producing an effective team project is with the team members. Although writers and HR lecturers can point the way towards more effective team working, it would be an oversimplification to advance the view that all that is required to become proficient in team working are a few HR textbooks and a set of lectures. Team working requires the acquisition and practice of a set of interpersonal attitudes, knowledge and skills. Hence, the development of values such as tolerance of diversity, compromise and the counterbalancing pleasant assertiveness are practical skills, which are encouraged by well-managed, teamwork projects. People learn and develop through the action of teamwork participation (Revans 1982). Although theory is useful to inform our understanding, it is through practical experience that individuals gain the ability to work with other people in teams, so this chapter provides a variety of personal and team developmental exercises.

THE HR APPLICATIONS OF TEAMWORK

In contemporary organizations, professional and departmental delineations are likely to be less prevalent than in traditional forms of management structure *(see Chapter 2 for matrix structures and integrated HR)*. Teams usefully function more effectively if some developmental HR strategies have been employed to nurture their development. Unfortunately, less experienced managers, and indeed more mature professionals, may mistakenly regard such proactive support as unnecessary or, worse, just as a matter of common sense. Developing people's team-working attitudes, knowledge and skills is undoubtedly good sense. Regrettably, it is not so commonly employed. If you are an academic, manager, or student, ask yourself how much time has your organization or university invested in developing your team aptitudes.

Working with other people can undoubtedly be stressful and sometimes differences of opinions will occur, hopefully without the need to refer to the HR specialist in the organization. Modern organizations use multidisciplinary teams *(see Chapter 2)* and sometimes there can be tensions and disagreements, so HR specialists and managers should be competent in understanding and resolving team member disputes.

Even within a supportive learning environment, I can say with reasonable certainty that each academic year there will be at least one student who will come to advise me that their team activities or team project are not going as well as they would like and that it is not their fault. Once people graduate and find employment, the team-working challenges in organizations are similar, except that if projects are not completed correctly, or fail to meet the required standards, there are unlikely to be second chances by way of a resit coursework submission. However, working with other people is an inevitable part of organizational life, so it is constructive to acquire the appropriate attitudes, knowledge and skills in a safe learning environment, such as a business course. This can save a lot of unnecessary 'experiential learning' later in professional life.

In college or university, the main object of interest is the students' development, whereas organizations tend to prioritize more task-oriented outcomes. To put the case in the clearest way, it is probably better to learn about working in teams with an empathetic tutor overseeing proceedings than a potentially unsympathetic employer who is likely to be more concerned about getting the job done than nurture your personal development. It is worth noting, however, that since work is completed by people, the best way managers can ensure that work is completed to a high standard is to train and develop their team of people to be more effective both individually and as part of the organization. This is one of the many reasons that post-experiential courses such as an MBA can make a valuable contribution to management development – provided that the mature student enters the programme with a positive attitude to learning and developing his or her attitudes, knowledge and skills.

● HR AND TEAMWORK: ATTITUDES, KNOWLEDGE AND SKILLS (AKS)

The sections that follow are organized under the headings *Attitudes*, *Knowledge* and *Skills*. This is to link your learning to experiential activities, so you are encouraged to do the self-evaluations and exercises as you progress. This approach recognizes that it is a combination of attributes that enable people to succeed in cooperating and working with others.

Attitudes

If we subdivide team working into attitudes, knowledge and skills (AKS) it is evident that the right attitudes are going to be a decisive factor in whether or not a team succeeds. Unless people actually try to make a team function effectively, it is likely to encounter difficulties early on, no matter how knowledgeable and talented they are. The American writer Stephen Covey (1999, p. 31) has challenged some of the conventional thinking on organizational behaviour by asserting that we can only achieve quantum improvements in our lives by moving from a focus on our behaviour to the paradigms from which our attitudes and behaviours are formed. Later in this section there is an opportunity to answer an attitudes questionnaire, which can be used to facilitate personal reflection.

The area of attitudes is a challenging one for those professionals interested in improving the performance of people in organizations because, of the three key areas, attitudes are likely to be the most difficult to alter. This presupposes that the individual employees begin by wanting to work together in a team at all. Hence it is worth acknowledging that there can be no set formula or any one theory that can provide the perfect solution to achieving high performing teams in all situations. Instead, a team-working situation should be regarded as an opportunity for ongoing personal development. HR professionals often refer to 'continuous development' in learning. This is particularly the case in team working. *There is always something new to learn about working with other people.*

Emotional intelligence

In recognizing that attitudes are important, members of a work team should begin by reflecting on their own motivations and commitment to the team project. Organizations operate by the consent and cooperation of many individuals, so any policy or project relies on the willingness of colleagues to work towards agreed aims and objectives. Even a good idea can fail if it lacks the support of colleagues because polite resistance is as likely to scupper a good plan as outright rebellion. Learning to work in project teams is a key factor in developing the kind of attitudes that are likely to equip us to work with other people in the workplace, recognizing and respecting diversity *(diversity is discussed in Chapter 6).*

During the past few decades, there has been a wide range of academic research that has critically evaluated the question of whether teams can outperform individual decision making (Hoffman and Maier, 1961; McGrath 1984; Vollrath et al., 1989; Davis, 1992; Guzzo and Dickson, 1996). When viewed collectively, the research evidence tends to indicate that team performance usually depends upon how members interact and their abilities to elicit the best from each other. This is a key aspect of emotional intelligence. Whilst it may be true that one highly talented individual may sometimes outperform a team, his/her work is less likely to be adopted in an organization where colleagues have had no opportunity to influence the outcomes or decisions. This is not to say that a committee should form every decision. Leadership should and indeed has to be recognized in both organizations and working teams. The fad for 'coordinators' instead of team leaders can leave teams effectively directionless.

There is also growing evidence to indicate that what has come to be described as 'emotional intelligence' can have far-reaching influences on how successful a person's professional career might be (see Goleman, 1995; Martinez, 1997; Davis et al., 1998; Fisher, 1998; Huy, 1999). It may therefore be proposed that emotional attributes such as self-awareness, self-discipline, commitment and empathy can be more relevant to working successfully with other people than intellectual muscle power, or IQ. This means that people who are able to display the appropriate attitudes are more likely to be hired and more able to gain the approval of others to progress in their career. Hence, the approach we take to team-working situations can have an influence on our own professional success and relationships with others. Conversely, leading teams is more that merely seeking popularity. Effective emotional intelligence harnesses the resources and diversity of teams to achieve aims and objectives.

Social loafing

A negative and ultimately self-defeating attitude to teamwork is called 'social loafing' (see Latane et al., 1979; Earley, 1989; Erez and Somech, 1996). Although a person who uses colleagues to do their work might consider himself or herself to be 'emotionally intelligent', this behaviour is likely to have negative consequences. Supervisors and colleagues soon recognize individuals who simply avoid contributing to the work, which can eventually isolate the loafer. In organizations, team failures inevitably have consequences for every team member because a project of work will not have been brought to a satisfactory completion. The extent to which any one member contributed more or less to that failure is ultimately of less importance than the fact that the team failed. A business course is therefore an excellent opportunity, whether for undergraduates or post-experience professionals, to enter into a safe learning area to improve their self-awareness and team-working attitudes. Although there may be some students or employees who would prefer to pursue their own agenda over that of their team, in reality no one person can achieve much without learning the attitudes, knowledge and skills of working with other people.

Exercise 3.1

EVERYBODY, SOMEBODY, ANYBODY AND NOBODY

Over the years I have worked with some successful project teams in both commerce and more recently in universities. The challenge of successful team management often begins with individual commitments to begin the work in time and make a full contribution to the aims of the team. It is therefore prudent to agree a statement of aims and targets early in the team's activity schedule. This approach also provides an opportunity for team members to recognize each other's areas of strength, so that future work can be distributed according to the members with the most appropriate knowledge and skills. Without such forward planning, important tasks may be left inadequate time for completion. This avoids the problems caused when Everybody, Somebody, Anybody and Nobody do not work as a team.

There are four people named Everybody, Somebody, Anybody and Nobody. The team had an important project, which Everybody in the team was responsible for completing on time. However, Everybody was sure that Somebody would do it. Anybody could have done it, but Nobody actually got on with the work.

Somebody got angry about the team's poor performance because it was Everybody's job. Everybody thought they could have done better without Anybody else. In fact Anybody could have done the work, but Nobody realized that Everybody was waiting for Somebody to do the project for them.

In the end, Everybody blamed Somebody when Nobody did what Anybody could have done.

Discussion questions

Think about the teams you have been or are a member of and consider the following questions:

1   How well do you think the team organized itself from the start of the project?

2   Do you think the team membership's responsibility is to improve performance or is it somebody else, such as a manager, training facilitator or lecturer?

3   To what extent would you describe yourself as an active member of your team?

4   If some members are less active than you, what steps have you taken to encourage more involvement in the team's activities?

Exercise 3.2

TEAMWORK ATTITUDES QUESTIONNAIRE

Think about your attitudes to a current team project or seminar group activity. Alternatively, use the questionnaire to reflect on employment situations (full or part time) where you are required to work with a few colleagues. Try not to sit in the middle by using a lot of 4s as an answer.

1	Strongly agree	5	Slightly disagree
2	Mostly agree	6	Mostly disagree
3	Slightly agree	7	Strongly disagree
4	Neither agree nor disagree		

1   This team project is important to me.

| | 1 | 2 | 3 | 4 | 5 | 6 | 7 |

2 I want everybody in this team to do well.

1   2   3   4   5   6   7

3 I like the people in my team.

1   2   3   4   5   6   7

4 I would be willing to put a lot of time into making this teamwork
project a success.

1   2   3   4   5   6   7

5 My own expectations for the project and those of my teammates are
similar.

1   2   3   4   5   6   7

6 I am proud to be part of this team.

1   2   3   4   5   6   7

7 I would prefer to be doing this project work on my own.

1   2   3   4   5   6   7

8 I would prefer to be doing this project work with a different team of
people.

1   2   3   4   5   6   7

9 The team's standards of work are unrealistically high.

1   2   3   4   5   6   7

10 I have other, more important work to do than this team project.

1   2   3   4   5   6   7

11 Other members of the team really value my contributions.

1   2   3   4   5   6   7

12 I find it difficult to agree with other members of the team about the
way we should conduct the project.

1   2   3   4   5   6   7

Discussion questions

1 From answering the questionnaire, do you sense that your team-working
experiences are mostly positive, neutral or negative? For example, if your
answers to the questions 1–12 are 1,1,1,1,1,1,1, 7, 7, 7, 7,1 and 7, then you
are very satisfied with the team project you are working with because you
selected all the most positive answers. Think about any questions you

awarded a 4 and consider whether you actually feel more or less positive about that particular aspect of teamwork, unless you really don't care either way. If that's the case, then what are the reasons for your absence of enthusiasm?

2 What can you do to improve your team performance?

3 Do you enjoy or not enjoy team working? Think about your contributions to your team and where these could be improved, both interpersonally and in work contribution.

Knowledge

Adaptive management

Knowledge of team dynamics can provide students, HR professionals and general managers with a more informed approach to team working. It may also help us in recognizing situations and stages as they occur and perhaps even anticipate difficulties before they arise. This section will consider the key elements of team working in conjunction with practical self-evaluation and teamwork exercises.

To begin with, it is useful to recognize that teams move through different stages of development. In this respect, the work of Tuckman (1965) is particularly interesting because he outlined what tends to go wrong as well as right in teams and that there are stages of progression of which teams should be aware. However, the key with using models is to recognize that they act as guides and should not be regarded as a prescriptive reality. As with so much of HR and management, it is less about mechanistic processes and more about adaptive responsiveness to new situations. In other words, models and theories cannot replace the requirement for you to make situation-specific decisions. What studying HR management can do is expose you to a range of possibilities and tools to use. The rest is up to you and the situation-specific learning you gain is interacting with fellow students in teams and in the workplace.

⬤ TEAMWORK: WHAT TO EXPECT

The research by Tuckman (1965) and Tuckman and Jensen (1977) analysed team development, setting out five stages. However, it is important to note that while the theory may be elegantly subsectioned, human relations rarely conform precisely to a prescriptive set of stages. While Tuckman's work does provide us with a useful 'map', each team's experiences may turn out to be more or less 'stormy' than the theory indicates. Hence, it is quite possible for a team to regress from performing to storming, while occasionally a team may become so dysfunctional that it ends up achieving very little. However, acquiring knowledge of the potential difficulties of teamwork should enable team members to work more constructively towards completing their assigned task.

Tuckman's Stages of Team Development

1 *Forming* – finding out about task and team
2 *Storming* – internal conflict develops
3 *Norming* – team conflicts are settled and cooperation develops
4 *Performing* – teamwork objectives are achieved
5 *Adjourning* – teams that have worked together well may have fond memories of the experience and gladly work together on another project.

First Impressions

How long does it take you to form an opinion of a new person you have just met? Not long. I have studied this with groups of students from many nationalities and the answer is usually less than one minute. Furthermore, the untrained person is more susceptible to continue reinforcing their original perceptions. When people are presented with someone new, they reference back to previous experiences to categorize the new person – a process known as 'stereotyping'. This is a psychological process by which humans categorize the complex world (see Devine, 1989; Hilton and Von Hippel, 1996) *(stereotyping is discussed in relation to recruitment in Chapter 7)*. Unfortunately, whilst stereotypes may be a convenient means of categorizing the world around us, it cannot help with the enormous diversity that is humanity. The key here is to be aware that you have stereotypes and then alter your perceptions in response to the real person, as opposed to the stereotype you have met.

Consequently the early, *forming stage* of a team's development is important. It provides team members with an opportunity to get to know each other and exchange pleasantries. It can also be a pivotal moment for the team because we do not get a second chance at making a really good first impression. It is helpful to enter this early stage prepared to listen as well as contribute to the forming conversations.

Open Questions: Forming Teams

It can be easier to open a conversation with new people by using the open questions approach, whereby conversation is shaped around questions beginning with; where, which, when, what, who, how. These types of question encourage more dialogue than a simple yes or no answer.

For example:

● *Which pathway/programme/degree are you on?* The modularization of many courses can mean that team members have other study commitments, which may influence the timetabling and schedule of work for your team project. It is better to anticipate and plan for the factors such as team members having other assignments to submit, than encounter difficulties with timing and priorities later. Although this recommendation is addressed towards business project management, it also provides a valuable transferable skill for the workplace where colleagues often have to manage several projects at one time.

● *Where can the team contact you?* This can establish the practicalities of the most convenient places to arrange team meetings. On this point it is as well to consider the environments that are conducive to study discussion. Also, be sensitive to team members who may not care to meet in bars, or at times of religious significance. Establish communication early on by agreeing on whatever method – telephone, email, meetings – is the best way to maintain regular contact.

● *When is the most convenient day to have meetings?* Many students work their way through college, so teams need to plan their meeting times. Usually the best time is when you are all together for a timetabled seminar. Many course leaders design a period of team working within the allocated session time to facilitate teamwork meetings. Be flexible and agree a realistic schedule to which the team can adhere. On some courses, the lecture and seminar programme has allocated time in the timetabled session for teamwork. Check this with your course tutor.

● *What are our objectives in terms of results?* The aims of the team are relevant to the eventual outcomes. The objectives should be specific and above all realistic and agreed by all the team members. Once the objectives are agreed, write them down and give every team member a copy to sign.

● *How are we going to achieve our objectives?* The team also has to set out a clear commitment to achieving the agreed objectives and prepare a schedule of work for the whole project. The motivation to succeed has to come from inside the team. It is not usually necessary to produce a complicated work proposal. I have seen teams produce superb flow diagrams to support their projects and subsequently fail to complete the work. Nevertheless, a plan of work stages is useful at this point.

● *Who is to be given responsibility for elements of the project?* Unless individuals are given specific tasks relating to each work stage, the team may drift along for weeks in misplaced complacency that someone is doing something, when in reality no one is doing anything! This is social loafing (Latane et al., 1979), whereby the feckless members may rely on their more conscientious teammates to eventually get the work done.

TEAM-WORKING ACTION PLAN
Setting agreed goals and monitoring progress

How a team is set up in the initial stages can have a considerable influence on how it progresses later. Remember that even if you are working with people you already know, it is still important to set an agreed set of objectives before the project commences. According to West (1994, p. 98), it is important to establish team goals in the initial stage of the team formation. My experience of working with numerous student teams would also support the view that those who fail to plan from the start may fail to achieve their full potential.

Remember to include **everyone** in the task allocation, then create a simple diary of what needs to be done and by whom. For example:

Action	By whom	Date
1		
2		
3		
4		
5		
6		
7		
8		
9		
10		
11		
12		
13		
14		
15		

Team Tensions and Disagreements

As the term *storming* suggests, research into team dynamics anticipates the possibility of conflicts arising within the team. To some extent, unnecessary storming can be avoided by careful preparations in the initial stage of the project. However, the best-laid plans can go astray, so some adjustments are likely to occur. Although it can be tempting to seek validation for individual positions from outside the team, it is more helpful to resolve difficulties within the team members. In the final analysis, it is the team's responsibility to complete a task so the strains and stresses are better resolved internally. It may be more emotionally comforting to blame another person for the team's difficulties, but the sometimes unpalatable truth is that it is more likely that communication failures and problems are the whole team's responsibility.

The storming may be the result of disputes regarding objectives, meetings and task allocation. It is for this reason that each member of the team should have a copy of the agreed objectives and the work diary as a starting point for discussions. It is also helpful for team members to recognize and remind each other that the purpose of working together is to complete a team project. If the project is not progressed successfully, everyone fails.

Teams Making Progress

After some adjustments and if interactions are conducted in an atmosphere of mutual respect, teams should be able to resolve difficulties and improve cooperation. Team members are usually more willing to work with each other and cooperate towards commonly agreed goals. However, the extent to which differences are subjugated to the team objectives depends on the extent to which each team member values the team and its plans. If team members regard the project as important, they are more likely to invest their knowledge, skills and time to help the team succeed. Conversely, team members may regard the project as so important that they are unwilling to compromise with other members. As discussed earlier, in matters of applying HR to team working, it is important to recognize the situation-specific nature of the team project.

Remember to maintain a dialogue and respect the diversity of your fellow team members. Although teamwork can be frustrating at times, success depends on the mutual consent of members to work together effectively.

Getting the Job Done

The earlier discussions and preparations should now deliver results and the diary of responsibilities and work schedule should help to keep the work on track. However, be prepared to make adjustments to the work in progress. Do remember to allow for contingencies. For example, computers do sometimes crash, appointments may be delayed and research can take longer than anticipated. Build 'contingency time' into the schedule so that the final project date can be fulfilled. When a team project goes to plan, it can be a rewarding and developmental experience.

Farewells

After a successful project, the members should have gained improved attitudes, knowledge and skills relating to working with others. Team members may look forward to working together again. The experiential learning they have attained from their first project should enable them to move more swiftly into the performing stage the next time they work together. However, a note of caution. Although there is something to be said for the adage, 'If it isn't broke, don't fix it,' sometimes working with new people can expose you to new learning opportunities. Well-established teams have the advantage of familiarity, but also have the potential to become complacent and even slip into groupthink, which will be addressed later in this chapter.

● THE ROLES WE PLAY IN TEAMS

It is helpful to recognize that as well as different stages in team development, we also tend to perform differing roles when working with other people. The research work by Belbin (1981, 1993, 2000) identified a set of different, but equally valuable team roles. Each of the roles provides the team with potentially different attitudes, knowledge and skills, which can combine to promote a more effective team-working situation. Belbin's research indicated that each team member could adapt to more than one team role, so it is not necessary to have a representative for every team role.

Equal in Value

The team roles help members to recognize that it is probably counterproductive to insist on equality of contributions because each person has different abilities. To use two simple examples, in an Olympic team the weightlifters are not required to run races and in football teams the goalkeeper is not generally expected to score goals. Alternatively, it is perfectly reasonable to argue that team members should gain experience of areas in which they do not have confidence in order to build their personal skill base. Where practical, it can be less pressurized and more constructive for students to gain new skills within controlled seminar activities, providing formative development, rather than in the workplace.

It is also important to read and understand theoretical models because they provide us with metaphors to categorize and make sense of the world. However, abstract models cannot give you all the attitudes, knowledge and skills to understand the complexity and diversity that is humankind. Everyone is on a learning and experiential journey. The reality is that all humankind does not fit into a set of predetermined categories. Instead, while metaphors can be a useful starting point, it is important to adjust our perceptions in response to each person we meet. So, I hope the notes below will help you to translate the model of team roles into some useful aids to your team's practice.

Critical Evaluations and Summary of Team-working Roles

Team roles provide us with generalizations that can help but certainly cannot define us all. The people of our diverse and multicultural world are not contained or constricted into a set of predefined roles. Instead it is useful to consider the team roles as signposts that provide a guide. It is the responsibility of each individual and team to make his or her team-working journey a success. Review the descriptions below and think about which most apply to yourself. Then ask your work colleagues or teammates to describe which they think most identifies your team behaviour. It is also quite possible that you may display different behaviours according to the mix of other members you are working with.

The reality of team working is that tasks have to be distributed so that everyone does something, although not everyone has to work on every aspect of a project. For example, one student may go to the learning resources centre to collect information, a resource investigator. Another may plan and organize the team's meetings, a team worker. Yet another will act as facilitator to the meetings, ensuring that each person has a fair hearing, the chairperson. The leadership and drive may come from someone who enjoys giving directions and shaping the project, a shaper. Creative ideas may come from someone who sits and reflects, a plant, while the finisher may oversee the final project details and so forth through the team roles. It is likely that one person may fulfil two or more of these team activities, so it is worthwhile investing time initially identifying what knowledge and skills are available to the team.

AKS in Team Roles

Teams should identify and allocate tasks to the persons best equipped in terms of attitudes, knowledge and skills. So a *chairperson* role requires someone who is enthusiastic, pleasantly assertive and self-confident. It also calls for impartiality and the ability to consider alternative points of view and approaches. The chairperson in a team also needs to have the trust and confidence of other members. The chairperson role is more to do with big picture 'strategic thinking' rather than day-to-day operational management. Conversely, the *company worker* denotes a person who is hard working and conscientious. In general, a company worker will present a high degree of self-control and commitment to achieving team objectives. Teams require coordination and so a *coordinator* displays tolerance and draws people towards cooperation. The coordinating role encourages team members to participate and work together. The person in this role tends to be of a calm disposition and thereby provides a helpful influence on team proceedings. If your team requires momentum, this is likely to come from a *shaper*. The shaper tends to be energetic, enthusiastic, extrovert and task-oriented, and may also be impatient and argumentative, thus provoking discussion and critical evaluation of ideas. The *plant* role is more reflective and creative. In some cases, this creativity can become individualistic and intellectual, although not necessarily a team player. An example of this might be a committed research academic, who may be better at researching new possibilities than managing programmes or communicating with students. The *resource investigator* is willing and capable of seeking out information from outside the team. She or he generally displays good communication and social skills and is capable of working independently on a specific external assignment. The *monitor evaluator* tends to be a logical, rational person, who may appear aloof, even detached, yet is capable of evaluating conflicting ideas dispassionately. The *team workers* are persons who provide the all-important morale boost to teams by being socially sensitive to the needs of others. Team workers tend to be diplomatic and keen to encourage other members to focus on common objectives rather than differences. Finally, if you have ever been in a team where the finish of the project lacked refinement, perhaps the *finisher* role was not adequately provided. This kind of role focuses on attention to detail. It requires a calm, controlled and focused approach to the detailed aspects of the team's work, particularly task completion. The finisher may irritate other team members with constant references to detail.

I'm a Person, Not a Team Role!

We are all much more unique and special than any set of predetermined team roles. One of the values of discussing team role theory, rather than just seeking a 'team label', is that it serves to remind us that the organizational manager needs to *value diversity*.

Each role is different and in its own distinct way provides an important contribution to the team's objectives. The simplest analogy would be that of a sports team; there is no point in having a team of exclusively midfield players or goalkeepers! Yet team members also need to be sufficiently flexible to adopt additional roles where necessary. It is self-defeating to say, 'that's not my role, so I won't help my team'. Team members should also be able to recognize the potential stresses that can arise when significantly different personalities come together.

Respect for diversity is of paramount importance in effective team working. This also cautions employers that the practice of selecting all employees from similar backgrounds and personality profiles may be counterproductive to attaining organizational effectiveness *(diversity in the workforce is discussed in Chapter 6)*. Although similar people may tend to agree with each other, they also tend to have similar weaknesses and are consequently less inclined to challenge assumptions and critically analyse team decisions.

The advantages of teams containing a combination of team roles is that results can be achieved that would be difficult to complete individually. For example, although a shaper might be irritated by the pedantic interjections of a finisher, the former provides momentum to the project, while the latter ensures quality. It is therefore possible that, left to his/her own devices, a shaper might complete the project sooner, but possibly miss a number of errors, while the finisher might delay reasonable progress while s/he reviews and refines every detail of the work.

⬤ GROUPTHINK

The research by Janis (1982) and Aldag and Fuller (1993) postulated that it is possible for teamwork to fail for a number of reasons where members ceased challenging ideas or refused to consider alternatives, hence groupthink. In essence, it may be possible for a team to become too cohesive and insular to internal and external criticism so that no one within the team criticizes decisions. In an extreme form, people can subsume their individuality beneath the constraints and dictates of the team's leadership. More commonly, team members may hold leaders in such respect that they are disinclined to offer alternatives. Additionally, in hierarchical organizations or where employees have low job security, there may be a greater chance of groupthink difficulties because employees may be disinclined to challenge the status quo. Hence, people are less likely to risk asserting themselves in situations where those in authority are more likely to penalize them for doing so. This means that factors such as organizational culture and structure, norms and values can influence how people work in teams, and their willingness to offer alternative solutions to the established viewpoint *(employee relations/job security is discussed in Chapter 4)*.

It is therefore important for HR professionals to view organizations holistically, so that the development of teams is considered in the context of the other forces working on and influencing people's behaviour.

PRACTISING HRM

THE *TITANIC* SCENARIO

It is often helpful to use a situational model to understand a concept such as groupthink in action. For this purpose, I describe groupthink behaviour as the *Titanic* scenario. The famous early twentieth-century ship was regarded as being the most technologically advanced of its day. According to records, the *Titanic* was divided into 16 watertight compartments and 15 transverse bulkheads that extended far above the water line, with watertight doors. These doors could also be closed from the bridge by an electrical switch. This would 'make the vessel practically unsinkable', according to official pronouncements (from Public Records Office documents). The technological excellence of the *Titanic* encouraged heightened confidence in the ship's officers who, in the pursuit of greater prestige and success, thought it expedient to drive this powerful ocean liner at full speed through an area known for icebergs. The telegraph warnings of ice, falling temperatures and weather conditions that would make spotting floating ice difficult did not deter the captain from pursuing a fast maiden voyage time to New York. Indeed, Captain Smith was a highly regarded and experienced officer of the White Star Line. The officers on the bridge at the time of the collision, First Officer Murdock (lost), Fourth Officer Boxhall (survivor), Sixth Officer Moody (lost), and Quartermaster Hitchens at the wheel (survived) (from United States Congressional subcommittee hearing, 1912, p. 1150), did not prevail on their captain to slow down the ship's speed. The deference, or unwillingness, of the other officers to request a reappraisal of the captain's decision to continue the current course and speed indicate that elements of groupthink may have had a role in the disaster.

For today's organizations, the constantly changing environment in which they operate allows little place for polices formed around 'continuing current course and speed'. The *Titanic* is arguably a classic example of where a combination of external and internal factors can lead to a team making the wrong decisions because alternatives are given too little credence.

If an organization/department/team has a record of success and a strong management culture and structure prevails, it can be difficult for people to raise concerns or offer alternative policies. This is not to devalue the importance of strong leadership qualities, but rather to emphasize the value of listening to other viewpoints. While it is difficult to innovate in a risk-adverse environment, risk taking needs to be tempered by counterbalancing evaluation and reflections on the potential downside. In the case of the *Titanic*, the potential gain in prestige of arriving in New York a few hours earlier should have been balanced against the possible losses caused by the possibility of a collision. It is therefore evident that team roles and the diversity which, different people can bring to a team *(diversity is discussed in Chapter 6)* can be a substantial asset to performance. Furthermore, storming (Tuckman, 1965), if conducted constructively, can avail teams of valuable opportunities to consider different approaches.

So it can be said that groupthink becomes more likely if:

1   Members of a team have an illusion of invulnerability.

2   Assessments of performance are overoptimistic.

3   Normal precautions are ignored and a high risk-taking approach is adopted.

4   The team tends to ignore warning signs.

5   Opposition or dissent to the accepted viewpoint is dismissed.

6   Team members who persist in challenging accepted values are regarded as disloyal.

DISCUSSION QUESTIONS

1   What do you understand by the term groupthink?

2   Why do you think teams can become overconfident?

3   What steps can be taken to lessen the occurrences of groupthink?

4   Consider whether a team you are working with may have groupthink tendencies. What can team members do to challenge groupthink complacency?

● EQUALITY

For teams to work effectively, the members have to able to share the responsibilities and benefits of its achievements. A common management mistake is to treat team members as individuals with regard to the allocation of tasks, promotions, rewards and performance management. The consequences are that individuals are less likely to cooperate as a team when they can expect to receive rewards based on their individual contributions. The counterpoint to this is that certain individuals may take teamwork to mean less work. However, providing clear objectives are set from the outset so that each member knows what is expected of him/her, it should be simple to identity social loafers early on and deal with them.

Members of a team should share the rewards and responsibility for the team's successes or failures. For example, the success of contemporary Japanese companies was supported by a realization of the value of cooperative team working (Procter and Mueller, 2000). If members ascribe all successes to themselves and all failures to the other members, a team is likely to become dysfunctional. Thus, competition rather than cooperation ensues, hindering the team's ability to operate effectively. If an organization sets individual performance-related targets, teams are less likely to be as effective because personal aims and ambitions become more of an issue than if the performance targets are set for the whole team *(performance and rewards are discussed in Chapter 10)*.

● SKILLS

Translating Attitudes and Knowledge into Actions

In the first two areas, attitudes and knowledge, you have studied how to approach teamwork and evaluated key areas of contemporary management thinking on teamwork. However, the next step is to convert attitudes and knowledge into practical skills.

Operational managers and HR professionals are more likely to be interested in how theories and models can be translated into useful practices (Currie and Procter, 2003). This pragmatic approach to teamwork applies to all sectors, public, private or not-for-profit. The AKS approach recognizes this, hence the following skills section concentrates on translating the work of the first two stages into action plans for improving team performance.

Motivations for Joining a Team

The manager and HR professional should recognize that people have diverse motivations for asking to join a team. However, as discussed earlier, differences can be a potential advantage, if they can be harnessed to achieving commonly agreed team objectives. Some motivations include:

1 *Empathy with the team's aims*. A sense of affiliation to the team's aspirations. This may be particularly relevant in not-for-profit organizations working with unpaid volunteers.
2 *Interest in the task*. People are often attracted to doing interesting work.
3 *A need for security*. The teamwork may provide a safe environment within an organization.
4 *Increased self-esteem*. Involvement in a successful team project can build individual self-image.
5 *Friendships*. Team workers can enjoy the social integrity of a well-organized team.
6 *Status*. Association with successful team projects enhances individual status. Other people are more likely to invite successful team players to join their projects.

7 *Power.* Involvement with an important or high profile project can enhance personal influence and power in an organization.

8 *Ambition.* A stepping stone to other personal aims.

The initial motivations are probably less important than the subsequent commitment to work towards agreed objectives and helping the team to achieve its potential.

PRACTISING HRM

TEAM BUILDER'S ACTION PLAN

It is constructive to begin with a short appraisal of potential team member's key areas of knowledge, interests and dispositions *(appraisals are discussed in Chapter 8).* It is then helpful to construct teams of diverse personalities, thereby lessening the potential occurrences of groupthink, while appreciating that people with differing perspectives need to be tolerant of each other.

1 Include a range of team roles when selecting team members.

2 Establish and agree team goals and objectives.

3 Agree the level of commitment and performance necessary to achieve the goals and objectives.

4 Agree individual tasks with a timetable.

5 Regularly monitor progress against agreed objectives.

6 Critically evaluate team's overall performance.

7 Team-based rather than individual rewards encourage cohesion.

8 Review final outcomes for areas of improvement.

● MANAGING TEAM DIFFICULTIES

It is quite possible, even likely, that teams will experience some difficulties (Hackman, 1994; Rayner 1996). There are also likely to be differences, both minor or major, whenever a group of people, with their own perspective on events and priorities, come to work together. This can be healthy and helpful, providing that individuals respect each other's contributions and retain their commitment to the overall success of the team project. The following should be considered if difficulties do occur.

1 Review the team builder's plan, above. Have any steps been omitted? For example, a lack of agreement on specific goals early on can lead to difficulties later.

2 Do any members have unresolved conflicts? These will need to be

discussed by the people involved. Individuals may not be the best of friends, but they still have to work on the team project. Try to concentrate on common goals, not differences, whenever practical.

3　Endeavour to resolve problems within the team. Externally imposed solutions may be resented by some of the team members, who will still have to continue working together.

4　Have regular meetings to discuss progress and resolve difficulties as soon as possible. Problems between individuals tend to become more intransigent if left unresolved.

GROUP ACTIVITY

AKS TEAM-WORKING REVIEW

1　Discuss the work on the AKS of teamwork.

2　Consider your answers to the attitudes questionnaire and any implications this might have to how you work in a team.

3　Think about the team roles and reflect on which of these you tend to feel most comfortable with. In general, people are capable of fulfilling more than one role.

4　If you are working in a team already, consider how what you have learnt can improve the way you work together.

5　Form a small group to discuss the place of team working in organizations.

PRACTISING HRM

SHACKLETON

If the idea of being part of a team sometimes appears daunting, imagine what it might be like if your life depended to it! In 1914, an explorer named Shackleton led an expedition bound for the Ross Sea, part of the South Pacific. The weather that year was particularly poor and his ship became stuck in ice and was crushed. Shackleton then led his party across the ice floes, hauling small boats over the ice. When the ice melted, Shackleton got his team to row the boats to safety on Elephant Island. In such difficult conditions, it is not surprising that some of the team expressed different views as to the best course of action. Shackleton listened to advice, but was firm in focusing the team on the common goal of survival.

Elephant Island was too isolated for the explorers to be found quickly, so it was agreed that a small group would leave its relative safety to find help. Shackleton selected a team of six crew to sail to the nearest inhabited island. They travelled 800 miles in a 22ft rowing boat, and successfully navigated their way to the tiny island of South Georgia. The team then had to cross the island's mountains to alert rescuers. After they had reached safety,

Shackleton accompanied another rescue team back to the group on Elephant Island.

It is worth noting that the men on the expedition were not selected from a special elite army regiment of exceptionally physically fit soldiers, but ordinary sailors and explorers. Hence, a lot can be achieved with average people and good teamwork. Writing about the relevance to modern organizations, Kinnes (2001) observed that the adventurer's leadership skills are now studied in business schools. In the film by Channel 4, broadcast on 2 and 3 January 2002, Shackleton is shown leading a team of men in atrocious conditions. In fact, all 28 men survived the expedition. Their survival was arguably, in large measure, due to Shackleton's effective leadership and teamwork.

The party of explorers faced real dangers to life, yet there are significant parallels to organizations. To survive in a difficult and rapidly changing organizational environment, leaders need to be able to adapt their plans and bring out the best in the people, while remaining focused on the longer term objectives so that the organization survives and goes on to greater successes. The most successful teams are therefore not necessarily the ones with all the most able people, but rather those that can work effectively together.

I have provided an imaginary list of 'excuses' that Shackleton's team members might have offered and applied them to contemporary work situations:

- *'The task is too difficult … I'd rather be in the Mediterranean sunshine instead of an ice field.'* Unfortunately, we do not always get the easiest circumstances, so teams have to work together and produce new solutions to resolve difficulties.

- *'Some of the team members aren't as "able" as I am.'* Shackleton did not have the luxury of 'expelling' weaker team members. Instead he worked at getting the best from the people he had available. No one team member can successfully complete all the tasks, so it is important to focus on getting the best performance from each person.

- *'The team members don't always get on well.'* When the task is really important, personal issues should take second place; it can sometimes help to explore what people have in common, rather than dwell on their differences.

In the Shackleton case study, the advantage to the individual team members was obvious, if they worked together effectively, they would survive. The counterargument is that people may become even more dogmatic about what they believe to be right when the teamwork represents something of high personal value. If the team of explorers had not worked together, it is unlikely that any of them would have survived. Augments about who might have been more or less to blame for the team's inadequacies would hardly be relevant.

SEVEN POINTS WE CAN LEARN FROM SHACKLETON'S TEAM MANAGEMENT

1 Express a positive belief in the team's abilities to complete the task successfully.

2 Take time to talk to and encourage small groups and individuals. Support team members who are experiencing difficulties.

3 Encourage members who have become disillusioned with the project's aims or even lost hope that it is achievable.

4 Listen to alternative suggestions. Adapt plans to incorporate good ideas.

5 Take firm action, where necessary, to maintain performance levels.

6 Respond to unfavourable changes in the 'environment' by initiating effective changes.

7 Resolve to maintain commitment to the team's key objectives, even when difficulties arise.

DISCUSSION QUESTIONS

1 What do you most like about working with other people?

2 What do you least like about teamwork?

3 Make a list of the attitudes, knowledge and skills that you think are most useful to successfully working in teams.

4 List the attitudes, knowledge and skills you believe you can bring to a team project.

5 After personal reflection or discussion with someone who knows you well, make a note of at least one area you need to develop in order to improve your performance in a team-working situation. Looking at the case study above, it might be interesting to think about the teamwork problems Shackleton may have faced.

⬤ CHAPTER SUMMARY

The modern organization requires flexibility and cooperation between people who can form and reform into high performance teams. A key HR initiative should be to encourage and assist the development of attitudes, knowledge and skills that enable people to achieve more, by working with others. There are challenges for organizations as well as advantages to team working. The encouragement of diversity within organizations can broaden the range and richness of experience available to team projects and reduce the possibilities for groupthink.

Conversely, people with differing personalities and opinions should follow the team builder's guidelines to avoid unnecessary negative conflict, while recognizing that those differences can be advantageous, if harnessed towards the achievement of common objectives.

The HR professional can promote more effective team working within an organization by recommending initiatives that create an environment where cooperation between colleagues is more likely to flourish. Hence, factors such the distribution of rewards can assist (team-based rewards) or detract (individual performance-related reward) from the teamwork performance. Furthermore, a secure employment environment is likely to be more conducive to collaboration and creativity than organizational environments where people are less secure. Thus, as with other HR activities, teamwork development should be seen as part of an integrated programme of employee developmental initiatives.

● REFERENCES

Aldag, R. J. and Fuller, S. R. (1993) Beyond Fiasco: A Reappraisal of the Group Think Phenomenon and a New Model of Group Decision Processes. *Psychological Bulletin*, **113**.

Belbin, R. M. (1981) *Management Teams: Why They Succeed or Fail*. London: Heinemann.

Belbin, R. M. (1993) *Team Roles at Work*. Butterworth-Heinemann: London.

Belbin, R. M. (2000) *Beyond the Team*. Butterworth-Heinemann: London.

Channel 4, Shackleton. Broadcast on 2 and 3 January 2002.

Covey, S. (1999) *The Seven Habits of Highly Successful People*. London: Simon & Schuster.

Currie, G. and Procter, S. (2003) The Interaction of Human Resource Policies and Practices with the Implementation of Team Working: Evidence from the UK Public Sector. *International Journal of Human Resource Management*, **14**(4).

Davis, J. H. (1992) Some Compelling Intuitions about Group Consensus Decisions, Theoretical Empirical Research and Interpersonal Aggregation Phenomena: Selected Examples 1950–1990. *Organisational Behaviour and Human Decision Processes*, **52**.

Davis, M., Stankov, L. and Roberts, R. D. (1998) Emotional Intelligence: In Search of an Elusive Construct. *Journal of Personality and Social Psychology*, October.

Devine, P. G. (1989) Stereotypes and Prejudice: Their Automatic and Controlled Components. *Journal of Personality and Social Psychology*, **56**.

Earley, P. C. (1989) Social Loafing and Collectivism: A Comparison of the United States and the People's Republic of China. *Administrative Science Quarterly*, **34**.

Erez, M. and Somech, A. (1996) Is Group Productivity Loss The Rule or the Exception? Effects of Culture and Group Based Motivation. *Academy of Management Journal*, **39**.

Fisher, A. (1998) Success Secret: A High Emotional IQ. *Fortune*, 26 October.

Goleman, D. (1995) *Emotional Intelligence*. New York: Bantam Books.

Guzzo, R. A. and Dickson, M. W. (1996) Teams in Organisations: Recent Research on Performance and Effectiveness. *Annual Review of Psychology*, **47**.

Hackman, J. R. (1994) Trip Wires in Designing and Leading Workgroups. *Occupational Psychologist*, **23**.

Hearing before a Subcommittee of the Committee of Commerce, United States Senate (1912) *Titanic* Disaster. Pt 15. *Digest of Testimony*. Washington: Government Printing Officer.

Hilton, J. L. and Von Hippel, W. (1996) Stereotypes. *Annual Review of Psychology*, **47**.

Hoffman, A. B. and Maier, N. R. F. (1961) Quality and Acceptance of Problem Solutions by Members of Homogeneous and Heterogeneous Groups. *Journal of Abnormal and Social Psychology*, **62**.

Huy, Q. N. (1999) Emotional Capability, Emotional Intelligence and Radical Change. *Academy of Management Review*, April.

Janis, I. L. (1982) *GroupThink*. Boston: Houghton Mifflin.

Kinnes, S. (2001) Shackleton. *Sunday Times*, 30 December.

Latane, B., Williams, K. and Harkins, S. (1979) Many Hands Make Light Work: The Causes and Consequences of Social Loafing. *Journal of Personality and Social Psychology*, June.

McGrath, J. E. (1984) *Groups: Interaction and Performance*. New York: Prentice Hall.

Martinez, M. N. (1997) The Smarts that Count. *HR Magazine*, November.

Newell, H. and Scarbrough, H. (2002) *HRM in Context. A Case Study Approach*. Basingstoke: Palgrave Macmillan.

Procter, S. and Mueller, F. (eds) (2000) *Teamworking*. Basingstoke: Macmillan – now Palgrave Macmillan.

Public Records Office. *Titanic: 14th–15th April 1912. The Official Story*.

Rayner, S. R. (1996) Team Traps: What They Are and How to Avoid Them. *National Productivity Review*, Summer.

Revans, R. W. (1982) *The Origins and Growth of Action Learning*. Bromley: Chartwell-Bratt.

Tuckman, B. W. (1965) Development Sequences in Small Groups. *Psychological Bulletin*, **63**.

Tuckman, B. W. and Jensen, M. A. C. (1977) Stages of Small Group Development Revisited. *Group and Organisational Studies*, December.

West, M. (1994) *Effective Teamwork*. Leicester: British Psychological Society.

Vollrath, D. A., Sheppard, B. H., Hinsz, V. B. and Davis, J. H. (1989) Memory Performance by Decision Making Groups and Individuals. *Organisational Behaviour and Human Decision Processes*, **43**.

PERSONAL NOTES ON CHAPTER 3

Notes for seminars

_____

_____

_____

_____

_____

_____

_____

_____

_____

_____

_____

_____

_____

_____

_____

_____

_____

_____

_____

_____

_____

_____

_____

_____

_____

_____

_____

_____

_____

NOTES ON CHAPTER 3 CONTINUED

Notes for revision/reminders

_____
_____
_____
_____
_____
_____
_____
_____
_____
_____
_____
_____
_____
_____
_____
_____
_____
_____
_____
_____
_____
_____
_____
_____
_____
_____
_____
_____
_____
_____
_____

Chapter 4

Employee Relations and the New Psychological Contract

Learning outcomes

After reading and completing the activities in this chapter, you should be able to:

1 Appreciate the context and value of effective employee relation's strategy.

2 Understand the importance of providing HR policies that improve the implementation of change in modern organizations.

3 Critically evaluate organizational change processes.

4 Recognize the role of HR in managing employee relations.

5 Evaluate and apply the sociotechnical model to organizational change processes

6 Apply sector analysis to the application of HR reward management interventions and strategies.

7 Understand the value and place of organizational corporate memory.

8 Compare the old psychological contract with modern alternatives.

9 Evaluate the implications of change and psychological contracts in organizations.

10 Critically evaluate modern psychological contracts and the influence they have on HR policy and practice.

11 Recognize the importance of developing employability to enhance modern employee relations.

INTRODUCTION

People are an organization's most valuable asset. This is what most organizational mission statements usually state or imply. But how true is the assertion in practice? In this chapter you will explore the interrelationships between organizations and people and the expectations each may form of the other – the psychological contract. Employee relations and the management of expectations go much further than a list of policy documents and legislative requirements. Indeed, employee relations are also intertwined with personal and organizational expectations, often unwritten forms of custom and practice. This is part of organizational culture *(organizational culture is discussed in Chapter 2)*. Therefore employee relations encompass the complexities of human organizational interactions, sometimes falsely criticized as the 'touchy feely stuff' that some argue is subordinate to the 'real aims' (financial or other prescribed targets, performance indicators) of the organization. However, effective employee relations can help organizations to achieve their aims and objectives. It is therefore important for anyone who plans to enter a people management role and particularly those who aim to become HR specialists to appreciate the underlying issues regarding employee relations. The role of this chapter is therefore to explore the practical interventions that can be put in motion to encourage better dialogue and understanding of employee relations.

⬤ MANAGING EMPLOYEE RELATIONS

In earlier chapters, you read about the changing patterns of HR. Yet changing the way people do their jobs can have a huge impact on employee relations. Historically, many of the employment disputes, when large numbers of people went on strike, were often as much to do with changes in working patterns as they were to do with pay and conditions. The modern HR specialist should therefore recognize that changes to working patterns need to be introduced with care and consultation. But what is change? The sociotechnical theory (Trist, 1981) helps our understanding of the interdependency of activities and interventions that influence change in organizations. This is important to our understanding of HR because the sociotechnical theory can be applied to focus our attention on the influence that changes in an organization's activities can have on employees. For example, changes to technology will alter the nature of how tasks are conducted, which in turn influences the way people work and the organizational structure (Figure 4.1). In all cases, changes have an impact on people, so employee relations is relevant to any change management initiative.

According to Reid and Barrington (2000, p. 21), the sociotechnical theory proposes that management should learn how to understand and adjust to changing relationships between people, tasks, technology and structure. It is therefore helpful to review the kinds of internal changes which have occurred in an organization and to what extent the appropriate HR initiatives have been put in place to prepare staff to manage the new technology, tasks or structures effectively. For example, if an organization has introduced new technology but neglected to invest sufficiently in staff training, it is less likely to be as effective as planned. It may sound obvious, but people become accustomed to doing their work in a certain way. New technology and new software means that they have to change the way they work and that can be stressful. If the employees were not consulted about the new developments, they may question the value and benefits of the new intervention.

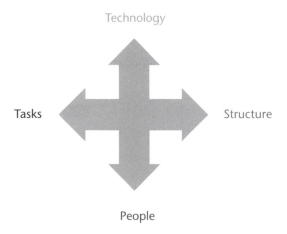

Figure 4.1 The interrelationships of change

EVALUATING CHANGE

Exercise 4.1

1 Select an organization to study where a change in tasks, technology, people or structure has occurred or is about to occur.

2 Apply the sociotechnical model to highlight areas that have changed or could change in the near future.

3 Evaluate what changes may arise in the way people work.

4 Discuss what HR managers can do to help workers to adapt to the changes.

 DOWNSIZING

The term *downsizing* has come to be recognized as the use of staff redundancies to improve short-term profitability by reducing the payroll costs. When downsizing is used to remove whole groups of employees, such as junior or middle managers, it is referred to as *delayering,* because whole layers of the organization's structure are removed. The use of downsizing or delayering staff numbers as a means of reducing costs has been criticized by the eminent management commentator Henry Mintzberg. During a radio interview by Peter Day (1996), he predicted that a lot of delayering may turn out to be another form of what happened in years past when organizations got rid of research and development (R&D), thereby saving money in the short term but jeopardizing the organization's future. The reason for this is that downsizing can have a debilitating impact on employee relations and motivation. In the modern workplace, where fewer people are often required to cope with larger workloads, the lack of long-term secure employment also places more stress on organizational cohesion. This is simply because commitment is a two-way street. When staff see their organization routinely expelling its unwanted employees, the survivors are less likely to give their whole unconditional commitment to the service and wellbeing of that organization (see Figure 4.2).

Reduce staffing levels   **Reduce short-term costs**   **Reduce morale**   **Reduce performance**

Figure 4.2 Interrelationships of downsizing and performance

The HR professional should endeavour to be in a position to advise colleagues of where and why tensions and difficulties in employee relations may arise, and how to avert unnecessary employee relation conflicts wherever possible. This kind of proactive approach to HR can also avoid unnecessary conflicts and sometimes costly litigation. Furthermore, the law tends to be a reactive intervention, which seeks to redress employment abuses by punitive sanctions. It is more constructive for organizations to address employee relations proactively, which are in any case likely to be more complex than simple adherence to legal requirements. Effective employee relations should therefore aim to create a work environment where issues can be discussed and resolved long before individuals feel the need to turn to their lawyers. The experience I gained in management, consultancy projects and working in a voluntary role as a chair of governors has encouraged my belief in constructive engagement for employee relations over adversarial management and litigation. Internal and external forces are constantly altering the modern workplace, so that what employees do and how they do it can change very quickly. For the most part, there is consensus about the importance of training as a means of helping organizations in the development of sustainable performance based on their human resources (Aragón-Sánchez et al., 2003).

As discussed earlier, in the sociotechnical theory, changes in one part of the organization influence other areas. Therefore downsizing is likely to have a broader impact, affecting more staff than just those who are directly involved. Additionally, any change is likely to be perceived differently by the various interested parties. To use a simple example, a recommendation to replace a tea person with a vending machine might seem to be a cost-effective change to the office services manager; to the tea person it means unemployment, and an act of ingratitude after many years service; and to the office staff an unwelcome reduction of employee benefits. It may even transpire that when the redundancy package for the tea person and the complaints from staff are considered, the change to a vending machine may not be such a good idea after all. This should not be taken to mean that changes of service provision should be avoided, but rather to indicate that even a relatively simple change process requires consultation and discussion with all the interested parties.

A change in working patterns and especially job security also has implications for the levels of trust between management and staff. Legge (1995, p. 90) observed that apart from sacking inadequate individuals, HRM provided a new rhetoric to obfuscate mass redundancies with euphemistic language including 'out-placing', 'downsizing', 'rightsizing', 'headcount reduction' and even 'workforce reprofiling'. Of more concern is that the act of sacking employees for short-term cost reduction was even represented as a positive act. In some cases, the unwanted employees may be paid a sufficiently large redundancy payment to soften the impact of being unemployed. Alternatively, if the job market is buoyant, people with strong transferable attitudes, knowledge and skills may actually welcome a redundancy package because they have the employability to secure employment elsewhere. However, even in the most auspicious circumstances, downsizing is likely to change the sense of commitment and trust among those employees who survive the redundancies. Research by Sahdev (2003), in large organizations where downsizing has taken place, found evidence to indicate that downsizing can result in many negative outcomes including the loss of motivation, skills, learning and innovation. This then leads us to the next employee relations' issue, survivor syndrome.

● SURVIVOR SYNDROME

The effect of those employees who survive a round of redundancies may be to react by withdrawing their emotional commitment. Newell and Lloyd (2002, p. 179) observed that in terms of organizational effectiveness and efficiency, research suggests that job insecurity can lead to employees having lower levels of commitment, being less willing to accept change, more resentful of imposed change and more secretive and competitive. These kinds of responses are the antithesis of the cooperative team-working culture needed to sustain an organization in the medium to longer term.

During the 1990s, my work in management consultancy drew me to question the veracity of downsizing and the resultant job insecurity. Commenting on the issue of job insecurity in *The Times* (Nieto, 1992, p. 23) I observed that the message conveyed to those who survived downsizing programmes was more likely to be negative than to inspire people to greater effort, resulting in less commitment, confidence and creativity and more self-protection. The reality is that insecure employees are likely to become risk-averse and consequently the organization may suffer from diminished innovation and employee initiative. Although downsizing may provide organizations with a temporary boost to profits, in that the largest share of costs are employee salaries, this can soon be overtaken by the loss of morale and the competitive survivalist culture which such a short-term management strategy is likely to cultivate. Furthermore, if the prevailing organizational culture becomes less optimistic, some employees are likely to seek jobs elsewhere. Ironically, it is probably the most capable people with the best CVs who are most likely to be able to find new jobs quickly. These are the very people whose attitudes, knowledge and skills would be most valuable to an organization seeking to bring about successful changes in its management practices.

The HR professional recognizes that when one person is made redundant someone else will have to do the work of their absent colleague. The loss of experienced workers can also be detrimental to the organization's stakeholder networks. People work with people and established relationships can be difficult to replace. The real cost of downsizing can continue long after the displaced employees have gone.

PRACTISING HRM

RESEARCHING ORGANIZATIONAL PERFORMANCE AFTER DOWNSIZING

Activity A is for HR students conducting primary research projects.

Activity B is for students conducting secondary research work such as case studies and library searches.

ACTIVITY A

If you are researching an organization for your course, consider asking employees about whether there have been significant redundancies in the organization and their attitudes towards the organization and its management. You may find it helpful to supplement your own primary research questions with the questionnaire below.

Listed below are a series of statements that represent possible feelings that individuals might have about the company or organization for which they work. With respect to your own feelings about the particular organization for which you are now working, please indicate the degree to your agreement or disagreement with each statement by circling one of the alternatives below each statement.

1	Strongly disagree	5	Slightly agree
2	Moderately disagree	6	Moderately agree
3	Slightly disagree	7	Strongly agree
4	Neither agree nor disagree		

1   I am willing to make a lot of effort beyond that normally expected in order to help this organization to be successful.
   1   2   3   4   5   6   7

2   I am positive about this organization in the conversations I have with people.
   1   2   3   4   5   6   7

3   I feel very little loyalty to this organization.
   1   2   3   4   5   6   7

4 I would accept almost any type of job assignment in order to keep working for this organization.

| 1 | 2 | 3 | 4 | 5 | 6 | 7 |

5 I find that my values (what is important to me) and the organization's values are very similar.

| 1 | 2 | 3 | 4 | 5 | 6 | 7 |

6 I am proud to tell people that I am employed (or work as a volunteer) with this organization.

| 1 | 2 | 3 | 4 | 5 | 6 | 7 |

7 I could just as well be working for a different organization as long as the kinds of tasks and pay were similar.

| 1 | 2 | 3 | 4 | 5 | 6 | 7 |

8 This organization really inspires and encourages me to do my very best work.

| 1 | 2 | 3 | 4 | 5 | 6 | 7 |

9 It would take very little change in my present circumstances to cause me to leave this organization.

| 1 | 2 | 3 | 4 | 5 | 6 | 7 |

10 I am very happy that I chose this organization to work over others I was considering joining.

| 1 | 2 | 3 | 4 | 5 | 6 | 7 |

11 There's not much to be gained by staying with this organization for too long.

| 1 | 2 | 3 | 4 | 5 | 6 | 7 |

12 I often find it difficult to agree with this organization's policies on important matters relating to employees.

| 1 | 2 | 3 | 4 | 5 | 6 | 7 |

13 I really care about the fate of this organization.

| 1 | 2 | 3 | 4 | 5 | 6 | 7 |

ACTIVITY B

Alternatively, if you choose to conduct secondary research, consider selecting from the quality press reports on your learning resources centre information base an organization where a significant downsizing programme has taken place in the past few years. Then look for more recent reports about the organization's financial and employee relations performance.

DISCUSSION QUESTIONS

1 From answering the questionnaire, do you sense that your, or your respon-

dents' employment experiences following downsizing are mostly positive, neutral or negative? For example, if your answers to questions 1–13
are 7, 7, 1, 1, 7, 7, 1, 7, 1, 7, 1, 1 and 7, then you or the respondent are
likely to be very satisfied at work because all the most positive answers were
selected. Think about any questions you awarded a 4 and consider whether
you actually feel more or less positive about that particular aspect of work.
Further qualitative (face-to-face interviews or group discussions) work
could be necessary to establish more in-depth personal preferences *(see
Chapter 11 for project and research methodology)*.

2 Has the organization reaped large benefits, remained the same or deteriorated since the redundancies? Discuss the significance of what you find
with regard to the possible implications for future HR policy.

⬬ CORPORATE MEMORY

| People join organization | Learn and add value | Leave | New people relearn | Leave |

Figure 4.3 Corporate memory loss

As with many aspects of HR, it can be difficult to quantify the exact consequences of downsizing mature staff or encouraging the early retirement of experienced employees. For example, employees will have formed networks of
contacts, both internal and external, and those interpersonal relationships can
help the smooth operation of an organization (see Figure 4.3). It is also difficult
to quantify experience, except that it can provide a corporate memory of what
has been tried before and thereby prevent costly repetitions of corporate history.
The government minister for the Department for Work and Pensions in Britain,
Ian McCartney has commented that:

> We don't want to do as we did in the eighties, when we wiped out the corporate
> memory of organizations by sacking workers who were over 50. We lost a lot more
> than just individuals. People have ambition, and deserve recognition and respect –
> that's true of whatever age they are. I don't think younger and older workers have
> different attitudes to work. All workers want to be recognized by the company. (Cited
> in seniorsnetwork.co.uk, 2002)

A balanced workforce profile representing a broad diversity of people may also
help an organization to relate more effectively to its own diverse stakeholders.
It is also likely to provide a richer range of ideas and approaches to organiza-

tional life *(employee diversity is discussed in Chapter 6)*. Although the British government has (at the time of writing) no plans to introduce legislation banning age discrimination against older workers, it is interesting to note that the US has had legislation in place for some time. The European Union (EU) is currently considering possible legislation, so this may alter the legal position in Britain if and when the legislation is passed.

The corporate memory also underpins the stories and history of the organizations. These inform new employees of what fate is likely to await them. In much the same way as certain product brands have a reputation for reliability, so organizations can build a reputation as being a reliable employer. This leads us to psychological contracts.

WHAT IS A PSYCHOLOGICAL CONTRACT?

By law, organizations are required to provide a written, explicit employment contract. However, the psychological contract is different. It is the unwritten implicit expectations. Employees recognize those activities that are explicitly required from them and those which are implicitly expected. In return, employees receive explicit pay and benefits and implicit rewards that they have come to expect through custom and practice. These additional unwritten rewards may nevertheless form a major factor in determining employees' perceptions of an organization. The psychological contract focuses on the exchange of perceived promises and commitments. In a research paper reporting on a survey of 1306 senior HR managers, Guest and Conway (2002) explored the management of the psychological contract. Three distinct and relevant aspects of organizational communication were identified, concerned with the initial induction of new employees, regular updates on what the organization was doing and longer term strategic information. The use of communication enabled managers to be, and be seen to be, more transparent in their employee relations so that psychological contracts were breached less frequently.

The Old Psychological Contract

Traditional twentieth-century bureaucracies usually provided a predictable and secure environment, whereby employees were implicitly assured of continuous employment. The psychological transaction was a safe and secure job in exchange for less pay than might be obtainable in more risk-taking, entrepreneurial organizations. The traditional bureaucracy essentially set out a rule book approach to employee rights and responsibilities, leaving less room for ambiguity and insecurity of employment tenure. This security, as described by Weber, represented a transaction whereby entrance into an office is considered to be an acceptance of an obligation to serve the management in return for a secure existence (Eisenstadt, 1968, p. 69). It is therefore arguable that the old bureaucracies were more able to promulgate compliance, where the expectation was for long-term secure employment in return for loyal compliance to the bureaucracy's idiosyncrasies. Thus, within such an employment environment, it was tacitly accepted that providing employees kept within the bureaucracy's rules, they might reasonably expect long-term secure employment. This was a key element of what was latterly described as the 'old psychological contract'.

By the late twentieth century, the rate of change in the business environment, and increasing globalization, precipitated a faster rate of change that began to challenge the structure of both large public and private bureaucracies in which protocol and consistency tended to be exalted over more risky innovations in policies, products and services. In their persistent commitment to accountability and regulatory conformity, the old bureaucracies tended to stifle the kind of new risk taking that modern organizations needed to progress and respond quickly to their external environment. During the early part of the twentieth century, this was less important because there was less competition and product choice. For example, in the early days of car manufacturing, the Ford motor company did not feel the need to give customers a choice of colour, every car was black! The vastly expanded consumer choices of the modern world means that organizations have to respond rapidly to changing demands, and bureaucratic forms of hierarchy are less able to adapt to such a dynamic environment where a new product can be out of date in months rather than years.

These changes in the business environment have had consequences for the employment security enjoyed within traditional bureaucracies. It would, however, be a mistake to regard the old psychological contract as a barrier to progress. Indeed, the security of knowing employment is not likely to be snatched away can actually stimulate innovations because employees can take a longer term perspective on project developments. Conversely, an insecure worker may be less likely to take chances and challenge the status quo if his/her tenure of employment is precarious.

The New Psychological Contract

The idea of a job for life with one employer, which underpinned the stability of mid-twentieth-century's bureaucracies, was certainly being eroded by the 1980s and 90s. Hence, these unwritten agreements – psychological contracts – have changed. In the past, employees expected long-term secure employment in return for long-term loyalty. However, the nature of work and organizations has changed so that some organizations need to employ fewer core workers, and more people on the periphery of the organization in short-term contracts.

The contemporary alternative to a job for life may be employability, yet this represents the antithesis of the old psychological contract. The new psychological contract encourages a relationship that implicitly recognizes its short- and medium-term duration so that commitments by both parties may be adjusted accordingly. The opportunity facing modern HR professionals is therefore how to create a working environment where innovation flourishes and employee relations are at a level where their commitment can contribute to the longer term success and performance of the organization. To counterbalance any mistrust that may overshadow such working relationships, Bagshaw (1997) argues for a climate of 'mutual investment', with 'congruence' between the goals of employees and employer. However, Nieto (2003) found that it may be more diffi-cult to attain corporate congruence in modern diversified organizations, where the needs, interests and aspirations of workers, full time, part time, short contract or consultancy, to list but a few, are unlikely to be similar. Additionally, the diver-sified socioeconomic groupings within the workforce add greater complexity to these internal differences. Instead, it may be that the only real 'job for life' is ensuring that, if this job ends, the employee has sufficiently updated attitudes, knowledge and skills to secure new employment. Hence, employability may be the new security.

This state of a person's sense of employment security can influence the way he/she behaves in an organization. Research by Hofstede (1994, p. 125) found that, where insecurity occurs, which he labelled 'uncertainty avoidance', there can be a suppression of deviant ideas and behaviour and a resistance to innovation. Hence people who are on short contacts, or permanent staff who feel in danger of redundancy, are less likely to take creative chances and more likely to be compliant. Some organizations may, of course, consider compliance to be desirable. However, while a comfortable groupthink culture might be easier to manage, it does not necessarily produce the kinds of new ideas and energy associated with more inno-vative situations. One of the dangers of avoiding new ideas and initiatives is that an organization can be quickly left behind in a competitive market environment. Although this appears to be more relevant to commercial companies, it is also rele-vant to public sector service providers and the not-for-profit sector. Thus, the university that is not innovative in the courses it delivers may not recruit as many students as it would like, while the charity that fails to present its case to the public may not receive the donations it seeks. In any sector, an organization can only be as good as the people it employs and the motivation, innovation and commitment to performance that they collectively produce.

Psychological Commitment

Employee commitment is arguably of key importance to managers interested in developing successful organizations. The extent to which employees express commitment towards their organization is also likely to be relevant to long-term performance or profitability, depending on whether the organization is a not-for-profit, public sector or commercial company. According to Womack (2002), net profit margins rose in businesses where employees described themselves as committed to their organizations. Conversely, organizations with less committed employees saw net profit margins fall. Other key factors were employees' views of the development opportunities they were offered and whether or not they were empowered to do their work effectively. However, a whole range of other factors could have influenced the rises and falls of under 3 per cent. Correlation does not prove causation. Nevertheless, it is fairly reason-able to propose that a committed workforce is more likely to improve produc-tivity than a disaffected one. Therefore development opportunities, which improve employability and empowerment, giving people a real say over the way they do their jobs, can produce a more effective modern psychological contract.

In research conducted with 400 public sector employees, the Audit Commission in Britain found employees complaining of being overwhelmed by paper work and bureaucracy and being set too many targets (Womack, 2002). This resulted in employees leaving the public sector for the more lucrative, and often less micromanaged, for-profit organizations. If people become discouraged and lose their sense of trust and commitment to their organization, it may be difficult to change the negative organizational culture. Hence, managers who adopt an excessive emphasis on tasks, processes and targets may actually be demotivating their people and reducing productivity and performance. Even employability cannot guarantee that a person will get a new job and therefore be able to manage their personal expenses. In the end, people regularly have bills to pay so the security of continuous employment is a large plus for long-term stability.

Psychological Contracts and Change

The area of change management has major implications for employee relations. It is for this reason that many business schools include the implications of change and change management as part of their graduate and postgraduate courses. Although the subject area may be ubiquitous to business management courses, it is difficult to do the subject justice within the constraints of a lecture programme that has to cover a broad spectrum of topics. However, within specialist HR courses, it should be possible to engage in a more in-depth study of the implications of change and psychological contracts for employee relations.

Research, reviewed by Kessler in *People Management* (2002, p. 54), offered some interesting insights into psychological contracts. Drawing on survey evidence from 200 in-house and 100 outsourced employees working for the same airline on call centre work but with different employment conditions, the study found that outsourced employees were less loyal and more likely to quit. It was suggested that these differences might be traced to the less secure and more uncertain nature of outsourced employment, as well as to feelings among these employees that they were treated less equitably.

● MANAGING ORGANIZATIONAL CHANGE

In the world of work, each person will have their own aspirations and responsibilities, so change, any change, in their work situation can potentially enhance or threaten pre-existing expectations. Even an apparently positive change can be perceived as threatening if it conflicts with what employees believe to be in their best interests. Human beings are social in nature, so any disturbance to interpersonal routines and behaviours will elicit a reaction. Therefore what managers tend to encounter are two distinct factors: the first is the change process itself and the second is the reactions of employees to that change. The management of a change programme can be scheduled and project managed. However, employee reactions to any given change to their working patterns are less predictable. Kurt Lewin's (1951) theory, illustrated in Figure 4.4, postulated that there would be forces in favour of change and forces against. Change programme managers may elect to overcome resistance by insisting on the implementation of their plans. However, such a strategy is likely to increase resentment and resistance. At best, enforced change programmes produce reluctant compliance, which is far removed from the kind of committed cooperation that is more likely to occur if employees' ideas have been included through active consultations.

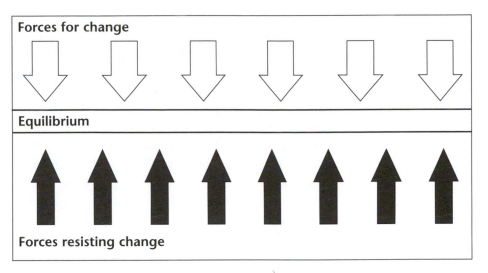

Figure 4.4 Forces for and against change

Three-stage Change Theory

Lewin also provided a three-stage model for implementing a change process. In the first stage, which he described as *unfreezing,* it is necessary to move the organization away from its current posture. Once employees recognized and accepted the need for change, the second stage, changing, can begin. This is followed by a third stage where the change is established in the organization and *refreezing* takes place.

The elegant simplicity of Lewin's theory requires further critical evaluation if it is to be helpful to HR professionals. To begin with, it is worth reflecting on how easy it might be to obtain the agreement of employees regarding a change process. Even if the recommended changes are beneficial, there is no guarantee that people will accept them. This means that the 'unfreezing' stage can take more time than might be originally planned. Next, the change process itself has to be carefully managed, with some positive incentives built into the process. It also helps if there are some identifiable interim benefits (easy wins) during the change process to stimulate positive support.

Finally, the term 'refreezing' needs to be critically evaluated within a twenty-first-century context. Whilst the mid-twentieth-century Weberian bureaucracies may have been able to 'refreeze' after change, the modern analogy might be more like 'slush'. Where changes in technology, employees, tasks and structure – the sociotechnical theory – are more frequent, the notion of 'refreezing' may not be an appropriate metaphor for modern change progression.

Exercise 4.2

EVALUATING CHANGE: WHY DO PEOPLE RESIST CHANGE?

Consider the following scenarios:

1 You are working on a team project with four other students, who are working very well. The tutor asks if you would like to change teams to gain experience of a wider range of team-working situations. Your course grades are based on the teamwork. Do you accept the change or decline?

2 The courses you selected for your final year were to be taught by a HR lecturer you have known since you began your course. The lecturer has been very encouraging and awarded you some first-class grades. Just before the semester begins, you hear that the lecturer has been given responsibility for a new postgraduate programme and a new tutor has been appointed to deliver your courses. How do you feel about the change?

3 The college you attend has just built a new, state-of-the-art business school on the other side of town. You live near the old college and most of your friends' courses will remain in the old building. You are told that as of the next semester all your courses will be taught in the new business school. No one asked your opinion about this change. What is your reaction?

4 You have just completed the first stage of an undergraduate degree with a college that receives its degree awards from a prestigious university. Your degree would therefore be from that university. However, your college has just decided to apply for independent status and renames itself by the local town where it is situated. How do you think the change might impact on the status of your degree?

Once you have answered and discussed the questions above, it should be evident that even changes which provide new learning opportunities or better working facilities (the new business school) may be resisted. A lowering of perceived status, the new college degree, may also demotivate people. It is therefore reasonable to expect that changes that will bring unemployment and insecurity to an organization are even more likely to meet with strong resistance.

It is arguable that twenty-first-century organizations should be prepared to continually develop, whereby refreezing is no longer appropriate. According to Bratton and Gold (1999, p. 274) technology, global markets, customer expectations and competition all contribute to support the view that learning is the only strategy to cope with a continuously changing environment. Similarly, Arnold et al. (1998, p. 493) found that change is an open-ended and continuous process of adaptation to conditions and circumstances. It may be argued, therefore, that modern HR should accept that change is a continuous process, or, as argued by Woodall and Winstanley (1998, p. 151), the learning organization may turn out to be a race without end, an aspiration rather than a final destination.

EMPLOYABILITY: TRANSFER OF EARNINGS AND ECONOMIC RENT

The move away from stable bureaucratic organizations to more flexible employment patterns has also transferred more of the responsibility for career development onto the employee. In the traditional bureaucracies, the employee could reasonably expect to remain in employment for many years. The more flexible psychological contract emphasizes employability over employment security. Essentially, it is the responsibility of the employee to ensure that they have the necessary attitudes, knowledge and skills to obtain a new job. In such circumstances, it is understandable for employees to respond by focusing on their own best interests before those of their places of work. This does not infer that an employee will not work conscientiously, but it must be more difficult to sustain long-term commitment where such loyalty is not reciprocated. The best security employees have is their ability to get another job, hence the term 'employability'. According to Begg et al. (2000, p. 189), earnings are the minimum payments required to induce someone to do a job. Economic rent is the extra payment a person receives over and above the minimum earnings required. By applying this economic model to employee relations, it is possible to calculate the difference between what a person earns and their value in the marketplace. In some cases, the person may be undervalued, alternatively, a person may not be able to command a comparable salary elsewhere. Clearly, the employee who is able to obtain alternative employment at a similar or higher rate of pay than his or her current job is in a stronger negotiating position than someone who cannot. Employability is essential to securing continuous employment, so investments in personal development are very worthwhile. When an employee leaves to take another position with more pay and greater responsibilities, it is helpful to question whether the former line manager had underestimated her/his potential.

People Do Not Leave Organizations, They Leave People

The term *organization* can isolate the human resources researcher from the obvious fact that organizations are no more or less than a set of individuals, each with their own hopes, dreams and aspirations. While senior managers may attempt to set policies in place, it is obviously the staff who are responsible for implementing them. Hence, it is not so much creating new initiatives and policies, which are the key to progress, but the interpersonal skills to gain the cooperation and support of the staff. However, some managers can find the breadth of human diversity difficult to accommodate, particularly in an organization where the management team seeks to rigidly control and direct its workforce. In his book on interpersonal skills, Hayes (1991, p. 169) observed two contrasting views of organizational interaction. In the first model, organizations are seen as well-integrated entities where everybody works harmoniously together in order to achieve a set of shared goals, whereas in the second model, organizations are seen as political organisms where individuals and groups attempt to influence each other in the pursuit of self-interest *(see Chapter 12 regarding personal communi-*

cations and priorities). A former director of a major retail company told me that at one point the senior management team was so embroiled in political infighting that the company was actually being managed by the middle managers. According to Thompson and McHugh (2002, p. 180), organizations can produce defensive behaviours and attitudes, which emphasize positional advantage and competitive struggles between generational, gender and professional groups to impress the corporate hierarchy. The problems associated with poor employee relations are therefore costly in terms of reduced performance and in the potential loss of capable people who choose to leave the organization. In political infighting, there are likely to be more losers than winners and even those who triumph are less likely to have retained the respect and personal commitment of their colleagues.

⬤ CHAPTER SUMMARY

It is important to recognize that HR initiatives and strategies are influenced by external and internal factors. The work in this chapter has provided relevant theoretical models, with which HR students can conduct research into organizations. Furthermore, the chapter has evaluated the influence on changing patterns of work on psychological contracts. The successful progress of a change initiative is dependent on the establishment and maintenance of sound employee relations and interpersonal relationships. HR professionals should also recognize that change processes are likely to encounter resistance and that it is more effective to consult with staff and gain cooperation than to impose changes. The new psychological contract of employment has replaced much of the security of tenure formerly retained by older bureaucracies. Modern workers should therefore invest in personal development to enrich their long-term employability.

⬤ REFERENCES

Aragón-Sánchez, A., Barba-Aragón, I. and Sanz-Valle, R. (2003) Effects of Training on Business Results. *International Journal of Human Resource Management*, August.

Arnold, J., Cooper, C. L. and Roberson, I. T. (1998) *Work Psychology* (3rd edn). Harlow: Prentice Hall.

Bagshaw, M. (1997) Employability – Creating a Contract of Mutual Investment. *Industrial and Commercial Training*, **29**(6).

Begg. D., Fischer, S. and Dornbusch, R. (2000) *Economics*. London: McGraw-Hill.

Bratton, J. and Gold, J. (1999) *Human Resource Management. Theory and Practice*. Basingstoke: Macmillan – now Palgrave Macmillan.

Day, P. (1996) Attacking the Organisation. BBC Radio 4. 8, 15, 22 and 29 May.

Eisenstadt, S. N. (ed.) (1968) *Max Weber on Charisma and Institution Building*. Chicago: University of Chicago Press.

Guest, D. E. and Conway, N. (2002) Communicating the Psychological Contract: An Employer Perspective. *Human Resource Management Journal*, April.

Hayes, J. (1991) *Interpersonal Skills: Goal Directed Behaviour at Work*. London: Routledge.

Hofstede, G. (1994) *Cultures and Organisations. Software of the Mind*. London: HarperCollins.

Kessler, I. (2002) Contracting Out and Market-mediated Employment Arrangements: Outsourcing Call Centre Work, *People Management*, 7 February.

Legge, K. (1995) *Human Resource Management. Rhetoric's and Realities*. Basingstoke: Macmillan – now Palgrave Macmillan.

Lewin, K. (1951) *Field Theory in Social Science*. New York: Harper & Row.

Newell, H. and Lloyd, C. (2002) Pharmco: Organisation Restructuring and Job Insecurity, in Newell, H. and Scarbrough, H. (eds) *HRM in Context. A Case Study Approach*. Basingstoke: Palgrave – now Palgrave Macmillan.

Nieto, M. L. (1992) Macho Talk at BET. *The Times*, 16 June.

Nieto, M. L. (2003) The Development of Life Work Balance Initiatives Designed for Managerial Workers. *Business Ethics: A European Review*, **12**(3).

Reid, A. and Barrington, H. (2000) *Training Interventions. Promoting Learning Opportunities* (6th edn). Wimbledon: CIPD.

Sahdev, K. (2003) Survivors' Reactions to Downsizing: The Importance of Contextual Factors. *Human Resource Management Journal*, **13**(4).

Thompson, P. and McHugh, D. (2002) *Work Organisations* (3rd edn). Basingstoke: Palgrave – now Palgrave Macmillan.

Trist, E. (1981) *The Evolution of Socio-Technical Systems*. Ontario Ministry of Labour. Ontario Quality of Working Life Centre.

Woodall, J. and Winstanley, D. (1998) *Management Development. Strategy and Practice*. Oxford: Blackwell.

Womack, S. (2002) British Workers 'Have Low Levels of Commitment To Employers'. *Daily Telegraph*, 3 September.

PERSONAL NOTES ON CHAPTER 4

Notes for seminars

PERSONAL NOTES ON CHAPTER 4

Notes for revision/reminders

Chapter 5

Managing Time and Life–Work Balance

Learning outcomes

After reading and completing the activities in this chapter, you should be able to:

1 Understand the attitudes, knowledge and skills required for successful time management.

2 Develop the skills to self-manage project schedules.

3 Critically evaluate the role of HR in improving employee life–work balance.

4 Interpret the situation-specific applications of the life–work balance in modern organizational HR strategies.

5 Recognize the role of HR professionals in recommending improved working practices that enhance performance and reduce unnecessarily stressful workloads.

6 Undertake and interpret a self-evaluation on time management.

7 Critically evaluate an organization's performance in time management and life–work balance policies and practices.

8 Present a case (individually or as a team exercise) of the benefits to organizational performance, of a healthier employee life work balance HR strategy.

● INTRODUCTION

In this chapter you will evaluate where HR initiatives can improve performance by actively enabling employee life–work balance and reducing counterproductive workloads.

Most of us would agree that we work to live, not live to work, so life comes first, and then work. With an increasingly diversified workforce (full time, part time, single parent, childless, mature returnees, contractors, self-employed, married, single), what each employee wants from work may be very different *(managing and motivating a diverse workforce is discussed in Chapter 6)*. This means that HR policies and practices should reflect those different needs. In the modern workplace, it has become increasingly evident that one size does not fit all, so there can be no one best practice for everybody.

The current discussion of life–work balance through both academic research and media interest has moved modern HR thinking on from the late twentieth-century debate centred on just the workplace. The modern HR approach recognizes that work is just one aspect of a person's life. A person is much more than an employee number. In harmony with the integrated HR philosophy of this textbook, the nature and design of life–work balance are person- and situation-specific initiatives.

Finding a Life–work Balance

For life and work to be more balanced suggests that, in some situations, the amount of weighting given to work may require some adjustment. The responsibility for selecting the key tasks and focusing appropriate resources towards them is another key HR strategic planning management skill. Towards that aim it could be worthwhile for managers to have a reminder on their computer, desk and diary which asks:

Desk Note: To which key area of this organization's
work does this task contribute value?

If the answer to the question is 'not sure', priorities should be reviewed.

People invest a lot of their time at work so it is makes sense for them to enjoy what they do and feel that it is useful and valued. My experience of working with organizations to develop time management plans is that a review of priorities is a valuable first step towards improvements in time management, performance and life–work balance. So, this chapter combines a review of the role of HR in workload planning, time management and life–work balance with practical initiatives that HR (and other management students) can apply to their workplaces and HR study projects.

Working Smarter, Not Harder

The level of process input does not necessarily have a positive correlation with successful outcomes. Can too much concentration on procedures detract from successful performance? It's an interesting question. The research evidence also indicates that working harder may not necessarily mean more productivity.

How do different countries compare in their productivity? In the National Institute's quarterly review, whose findings were discussed by Smith (2002) in the *Sunday Times*, research comparisons were made regarding the productivity levels in different nations. The review found evidence to indicate that Britain is over-working and underperforming. The overall results for comparative productivity found that, on an hourly basis, America is 26 per cent ahead, France 24 per cent and Germany 11 per cent. In the private sector, which is supposed, by some, to be one of Britain's strengths, the gap is even bigger. On an hourly basis, German workers in the market economy are 19 per cent more productive, those in France 22 per cent and those in America 39 per cent (Smith, 2002). Hence, the overall British performance compared poorly and is all the more disappointing when set in the context that British employees work longer hours than any of their major European competitors. Doubtless, there are some highly efficient private companies, public services and not-for-profits, while there are others that are less efficient. However, the research did indicate the need to reflect on working practices and for organizations to conduct further research into their levels of efficiency and performance. From a research perspective, it is also arguable that large quantitative studies across different countries may not be able to address situation-specific organizational issues. Notwithstanding debates on research validity, the National Institute's findings do raise some interesting questions. The employment trends in Europe, the USA, Asia and Australia suggest changes in employment demographics, with the workforce becoming older and more diversity of employment modes outside the traditional 9–5 of an office or factory. Can people work hard, but not be more productive? Does life–work balance influence workplace performance? It is for the HR student to critically evaluate the place and purpose of time management and life–work balance in an increasingly diversified workplace.

A TRIUMPH OF PROCEDURES OVER OUTPUT?

In the British public sector, a common criticism is that successive governments have interfered by prescribing how work should be carried out. Smith and Cracknell (2002) noted that the King's Fund, (a health think tank) attacked the torrent of pledges, policy documents, regulations, advice and guidance that has issued from the Department of Health, saying such interventions waste time and resources on the front line, demoralizing doctors and nurses. At the centre of such interference is a fundamental error in what sound management planning is about, namely to set out the overall objectives. The exact detail of how objectives are implemented should be the responsibility of local operational managers. An overtly prescriptive management regime demands that people work to rule, rather than do what is right; the assumption being that the 'rules' will represent the best approach to work in every situation. This kind of bureaucratic style of management planning can lead to a culture of compliance to processes, which may become a substitute for a commitment to results achievement. Alternatively, if targets are agreed via consultation and local managers have responsibility for implementation, they become responsible for what is actually achieved. This kind of approach is a shift of both emphasis and responsibility from process monitoring towards goal achievement.

If life–work balance is relevant, arguably it is just as important in public services and the voluntary sector, as it is to commercial organizations. For example, the principal of a successful secondary school told me that their process procedures and child performance tests were currently producing data that was unheard of in times past; although, on reflection, she also regretted the loss of the broader social and personal educational provision of times past. When she had entered the profession, her colleagues often voluntarily gave their time in the evenings and weekends organizing social and recreational activities for the children. The governmental officials who imposed the time-consuming data collection requirements were unlikely to have had such an outcome in mind; but more data versus personal and social development was in reality a choice that busy professionals had to make, given the increased demands upon their time.

The aim of HR managers in an organization, whether public or private sector, should be to enhance that organization's performance (Boselie et al., 2003), although the aims and objectives may differ from one sector to another. However, essentially the question is simply, what is the purpose of the organization? For example, does a school really want more paper work, more tests, more prescriptive micromanagement, or more time to invest in helping young people? The answer may appear obvious, but it is so easy for organizations to become embroiled in procedures and lose the focus of their key objectives. Excessive procedural control may be well intentioned, but can turn into a triumph of procedures over content. It is therefore imperative that HR and other senior managers discuss what the key objectives are so that management plans can be arranged to make it easier for people to achieve them. The objectives should also reflect the views of operational managers who, when all is said and done, will be responsible for turning the plans into real results. Once the overall objectives are established, the local operational decisions should be left to those most capable of assessing local needs, the managers and staff directly responsible for the local tasks. Managerial systems that overly depend on top-down directives tend to become too prescriptive and lack operational flexibility, which is essential in the modern environment where responding to changes needs requires flexibility.

HRM IN ACTION

TOO MUCH HOMEWORK

The British education system has probably sustained as much if not more enforced regulation and intervention than many other services. These reforms have arguably been in progress for many decades, but what has the increased employee 'homework' actually achieved?

INFORMATION FROM THE INTERNET – 7 JANUARY 2003

A survey of 70,000 teachers in England has found that one-third expect to quit the profession within five years because of the heavy workload, unruly pupils and government interference. More than half who took part in the survey, conducted for the *Guardian* and the General Teaching Council (GTC), said morale was worse than when they began teaching. Whist the government has addressed recruitment problems, there wouldn't have a recruitment problem if more teachers were retained, according to Carol Adams, chief executive of the GTC, an independent, professional body for teachers in England. Adams also noted that teachers had told her organization that if they could have a reduction of unnecessary paper work and some time away from the classroom to refresh and update their subject knowledge, they would stay in the profession. In the survey, teachers were asked to name three demotivating factors. Some 56 per cent picked 'workload including unnecessary paper work', 35 percent pointed to the 'target-driven culture' and 31 percent cited poor pupil behaviour and discipline. Of the third who expected to leave teaching in five years' time, just over half planned to retire, with the rest hoping to find new jobs. The GTC calculated that 28,500 teachers would leave within five years for a job outside education, almost as many as were recruited last year.

DISCUSSION QUESTIONS

1 Do you prefer to have some flexibility as to how you do your work or be closely monitored?

2 Discuss why excessive bureaucratic control and paper work can lead to demotivation.

3 How might management and employees better organize policies and procedures to remove unnecessary red tape (non-productive paper work)?

4 Do you think micromanagement (excessive management control and procedures) is a symptom of low trust? Discuss.

● MANAGING EXPECTATIONS

When you take on a new responsibility, think about what you do that can be removed. The reality of life–work balance is that the more time used on one activity, the less there is available for others. So we all have to make choices as to where we invest our time. Hence, finding an HR professional who can do everything might be a rather challenging recruitment assignment. It could be compared with trying to find an accountant who is also a salesperson and a qualified lawyer. The internal HR team needs to discuss, with management colleagues, those areas which they can deliver and those where some external input is required.

Imagine for a moment what the 'job description' for a hypothetical HR 'superperson' might include. (I would be the first to admit that what follows is not a full and definitive list of everything that HR professionals can be called on to do.)

However, let's try to think of what might be in the list, and perhaps you can add some other items.

The HR superperson can:

1   Assist the senior management team to plan the strategic direction of the organization.
2   Research the organization's environment and prepare industry comparisons on rewards and motivation to design policies which establish and retain good staff morale.
3   Design and then communicate HR policies to all sections of the organization.
4   Design staff evaluation procedures and appraisals so that training and other human relations requirements can be identified.
5   Provide, or facilitate via external providers, staff performance training so that people gain and retain leading-edge technical and managerial knowledge and skills, thereby enhancing organizational performance.
6   Study and identify staffing requirements so that the organization can be proactive in planning recruitment and retention strategies.
7   Design recruitment and selection campaigns that attract high-quality applicants and present the organization in a favourable manner to both internal and external stakeholders.
8   Interview and recommend potential new employees, liaising with managers to ensure a good team and organizational fit.
9   Provide up-to-the-minute employee relations legal advice on every issue from recruitment to dismissal and anything in between.
10 And so on and on. The HR person should also complete all the above tasks in an exemplary manner and without contravening EU working time directives!

(Nieto, 2001)

The reality is that no one is going to be able to achieve all the tasks listed above. So what are the priorities? What can be more suitably outsourced to a specialist firm or consultant? Which tasks should be deleted? One of the ways to identify areas of priority is through auditing time and work activities. Have a look at the exercise below and complete the time management audit.

PRACTISING HRM

WORK EFFICIENCY AUDIT

It is useful to analyse the key activities of a job role and examine what is essential, what is desirable and what is unnecessary to job performance. It is then possible to evaluate which activities tend to add little or even detract from efficient performance. If you are or have been employed, either full or part time in paid or voluntary work, it is helpful to review the work you did or are doing and create an efficiency audit.

List the tasks you were required to complete in your job under one of the three headings below. Once you have made the lists, estimate how much time was dedicated to each item.

Cumulate your allocations to a total of 100 per cent of working time.

ESSENTIAL TO JOB PERFORMANCE

Item	Percentage of time
	Subtotal of percentage

DESIRABLE TO JOB PERFORMANCE

Item	Percentage of time
	Subtotal of percentage

UNNECESSARY TO JOB PERFORMANCE

Item	Percentage of time
	Subtotal of percentage

Totals of time invested:

Essential to job performance _____ %

Desirable to job performance _____ %

Unnecessary to job performance _____ %

This exercise is also of practical value to HR specialists who are asked to appraise performance and design job descriptions, because it provides specific job information and encourages employee reflection on how and where they are investing their time. Team leaders and others responsible for directing workloads can also reflect on the findings and then discuss where the priorities should be. It is important to recognize that for every new activity, document, report, set of compliance requirements, inspection, observation, team review, presentation and accountability that people are asked to work on, they will be able to give less time to other tasks. The only part of a person's itinerary that is not flexible are the number of working hours available. Hence, the removal of unnecessary work can significantly enhance performance by releasing valuable time to invest in value-adding activities. The process of agreeing such priorities is best affected through consultation and mutual agreement. In most cases, the person who is actually doing the job will be best placed to identify the essential and desirable tasks.

FOCUSING ON VALUE-ADDING TASKS

Some of the demotivating factors highlighted by teachers in the earlier HRM in Action are likely to be shared with other professionals and organizations. For example, the waste of time caused by 'workload including unnecessary paper work' and 'target-driven culture' is a recurrent criticism of organizational management. These terms are in themselves open to different interpretations, because one person's unnecessary paper work may be another's essential data. However, irrespective of the merits or demerits of a particular bureaucratic procedure, it is more likely to be counterproductive if a significant number of employees regard it as unnecessary and are thereby demotivated in their work. Furthermore, procedures that are too rigid prevent diversity and flexible working *(managing and motivating a diverse workforce is discussed in Chapter 6)*. During research interviews for this book, senior managers interviewed from a variety of organizations expressed the view that most tasks may be successfully completed through a number of methods. Research by Bélanger et al. (2003) also indicated that it is more helpful to encourage a greater degree of employee self-regulation. It may be that people tend to work more effectively when they feel they have some control over how they complete their assigned tasks, instead of being compelled to comply with rigid internal or external compliance regulations.

Conversely, there are some areas such as health and safety, where rigid compliance to regulations is both compulsory and sensible. This would also clearly apply to all legislation on employment rights and responsibilities. For example, compliance with laws on racial, gender, religious, and disability discrimination is necessarily prescriptive and managers must comply in their employment policies. Furthermore, multinational organizations may also require practices to be implemented globally, and therefore, age discrimination, which is illegal in the USA, but not in the UK, may be regulated by some international organizations. The balance that needs to be established is between stakeholder protection and overbureaucratization.

DELEGATION: AUTHORITY WITH RESPONSIBILITY

If the HR associate who has been given responsibly for a particular recruitment project does not also have the authority to make decisions, they are in the frustrating situation of having to continually seek permission for every new initiative. In such circumstances, it is really the HR manager who has to make all the operational decisions, and who will consequently soon become overworked, stressed and inefficient, because they are actually trying to do their team's work for them.

Managers need be able to delegate *authority* with the *responsibility* for projects. The manager's ability and confidence to delegate work should flow from a considered appraisal of his/her key tasks and time management allocation. Once the task is delegated, the authority to manage the work should also be delegated as well as the responsibility for the outcomes. Managers monitor progress, but if this becomes a micromanagement of processes, then, in reality, managers have still retained the authority for the work. True empowerment of employees requires the delegation of both the responsibility and the authority to get on with the job (Rothstein, 1995). Trust and confidence in the attitudes, knowledge and skills of employees are key to successful delegation. Without trust, the manager will find it very difficult to allow his/her staff to get on with the work independently.

HRM IN ACTION

INTERVIEW WITH A SENIOR EXECUTIVE (1)

One of the privileges of academic research is to interview senior managers and ask questions about what they really think happens in their organizational environment. The short extract that follows is taken from transcripts of an interview I conducted with the chairperson of a leading consultancy.

Question: Modern research has found that Britain has longer working hours than any other European country, but our productivity per working person is lower. How would you comment on that as a senior executive of a large organization?

Answer: I think partly we don't invest in people [in Britain], although people will pay lip service to these situations. As a consequence, they don't invest in training or rewarding people as long-term assets. Short term, people are used and that actually affects people's deep down motivation so ultimately their productivity suffers.

On the management side there's a macho thing, regardless of whether its productive or not, people seem to feel they've got to put the hours in and be go-getters. I say to my people, if you find yourself working long hours all the time there are only two reasons why that happens. Either we have given you too much and you need more staff, or you cannot hold your job down. Now in your position you are expected to do whatever hours are necessary, but if it turns out that you are here till seven or eight o'clock every night, then you and I need to have a chat because maybe you need training or I need to give you some additional resources. There may be times when it is necessary [to work long hours] but if its ongoing then there's a problem. Its not good for people, and what's not good for them is ultimately not good for us [the organization]. It may be a short-term gain but has long-term consequences. The last point on the hours issue is that you cannot expect people to work ten hours a day and expect to get peak performance out of them. They end up doing the same amount of work but over a longer period.

DISCUSSION QUESTIONS

1 Why do you think managers 'pay lip service' to investing in people?

2 What connection does the interviewee make between short-term management and employee motivation?

3 Explain what you understand by 'a macho thing' regarding long working hours.

4 What kind of training might help a person who is regularly working excessively long hours?

5 Why do you think people who work long hours are likely to be less productive than those who manage their time more efficiently?

6 In what ways might a working environment that is 'not good for people' also be detrimental to the organization?

HRM IN ACTION

INTERVIEW WITH A SENIOR EXECUTIVE (2)

This was a particularly exciting study because the company, for which I had provided consultancy advice, had agreed to allow HR students access to conduct research for their team project. The company then decided to extend the research and had invited me in to discuss some of the HR issues. The initial study conducted by the HR students had indicated some dissatisfaction with HR and the company was following up the research with a larger qualitative staff survey. Initially the research focused on the European offices and would be extended worldwide within a few weeks of the interview below. The respondents requested that neither their names nor that of the organization should be identified, so details are marked **X** *(the protection of confidentiality for research respondents is discussed in Chapter 11).*

> **Question:** Please tell me about your survey results.
>
> **Answer:** We surveyed **X** hundreds of people in Europe electronically. There was quite a lot of commonality in the feedback. Training and development was the number one item.
>
> **Question:** Why do you think that was the case?
>
> **Answer:** We are a highly scientific organization so there is a thirst for knowledge and education from an academic perspective. The perceptions were that there's a desert in terms of training and development. But when you look at what training took place, it's quite interesting that there was a lot of training, except it wasn't marketed particularly well, it wasn't targeted.

Communications was another item, when we have an organization over wide geography, we sometimes have difficulties managing the boundaries between people.

Then the other issue was life–work balance, which was interesting because it's a very generic heading. What does that mean? What can we do to tangibly impact the substance of that topic but also the perception of employees?

When you look around the place, a couple of things mitigate against this topic [life–work balance] because of [the nature of] our work. Increasingly we are studying the output of what we do, rather than the service our employees provide in time and materials. So we have moved from an input to an outcomes emphasis.

Question: How does this link into the life–work balance?

Answer: When you are monitoring employees' hours, the opportunities to flex their time is limited. But the outcomes-based scenario lends itself to greater flexibility. If we sell what we are putting into the system, that's limited flexibility, limited individual discretion; if you sell the output, then you can flex that which you put in. If what we are measured on is a set of deliverables, then our client shouldn't care how we do that. So what we try to do is to drill down and say, what can we tangibly, practically do to address this life–work balance issue? We know there are environmental pressures for employees to perceive themselves in different roles.

Thirty years ago it wasn't so much of an issue even though people worked longer hours on the whole and with less holidays. It was an entirely different socioeconomic environment. Typically there was only one working spouse and now there are two. All these factors are put in front of our employees' daily: Are you working too many hours; as a working dad, do you get enough time with your children? All these things are really hitting working families. This isn't going to go away. We cannot have another survey where this [life–work balance] goes unaddressed.

We need to get to a point where we can do maybe three or four things tangibly, pan-European, where we can demonstrate that we are taking the feedback seriously and that the result of those actions enables employees to address their work–life balance issues. We have **X** people in this organization but we have immature processes for dealing with people. We haven't invested in the people processes and what our population is crying out for is some investment in the people processes so that they can access training and development, they can apply some sense of personal self to their work – whether that's taking some time off to play tennis or whether it's looking after or being with their child and that the company will foster either of those activities. Now the young 20 year old with no kids who works long hours can take some leave time off in a quieter period and that can mean going off to play tennis [tennis was given as an example of any social or recreational activity]. However, school holidays are predetermined so you don't have the flexibility when kids are off school or sick. I think in the family situation we need enabling policies because events [for employees with families] are outside their own discretion.

In terms of retention, it is good [for employees] to know that when they get into the situation it's available to them. Its like sickness, with our permanent health plan, I suppose about 0.2 per cent of our population ever comes into contact with it, but when they do they're glad that its there and then there's a knock-on impact so that people know if they get into that situation its available.

Question: What do you really value as an organization? What is it you want from people and what is it you think they want from you?

Answer: The valuing question is important because what we need to understand is beneath this generic heading of life–work balance. What does it mean for you? What would you like the company to do to facilitate more of or less of what is enabling you to feel your life is in balance? This could mean staff may like to have a concierge service available to take care of things such as family gifts, dry cleaning, car servicing.

DISCUSSION QUESTIONS

1   What does life–work balance mean to you? Is it possible that it can mean different things depending on a person's particular situation?

2   The executive discussed a shift from monitoring inputs (hours worked, work plans submitted,) to outputs (what teams achieved). What are the advantages and disadvantages of focusing on inputs or outputs?

3   If employees with family responsibilities can take time off, when necessary, is it also reasonable to encourage people without such responsibilities to take time to enjoy recreational activities?

4   How do you think a family friendly policy, or healthcare plan can be 'good' for retaining staff even if they don't have families or have a long-term illness?

5   To what extent, if at all, should an organization take responsibility for helping employees to manage their lives outside the workplace, with services such as childcare, and taking 'care of things such as family gifts, dry cleaning, car servicing'?

6　What are the advantages to an organization of having employees who feel that their 'life is in balance'?

7　What kinds of employment 'benefits' are or would be important in your choice of where to work?

● LIFE–WORK BALANCE: A PARADIGM SHIFT FOR HR?

To everything there is a season, and a time to every purpose. (Eccles. 3:1)

Modern HR professionals are likely to encounter a variety of issues arising from life–work balance, which differ according to the personal circumstances of employees, workers or volunteers. The conventional practices of reward management, which concentrated on financial remuneration and hierarchically structured benefits systems, may lack sufficient flexibility to sustain employee motivation and retention in a modern diversified workplace. It is possible that a paradigm shift in HRM philosophy may be required, away from employee relations, with its tendency to paternalism, towards a more empowering employee partnership (Nieto, 2003).

Both my research as an academic and working with organizations have encouraged me to think that the HR responses to issues of life–work balance vary considerably according to institutional sectors, individual organizational policies and historical practices. In comparing organizations from different sectors, I found that there were also variations in the definitions of life–work balance. For the research work, respondents included chief executives, who were seeking to develop a strategy, HR people grappling with how to translate strategic aspirations into coherent policies and the recipient employees. For example, in one in-company survey the majority of the respondents indicated that career development was of key importance. It may be that the demise of the 'job for life' culture in large organizations has heightened employee concerns about future employability when and if they feel it is time to move to a new employer. Modern workers recognized that a key aspect of life–work balance is the security of being able to gain access to a new job, thereby accepting the reality that a life without gainful employment is a luxury most of us cannot afford. Life certainly can become unbalanced if a person is unemployed, with all the stress and concern that unemployment can create for individuals and their partners.

The paternalistic, bureaucratic model of personnel management was biased towards inflexible policies and procedures regarding working patterns and rewards (Warren, 1999). Perhaps, but by no means always, the employee had more security of tenure, but at the expense of flexibility. This was possibly most typified by the 'clock in, clock out' approach to managing employee working practices, whereby the employees reconfigure their lives around the organization's procedures. In reality, the employees had little or no input or choice as to the terms of their contract. All employees, at least those on a given rung of a hierarchy, were offered the same terms and conditions of employment. This kind of structure is still common in twenty-first-century organizations. While such people management practices may be justified philosophically for their egalitarianism and pragmatically for procedural simplicity, difficulties can arise when human needs do not always fit neatly within mechanistic models of working.

The modern HR strategist has to address the differing needs of employees, and so design policies that offer a range of flexible benefits without becoming overly prescriptive. Indeed, according to O' Neill (2002), excessive control can be counterproductive to encouraging trust and improved performance. Different groups of employees also have differing needs; for example Tremblay (2002) found specific life–work issues for women in the teleworking environment. In Burke's research, the role of life–work balance in achieving positive emotional and physical wellbeing was found to be relevant to both men (Burke, 2000) and women (Burke, 2001).

The diversity of employee interests is supported in recently published research papers and media interest. Coleman (2000) reported on a survey of 2000 managers, with reference to family friendly policies, where the respondents indicated that both parents and childless employees needed more time to develop aspects of their lives outside the workplace. However, counterbalancing any unanimous tendency to legislate or prescribe universal solutions, Marrin (2003) highlighted research from the Institute of Directors, conducted between 1998 and 2001, which found that organizations were less inclined to employ women in their reproductive years. The conflicts of parenthood and managing a successful career are also discussed by Hinsliff (2002). This is clearly a contentious area for debate. In this respect, HR-trained professionals can and should exert a positive influence on recruitment policies and management practices, and emphasize the legal and moral arguments against any form of discrimination. Senior managers should also reflect on the value-adding attributes of a diversified workforce (*diversity is discussed in Chapter 6*).

It is unhelpful to restrict the discussion of life–work balance with overtly constrained definitions that do not reflect the reality or diversity in modern organizations. The term 'organization' tends to allude to twentieth-century models of working. However, this may not be completely relevant to loose form, flexible gatherings of knowledge and skills such as mixed combinations of contractors, consultants, researchers, full-time and part-time workers and self-employed people, who might all be cooperating on a specific project, then move on to other assignments.

Modern technology can mean that people have the opportunity to work from home. This means that the boundaries of work and personal life may become blurred for homeworkers, who could be working longer hours than they might within the more socially interactive environment of an office. Again, it is also entirely possible that outputs in some areas of work are improved by the synergy of social interaction, while others benefit from periods of uninterrupted concentration. There are balances to be explored in work too.

PRACTISING HRM

LIFE–WORK BALANCE QUESTIONNAIRE

The questionnaire below can be used to research life–work balance issues. Answer the questions as a seminar activity and discuss the results in a study group. If you are conducting primary research for a course, seek permission to circulate the questionnaire to employees in the organization.

1	Strongly disagree	**5**	Slightly agree
2	Moderately disagree	**6**	Moderately agree
3	Slightly disagree	**7**	Strongly agree
4	Neither agree nor disagree		

1 Life–work balance issues are important to this organization.

    1   **2**   **3**   **4**   **5**   **6**   **7**

2 I am happy with the balance of work and personal interests I have been able to achieve as an employee of this organization.

    1   **2**   **3**   **4**   **5**   **6**   **7**

3 My career is the most important aspect of my life.

    1   **2**   **3**   **4**   **5**   **6**   **7**

4 I would prefer to have more time to follow interests outside the workplace.

    1   **2**   **3**   **4**   **5**   **6**   **7**

5 I am prepared to work long hours when it is necessary to get a job completed.

    1   **2**   **3**   **4**   **5**   **6**   **7**

6 I regularly work longer hours than specified in my contract.

    1   **2**   **3**   **4**   **5**   **6**   **7**

7 Work pressures have contributed to creating difficulties in my personal life.

    1   **2**   **3**   **4**   **5**   **6**   **7**

8 I think my colleagues are happy with their life–work balance.

    1   **2**   **3**   **4**   **5**   **6**   **7**

9   My manager takes an active interest in helping me to achieve a sustainable life–work balance.

    1   2   3   4   5   6   7

10 My immediate manager has been supportive of my participation in
personal and career development activities.

    1   2   3   4   5   6   7

11 The three main benefits of the life–work balance policies of this organization are:

(i)

(ii)

(iii)

12 The three recommendations I would like to offer for the further development of the work–life balance are:

(i)

(ii)

(iii)

From answering the questionnaire, do you sense that your, or your respondents' life–work balance experiences are mostly positive, neutral or negative?
For example, if your answers to the questions 1–10 are 7, 7, 1, 1, 7, 1, 1, 7,
7 and 7, then you or the respondent are likely to be very satisfied with
life–work balance, because all the most positive answers were selected. Think
about any questions you awarded a 4 and consider whether you actually feel
more or less positive about that particular aspect of the life–work balance.
Further qualitative (face-to-face interviews or group discussions) work could
be necessary to establish personal life–work balance preferences *(see Chapter
11 for project and research methodology)*.

⬤ HOW INDISPENSABLE ARE WE?

One of the difficulties that some workers have in addressing life–work balance
issues, be they paid or voluntary staff, is that they believe their contribution is
so valuable that no one else could really do the work. Sometimes insecurity can
lead to 'presentism', where employees believe that being in the workplace for
long hours will raise their status with management and colleagues. This kind of
behaviour can soon deteriorate into a negative circle, where the longer hours

lead to more tiredness and stress which in turn reduce work efficiency and output. Whatever the emotional attachments, all of us will be replaced by someone else in the workplace eventually, through staff movement or ultimately retirement. It is more relevant to aim to have been a good steward of the responsibilities and hand them on to others in good order, than to hang on to a role because of imagined 'indispensability'.

Following my own advice on taking breaks from work, I recently joined a health club and on a particularly clear winter's morning I decided to go swimming for half an hour. The pool was empty and as still as a millpond. As I swam, the low winter light from the windows streamed into the water, creating an iridescent wave in front of me. It was really quite remarkable to see how much movement just one swimmer could produce in a pool. However, almost as soon as I got out of the water it returned to its still, flat position. The waves I had created by swimming were soon gone and this may be the case when we leave an organization too! Is it possible that individuals can overestimate the lasting influence they have on an organization? Perhaps no individual is, nor indeed ought to be, indispensable and should aim to enable others to take over as and where necessary. Conversely, the influence we can have on other people may be more enduring. Everyone remembers a teacher who helped them and perhaps that can be true of nurturing, empowering managers too. A complementary comment, a word of support or a friendly gesture can make a real difference to someone's day at work. As HR professionals we should endeavour to be a positive factor in the organization.

Be part of the solution, rather than part of the problem.

PRESENTING THE CASE FOR LIFE–WORK BALANCE

GROUP ACTIVITY

Design a short presentation (either as a team or individually) on the benefits to organizational performance of a healthier employee life–work balance HR strategy *(for presentation skills see Chapter 12)*.

CHAPTER SUMMARY

The starting point for the development of more effective time management and the achievement of sustainable life–work balance is an evaluation of current work priorities and tasks. By concentrating on the key tasks that add value to the organization's performance, people can be encouraged to invest their working time more effectively. This approach requires management to recognize the investment value of employees enjoying a healthier balance between their work responsibilities and personal lives. Unfortunately, this can sometimes be a challenge in itself because organizations are subjected and subject themselves to unnecessary procedures, which may add little or no value to the progress of their work. It is therefore important that HR professionals conduct audits into areas such as life–work balance and engage in constructive dialogue with colleagues with reference to the selection of work priorities.

Each person also has a responsibility to both themselves and their colleagues to recognize that it is not feasible to add more and more tasks to a job role without deleting or delegating some other elements of the work to others. HR professionals can therefore assist colleagues in re-evaluating work schedules and encourage them to direct time, energy and resources towards the most important tasks. In an increasingly diversified workplace, managers should consider the differing life–work balance requirements of their people. The one-size-fits-all approach to benefits and work conditions is less flexible and therefore obstructive to people contributing effectively in the modern work-place environment.

● REFERENCES

Bélanger J., Edwards, P. K. and Wright, M. (2003) Commitment at Work and Independence from Management: A Study of Advanced Teamwork, *Work and Occupations*, **30**(2).

Boselie, P., Paauwe, J. and Richardson, R. (2003) Human Resource Management, Institutionalization and Organizational Performance: A Comparison of Hospitals, Hotels and Local Government. *International Journal of Human Resource Management*, **14**(8).

Burke, R. (2000) Do Managerial Men Benefit from Organisational Values Supporting Work-Personal Life Balance? *Women In Management Review*, **15**(2).

Burke, R. (2001) Organisational Values, Work Experiences and Satisfactions among Managerial and Professional Women, *Journal of Management Development*, **20**(4).

Coleman, J. (2000) Childless Managers Need Work/Life Balance Too. *European Business Review*, **12**(6).

Hinsliff, G. (2002) High Flying Women who Refuse Family Juggling Act. *Sunday Observer*, 22 December.

Marrin, M. (2003) Flexitime for All Can Make a Women's Career Go Snap. *Sunday Times*, 5 January.

Nieto, M. L. (2001) Do Managers Need HR? *Network*, (4).

Nieto, M. L. (2003) The Development of Life–Work Balance Initiatives Designed for Managerial Workers. *Business Ethics: A European Review*, **12**(3).

O' Neill, O. (2002) Called to Account. *Reith Lecture*. BBC Radio 4, 17 April.

Rothstein, L. R. (1995) The Empowerment Effort That Came Undone. *Harvard Business Review*, January–February.

Smith, D. (2002) Productivity Sent Packing. *Sunday Times*, 3 February.

Smith, D. and Cracknell, D. (2002) The Gamble That Will Cost Us All. *Sunday Times,* 14 April.

Tremblay, D. G. (2002) Balancing Work and Family With Telework? *Organisational Issues and The Challenges For Women and Managers*, **17**(3).

Warren, R. C. (1999) Against Paternalism in Human Resource Management. *Business Ethics: A European Review*, **8**(1).

PERSONAL NOTES ON CHAPTER 5

Notes for seminars

_____

_____

_____

_____

_____

_____

_____

_____

Notes for revision/reminders

_____

_____

_____

_____

_____

_____

_____

_____

_____

_____

_____

_____

_____

_____

_____

_____

_____

_____

_____

_____

_____

Chapter 6

Motivating a Diversified Workforce

Learning outcomes

After reading and completing the activities in this chapter, you should be able to:

1 Identify the trends that have led to changes in the nature and needs of the workforce.

2 Appreciate the value of encouraging organizational diversity.

3 Critically evaluate strategies for motivating different groups such as contract workers, part-timers and mature employees.

4 Recognize the different motivational requirements of voluntary and public sector workers.

5 Examine the implications of demographic age profile trends.

6 Recognize the connections between the value of employee motivations and organizational performance.

7 Critically evaluate the role of HR-trained professionals in encouraging the development of more effective employee motivation initiatives.

8 Present a case (individual or group presentation) on possible approaches to motivating a diversified workforce.

● INTRODUCTION

In this chapter you will learn how HR is changing to adapt to the new trends and working patterns that are collectively described as a diversified workplace. You will also learn how to recognize organizational diversity and the implications it has for HR initiatives. This includes developing strategies for motivating diverse worker groups and appreciating their differing requirements. This is particularly relevant for the public and voluntary sector, where models designed for the for-profit environment may not be appropriate. One of the lessons I have learnt from leading seminars and lecturing for postgraduate programmes is that one of the most effective ways students learn about working with diversity is through practical exercises and self-evaluation. So in this chapter there are activities to encourage you to think about practical initiatives to enhance diversity. In reality no amount of theorizing or legislation can *make* people more tolerant. You have to think about diversity and practise it in your daily life.

How can HR professionals help to motivate a diversified workforce? Although it may be much easier to design prescriptive systems than to create open frameworks in which people have choice, there is a growing recognition in both academic study and among HR practitioners that more flexible approaches are required. According to an editorial review on modern HR by Wright and Brewster (2003) following the Learning from Diversity global conference held in Barcelona in June 2001, there appears to be an emerging consensus that the pursuit of best practice may be too restrictive. Instead the articles in the *International Journal of Human Resource Management*, December 2003, offered the alternative scenario whereby in HRM no one size fits all. Indeed, as each person has his/her own preferences and personal circumstances, so the best practice, one-size-fits-all approach can fail to reflect the needs of an increasingly diversified workforce.

Instead of the old paradigm of HR, which focused predominantly on full-time employees, new HR models need to be able to serve a more diverse set of workers. This includes full time part time, women returners, lately retired returners, portfolio workers, consultants, contractors and students working their way through university (Figure 6.1). This list is not exhaustive, yet it highlights that modern organizations are likely to contain people with a broad range of personal motivations, preoccupations and widely differing concerns and preferences.

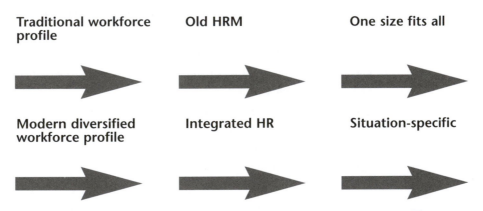

Figure 6.1 Evolution of diversified HR

Motivating a diversified organization is not going to be easy. Yet the benefits of a diversified workforce are the diversity of ideas and approaches that it brings to the organization (see Caulkin, 2001). Before reading further, have a look at Chapter 3 again and consider the opportunities and challenges created by teams and team working. Any student who was worked on a team project will have a story to tell on what went right or wrong. The workplace is a continuous team work project, so why is a diversified workforce challenging to motivate? In common with teamwork projects, it is important to establish a number of agreed aims and objectives at the earliest stage of a work project. Unless the people doing the work are committed to working together, their efforts are likely to be dissipated.

● INTEGRATED HR AND DIVERSITY

The breadth of modern organizational requirements makes it unrealistic for any one person to be an expert in all management areas. Indeed, within the complex global organizational environment, it has become increasingly unrealistic for even a team of HR people to be experts on everything from national and international cultures, employment laws, recruitment, appraisals, induction, employee cross-cultural team working, HR strategic planning and so forth. Instead, the HR professional can be more involved in developing strategies and then selecting outside expertise to assist her/him where appropriate, thereby diversifying HR input and provision. Hence, the role of HR professionals is, or should be, refocused towards providing recommendations and strategic support to colleagues and facilitating rather than providing services. For example, Friday and Friday (2003, pp. 863–80) have asserted that managing diversity begins by valuing diversity and them systematically incorporating policies into the organization in a strategically planned process. (Also see Nkomo, 1992).

In academia, we also ought to acknowledge that research operates on a different timescale to operational HR and so there can be time lags between the development of new management HR approaches and organizational implementation. For example, a manager often has to make a decision about how to best motivate a colleague in a moment, while a researcher has time to reflect on the outcomes of organizational interpersonal behaviour, often with the benefit of research materials from a set of interviews and questionnaires.

Notwithstanding the gap between theoretical discourse and practice, it would be sensible for modern HR students to recognize the value of addressing issues of diversity in the planning and development of managerial interventions.

The business student should also be aware that it is necessary to be empathetic to the broader needs of the organization, rather than just one job role, whether HR, IT, finance, marketing or law. This modern approach was recognized by Wind and Main (1998, p. 270) who observed that there are no business issues that are resolved in just one professional discipline. The challenges we meet in the workplace are more usually cross-functional. Therefore HR people can try to facilitate interdisciplinary cooperation across their organization, bringing people together to cooperate on cross-functional projects. In practice, this can also mean introducing external experts to facilitate elements of HR development programmes or enrolling staff on appropriate masters programmes run by universities. The advantage of these approaches is that the employee is exposed to a diverse range of other people, from different cultures and organizations in the private, public and charity sectors. The learning experience is further enhanced if the courses include teamworking assignments directed at real organizational issues. This kind of exposure to experiential and new theoretical approaches can be the genesis for new innovative management. It also encourages business schools to work closely with organizations, a symbiotic relationship benefiting everyone involved.

● DIVERSITY: CAN WE BE DIFFERENT AND EQUAL?

Everyone in an organization should be treated with equal respect and enjoy equal opportunities. Are all men, women (able bodied, disabled), cultures, races and religions equal in all organizations? I doubt it very much, but we are all responsible for improving the workplace environment. HR professionals have a responsibility to encourage tolerance and understanding of diversity (see Thomas and Thomas, 1990; Cox and Blake, 1991; Hall and Parker, 1993; Kossek and Zonia, 1993; Kopp, 1994; Williams and Bauer, 1994; Dawson et al., 1995; Farnham, 1997). However, overall, the research evidence indicates that the needs, ambitions and aspirations of a diverse workforce are unlikely to respond to one-size-fits-all HR strategies. For example, a family friendly policy could serve the needs of those men and women who have families, but not necessarily independent career women and men. If a person can have an afternoon off work for childcare, can childless workers have time off too? The temporary student employee is likely to have different commitments to those of a full-time employee. How can the organization gain the best performance from people with diversely differing needs and interests? Probably not by treating them all as if they were the same person. Instead, flexible pay and benefits packages can be designed to fit the person, rather than the person having to fit the package.

A director of a major telecommunications company BT noted that her organization had put in place policies to cater for the needs of its diversified employee requirements. Designing HR strategies for managing diversity whilst ensuring equal opportunities and meeting statutory requirements can be challenging (see Peasaud, 2003; Maxwell, 2004). However, there really should not be a contradiction between offering equality of opportunities while providing a flexible working environment.

The developments in computer and communication technology have increased the opportunities for greater employment flexibility. Handy (1995, p. 42) predicted that the office of the future would be more like a clubhouse for meeting people. This type of working environment could mean that some people could work partly or entirely from home, This could open opportunities for a greater diversity of employment, full time, part time, disabled, flexible hours, childcare, elderly relative care, than might be achievable in a traditional office environment. In these new working arrangements, motivation is a key issue because being separated from the stimulus of colleagues and regular social interaction could be demotivating. Thus homeworkers should have a place, real or virtual, to discuss their work and interact with colleagues.

PRACTISING HRM

WORKING GIRLS

It is interesting to research and study theoretical models, but seeing changing working patterns in real life can sometimes be a thought-provoking surprise.

In the situation on which this Practising HRM is based, I was lecturing on a CIPD course in London. The student cohort for the seminar consisted of 50 women, with ages ranging from early twenties to mid-forties and one male student. This was, admittedly, somewhat unusual and I was also conscious that presenting a session on changes in the workforce profile and women was likely to stimulate a lively discussion. The second part of the session was to be a facilitated discussion and I had planned to ask groups of students to reflect on their own workplace experiences and any issues that might arise from balancing a demanding career with childcare. So, to ensure that each group had a diverse group of people including those responsible for childcare, I asked the students: 'Could you please let me know if you are a working parent?' Of the 51 people in the seminar room, just two raised their hands. For a moment I wondered what to do next, with just two parents in the room. The following question areas produced a vibrant discussion.

⬤ To what extent, if at all, has your career influenced your planning regarding when to consider starting a family?

⬤ What facilities, if any, does your employer provide for staff wishing to work from home?

⬤ What policies does your organization have to support employees with caring responsibilities (children and other family members such as spouse or parents)?

⬤ In your experience, what changes in attitudes, if any, have occurred in your work environment to encourage employees balancing work with family or caring responsibilities?

⬤ If you are a working women, to what extent, if at all, do you think having a family would hinder your career progression?

⬤ If you do not intend to have a family, what workplace benefits would you like to see established for career men and women?

PRACTISING HRM

WHAT IS AN EMPLOYEE BENEFIT?

Make a list of the benefits employers can offer. Then consider how each element could be balanced with the others.

For example:
⬤ Flexible working hours or homeworking

⬤ Shorter holidays for more pay

⬤ Enhanced pension benefits for mature workers or earlier retirement

● RESPECT

The manager who is able to gain the respect of his/her team is more likely to achieve improved levels of motivation. Although some organizations tend to concentrate on performance management and rewards to elicit employee cooperation, the research evidence supporting the value of management and employee relations can be traced as far back as the mid-twentieth century. For example, the work of Max Weber, writing on bureaucracy, articulated the complexity in the interactions between managers and staff. Weber observed that materialistic interests and calculations alone could not provide stable employee and management relationships in organizations (Henderson and Parsons, 1947, p. 325). Whilst the workplace has changed, there are contemporary learning outcomes to be drawn from Weber's work. An employee–employer relationship, which is built on mutual trust, can enable each side to benefit from some flexibility to mutual advantage. For example, employees may be more willing to work additional hours or make an extra effort to support a manager who has responded favourably to their individual needs. Establishing a reciprocal relationship of respect may require some adjustments. For example, it is likely to be counterproductive for an employer to ask staff to work to the letter of their contracts. The ubiquitous catch-all clauses requiring staff to work additional hours as and when the employer may require need to be counterbalanced by some compensation to retain goodwill. The work of Weber accords with more recent writers such as Watson (1994, p. 171) who argued that workplace relationships should be founded on trust and reciprocity. According to Thompson and McHugh (2002, p. 276) a key measure of managerial competence is the ability to infuse motivation and commitment in others (also see Agarwala, 2003).

The implications for organizations of motivating a diversified workforce are challenging and sometimes difficult to reconcile with external pressures to reduce costs. In times of less certainty, why should employees perform in the best long-term interests of an employer who may not be able to reciprocate by guaranteeing long-term employment? It is, arguably, even more important for employers to provide professional development so that instead of a long-term employment guarantee, people can attain employability, equipping them to find another job, should the need arise. These kinds of proactive HR initiatives may also contribute towards encouraging improved motivational levels, although not every person will respond positively or necessarily reciprocate good treatment. People are complex and do not always respond the way theories claim they ought to. However, proactive developmental strategies are more likely to be conducive to sound work relationships than indifference or, worse, disrespect of worker diversity.

● AGEISM

The largest age group of people in the modern workplace is euphemistically described as the 'baby boomers'. This group represents the generations of people born after the Second World War (1939–1945) and during the prosperous 1950s and 60s. After that time, there was a fall in the number of children born in the affluent economies, and this is reflected in the twenty-first-century's workforce age profile. In response to the ageing workforce, governments have to rethink their policies towards the age of retirement. This is a difficult and emotive issue. It is indefensible for organizations to discriminate on the basis of a person's age. In the US age discrimination is illegal. However, should older workers be compelled to work beyond 65 before they may receive a pension? According to Sargeant (2004, pp. 151–66), there are important issues to consider regarding possible differences in the contractual retirement age, the pensionable retirement age and the abolition of the mandatory retirement age as a result of the EC's Equal Treatment Directive of 2000, and proposed Age Discrimination in Employment Regulations. While everyone should have the right to be treated without discrimination in finding gainful employment, the counterbalance is the availability of protected pension reserves, personal, corporate and state funded, that enable people to retire to a comfortable lifestyle following a lifetime of work. Employees who do work into their later years can bring organizations the benefits that are accrued through experience, although it may not be possible, practical or desirable for everyone to work into their seventies or eighties.

Snape and Redman (2003, pp. 78–89) evaluated the influence on employee attitudes of perceived age discrimination. The research was based on public sector workers and found that age discrimination occurred towards people who were considered 'too young' as well as 'too old'. Ageist discrimination was found to have a negative influence on employee morale. Employees who felt they had been discriminated against for being too old were also more inclined to retire earlier than they might otherwise have chosen. These kinds of outcomes are the antithesis of the kind of strategic workforce planning that should be occurring within the current demographic trend, where there are fewer younger people and an ageing workforce profile. Given that there are fewer young people, the forward-thinking organization should be encouraging and training people in the 18–30 age group. However, the core of the workforce is now the baby boomers (people in their forties, fifties and sixties), so organizations also need to retain their knowledge and skills. Furthermore, there are insufficient younger workers to replace such a large element of the workforce. One solution may be to encourage the migration of people from other parts of the world into the workforce. For centuries, industrial nations such as the US, Australia and the UK have long been accustomed to adopting people from other nations (see Cadbury, 2003). In Europe, this is likely be accelerated by the inclusion of more nations into the EU, whereby skilled workers can move more easily from one nation to another for employment opportunities. This also increases the diversification of the workforce and the rich variety of cultures and perspectives that they bring to organizations.

In common with other areas of discrimination, ageism can be the result of negative attitudes and perceptions. Hence negative characteristics may be erroneously ascribed to a person simply because they are over fifty or sixty years of age. Instead, it is much more equitable to evaluate individuals by their attitudes, knowledge and skills rather than their chronological age. Attributes such as flexibility, energy and enthusiasm that are sometimes ascribed to younger people are as likely to be found in the mature worker. Conversely, the younger graduate should not be discriminated against for not having any experience. Forward-thinking HR strategy can incorporate training and development programmes so that new employees, of whatever age, can enhance their knowledge and skills.

● CAN VOLUNTEERS BE MANAGED?

The nature of the voluntary sector is different from the private and public sectors, in that many of its key workers are unpaid volunteers. Although areas such as financial rewards *(see Chapter 10)* do not apply to volunteers, the evidence of modern HR is that there are many more elements to motivation than just pay awards. Indeed, in the absence of extrinsic rewards such as pay, the intrinsic rewards, the psychological fulfilment, become even more prominent. The first question to consider is why people volunteer? What do they hope to give and gain from the experience?

PRACTISING HRM

THE CHARITY WORKER

Think about a charity, where you might consider serving as a volunteer.

- ● Make one list of the knowledge and skills you could bring to the role.
- ● Then make a second list of what you think you could learn from the experience of volunteering.

Research into the motivations of volunteers of a large charity organization indicated that altruistic motives such as, 'working for a good cause' and 'giving something back to society' were balanced by personal needs such as a desire to meet people and forming friendships with co-workers. This is interesting because intrinsic motivators are not exclusive to the voluntary sector. Indeed, public and private sector employees usually express similar motivations. This therefore raises the question of what motivational characteristics are particular to volunteers (see Cnaan Ram, 1996; Osborne, 1996; Palmer and Hoe, 1997; Harris and Rochester, 2001).

Although volunteers do not receive pay, it should not be the case that they are regarded as less important than paid workers. Indeed, most charity organizations could not function without the active work of their voluntary workforce. A charity organization will also have a range of protections and benefits in place for paid employees, although these may not automatically be accorded to their volunteer colleagues.

In another study, a charity that provides aid relief abroad set about creating a formal set of HR policy documents. The purpose was to establish the responsibilities of the paid management staff and a 'volunteers compact', which set out the rights and responsibilities of the volunteer to the organization and vice versa. This included areas such as selection, induction, training, equal opportunities, expenses, health and safety, complaints procedures and termination. The documentation for these policies was created by the charity's head office, where there was some ambivalence as to whether it should be rolled out across the whole organization. For example, some of the volunteers had entered into service precisely because they were disaffected with what they perceived as unnecessary bureaucracy in other employment sectors. Any notion of being 'managed' could result in significant numbers of volunteers leaving the organization. Also the local paid managers did not necessarily have the HR knowledge and skills to implement the policy and could reasonably argue that they had more immediate concerns in delivering aid.

A consultation process was then initiated to resolve the impasse between the organization and its volunteers. This included discussions on what kinds of rights and responsibilities might be mutually acceptable to the charity and its volunteers. For example, should an unpaid volunteer have the right come and go as they please, or do they have a responsibility to commit to some workplace constraints? Central to any consultations was the notion of to what extent volunteers could or should be managed.

Exercise 6.1

THE VOLUNTARY SECTOR

1 What do you consider to be the main differences in voluntary worker motivations and employed worker motivations?

2 If volunteers are unpaid, does it also follow that they need not be managed?

3 If successful HR ought to be more about building cooperation than control through rewards and sanctions, to what extent should managing volunteers be no different from the best of HR management practices?

4 What are the advantages to a volunteer of having a document clearly stating his/her rights and responsibilities?

5 Why do you think some voluntary workers are resistant to any notion of being managed?

6 If HR is a situation-specific profession, how should HR professionals working in the voluntary sector adapt their management style to serve the needs of voluntary workers?

HRM IN ACTION

THE HR INITIATIVE THAT WENT WRONG

Patrick, a young and enthusiastic graduate, joined a large and successful organization where there appeared to be a range of opportunities for training and career development. The organization's personnel director was keen to develop a more proactive human resources function and encouraged Patrick to undertake an audit of HR activities and obtain feedback from staff as to which areas HR could improve its service to the organization. The results of the audit were a surprise to the management team. A significant number of the staff, team leaders and middle managers interviewed were, to put it mildly, scathing of the organization's recruitment, retention, training and remuneration policies. The personnel director was deeply concerned by the results of the research and recommended a root and branch reorganization and management development programme, recruitment, appraisals, rewards and life–work balance packages. Patrick was, of course, delighted that he could make such a significant contribution to the organization in his first HR job and he was fulsome in praising his employer.

Problems were, however, not far over the HR horizon. The value of the HR input was not shared by all the key opinion formers; indeed, a significant number of senior managers thought that the place of HR was to focus on operational matters and not to 'meddle' in management planning issues. There were some senior managers who saw little, if any, value in having an influential HR function. Indeed, some managers were openly hostile at the interference in their working practices. Some of the top management team argued that external providers could handle all the HR department's tasks.

Following a period of increasing discord between the HR director and the other top managers, and disheartened by the lack of commitment to a longer term development plan, the HR director moved to another organization. A new HR director was appointed to focus on compliance to industry and legal standards and enforce employee performance evaluations through competency standards and compliance documentation for each department. Patrick, who had put so much effort into improving the standards of service to the departments, now found his role firmly fixed in overseeing operational administrative tasks, including the overseeing of a variety of external providers who, in the absence of a strategic lead, focused on the compliance regime. In less than 18 months, most of the original HR team had moved to other organizations. The problems uncovered by Patrick's study became worse and employees resented the additional paper work imposed by the new HR director, which they felt was rapidly becoming a key part of the problem, rather than any part of a solution. The difficulties that employees experienced in communicating with the management team were aggravated by the use of the management of competency standards, which they believed, with good reason, had been imposed without consultation. Many of these problems were blamed on the HR team, who were regarded as distant and disengaged from the realities of the organization's core business activities. There was also an increase in employment disputes, some of which led to industrial action and legal actions.

DISCUSSION QUESTIONS

1 Why is it important to consult and involve senior managers in the preparations for any potential new HR initiative?

2 The HR audit results were a surprise to the operational management team. What can we infer this means with regards to staff and management communication and relationships?

3 What is likely to happen to staff morale if the management team do not make changes following the results of the audit?

4 Why do you think the managers were hostile to the results of the audit?

5 How might the communications and teamwork of managers and staff have been improved? *(team working is discussed in Chapter 3).*

6 Why should HR professionals make a real effort to understand the aims and objectives of their colleagues in the organization?

MOTIVATING A DIVERSIFIED WORKFORCE

Present a case (individual or group presentation) on possible approaches to motivating a diversified workforce in one of the following:

● A for-profit organization

● A voluntary sector organization

● A public service organization.

 CHAPTER SUMMARY

In this chapter you have reflected on the challenges and needs of the modern diversified workplace and critically evaluated the role of HR-trained professionals in encouraging the development of more effective employee motivation initiatives to meet the needs of a diverse workforce. This included an evaluation of the trends that have led to changes in the nature and needs of working people. The chapter has also encouraged case study evaluation of the kinds of strategies that HR professionals can employ for motivating different groups such as contract workers, part-timers and mature employees and volunteers.

● REFERENCES

Agarwala, T. (2003) Innovative Human Resource Practices and Organisational Commitment: An Empirical Investigation. *International Journal of Human Resource Management*, **14**(2).

Cadbury, D. (2003) *Seven Wonders of The Industrial World*. London: Fourth Estate.

Caulkin, S. (2001) The Time is Now. *People Management*, 30 August.

Cnaan Ram, A. (1996) Defining Who is a Volunteer: Conceptual and Empirical Considerations. *Non-Profit and Voluntary Sector Quarterly*, **25**(3).

Cox, T. and Blake, S. (1991) *Managing Cultural Diversity: Implications for Organizational Competitiveness*. The Academy of Management Executive.

Dawson, S., Mole, V., Winstanley, D. and Sherval, J. (1995) Management, Competition and Professional Practice: Medicine and the Marketplace. *British Journal of Management*, **6**.

Farnham, D. (ed.) (1997). Employment Flexibilities in Western European Public Services: An International Symposium. *Review of Public Personnel Administration*, **17**(3).

Friday, E. and Friday, S. S. (2003) Managing Diversity Using a Strategic Planned Change Approach. *The Journal of Management Development*, **22**(10).

Hall, D. T. and Parker, V. A. (1993) The Role of Workplace Flexibility in Managing Diversity. *Organizational Dynamics,* (22).

Handy, C. B. (1995) Trust and the Virtual Organization. *Harvard Business Review*, May–June.

Harris, M. and Rochester, C. (eds) (2001) Voluntary Organisations and Social Policy in Britain. Perspectives On Change and Choice. Basingstoke: Palgrave – now Palgrave Macmillan.

Henderson, A. M. and Parsons, T. (1947) *Max Weber. The Theory of Social and Economic Organization*. New York: Oxford University Press.

Kopp, R. (1994) International Human Resource Policies and Practices in Japanese, European and United States Multinationals. *Human Resource Management*, winter.

Kossek, E. E. and Zonia, S. C. (1993) Assessing Diversity Climate: A Field Study of Reactions to Employer Efforts To Promote Diversity. *Journal of Organizational Behaviour,* (14).

Maxwell, G. A. (2004) Taking the Initiative in Managing Diversity at BBC Scotland, *Employee Relations*, **26**(2).

Osborne, S. (ed.) (1996) *Managing in the Voluntary Sector: A Handbook for Managers in Charitable and Non-profit Organisations*. London: Thomson International Business Press.

Nkomo, S. M. (1992) The Emperor Has No Clothes: Rewriting 'Race' in Organizations. *Academy of Management Review*.

Palmer, P. and Hoe, E. (eds) (1997) *Voluntary Matters. Management and Good Practice in the Voluntary Sector*. London: The Media Trust and the Directory of Social Change.

Peasaud, J. (2003) In Good Company. How Can Organisations Encourage their Employees to Absorb and Adopt the Message of Corporate Social Responsibility? *People Management*, July.

Sargeant, M. (2004) Mandatory Retirement Age and Age Discrimination, *Employee Relations*, **26**(2).

Snape, E. and Redman, T. (2003) Too Old or Too Young? The Impact of Perceived Age Discrimination. *Human Resource Management Journal*, **13**(1).

Thomas, R. R. and Thomas, J. R. (1990) From Affirmative Action to Affirming Diversity. *Harvard Business Review,* (68).

Thompson, P. and McHugh, D. (2002) *Work Organisations* (3rd edn). Basingstoke: Palgrave – now Palgrave Macmillan.

Watson, T. J. (1994) *In Search of Management. Culture, Chaos and Control in Managerial Work.* London: Routledge.

Williams, M. L. and Bauer, T. N. (1994) The Effect of Managing Diversity Policy on Organizational Attractiveness. *Group and Organization Management*, (19).

Wind, J. Y. and Main, J. (1998) *Driving Change. How The Best Companies Are Preparing For The 21st Century.* London: Kogan Page.

Wright, P. and Brewster, C. (2003) Learning from Diversity: HRM is not Lycra. *International Journal of Human Resource Management*, **14**(8).

PERSONAL NOTES ON CHAPTER 6

Notes for seminars

_____

_____

_____

_____

_____

_____

_____

_____

_____

_____

_____

_____

_____

_____

_____

_____

_____

_____

_____

_____

_____

_____

NOTES ON CHAPTER 6 *CONTINUED*

Notes for revision/reminders

Chapter 7

Recruitment and Selection: An Integrated Approach

Learning outcomes

After reading and completing the activities in this chapter, you should be able to:

1 Appreciate the role of HR in developing recruitment and selection strategies.

2 Critically evaluate recruitment and selection methodologies.

3 Reflect on the recruitment implications of AKS in job analysis and design.

4 Appreciate the use of an integrated HR approach within organizational recruitment strategic policy development.

5 Design a recruitment and selection strategy where HR input is integrated into organizational performance.

6 Understand how to prepare and interpret CV information.

7 Evaluate and practise a simulated job selection interview.

INTRODUCTION

Whether or not you plan to follow a career in HR, anyone who has aspirations to move into a managerial role will benefit from improving their understanding of recruitment and selection. In most organizations, it is not only senior managers who are required to recruit and select staff. New managers can also expect to be involved in recruitment. In reality, any management role, in any function from sales and marketing to finance, can benefit from being more effective in recruitment and selection. However, without some background knowledge and training, recruitment and selection can be a daunting task. It is relatively easy to select a well-qualified person with a successful track record for a new job, but is he or she the right person for the situation? Is the person selected going to be effective in their new work environment? Does success in one organization necessarily determine success in a new situation, with a different set of colleagues? The 'safe choices' may also preclude less experienced new graduates, experienced older workers or people returning to the workforce following a time out whereby they can bring fresh perspectives to their workplace. It is arguable that to meet the needs of stakeholder diversity, organizations require more diverse workforces. Lets explore recruitment and selection with an open mind and a willingness to consider new approaches.

Legal Matters

The modern employment environment, both local and international, is regulated by stringent legal requirements. Employment legislation is constantly changing, so even well-informed HR personnel are not in a position to safely advise their organizations on employment legality. Always employ legal professionals to inform policy and procedures. However, the law cannot select the 'right' person for a job. Recruitment and selection is a specific set of attitudes, knowledge and skills and it is these you will learn by studying this chapter.

⬤ SELECT THE HR ELECTIVES: BECOME A MORE EFFECTIVE MANAGER

Selecting the HR electives of your degree pathway is a valuable preparation for the workplace and is also likely to increase your confidence in managing people, including recruitment and selection responsibilities. It is also often worthwhile for experienced managers to revisit their core recruitment strategies and reflect on whether they need to review their attitudes, knowledge and skills in this area.

The ability to understand the recruitment and selection process can also increase your knowledge and skills in applying for and successfully obtaining a new job, so there are personal as well as professional incentives for improving your performance in this area. It is for this reason that recruitment and selection is often offered on both undergraduate and postgraduate courses, because it is so fundamental to management that anyone can visit or revisit this area throughout their working career. In fact, any experienced manager who has hired the 'wrong' person will confirm how inconvenient and costly poor recruitment performance can be. It is equally possible that good candidates can be missed, people who could have added value to an organization, simply because they were filtered out by inappropriate selection schemes.

The purpose of this chapter is to address the area of recruitment and selection in a theoretical and practical manner. The overall method I advocate is an integrated approach, which by its nature is a flexible system, offering the opportunity to design organization- and situation-specific recruitment and selection solutions.

⬤ EVERY MANAGER IS IN HR

Modern functional managers (managers with responsibility for a section or team of staff) are being given more direct responsibility for HR activities. This has meant that the role of the traditional HR or personnel departments has been evolving from one which focused on operational implementation to a more consultative, facilitating role. During the research for this book, I observed a range of organizations including international businesses through to SMEs. In some cases, even SMEs (employing 20 or more people) did not have any specialist HR function. Even within larger organizations, there appeared to be a movement towards using more external service providers and smaller internal HR teams. This is not a reason to change your degree to another discipline, or start looking for a career outside HR! Instead, for graduates interested in HR, it is encouraging to recognize how many and varied the jobs are, including: consultancy, general management, training companies and, of course, traditional personnel departments. These changes in modern HR could be said to be increasing rather than contracting the opportunities for people with HR skills. The real difference is that the work of HR specialists is moving, or should be moving, closer to the needs of the organization and therefore becoming more strategically focused. There is a growing recognition that HR has a direct influence on productivity and financial performance (Huselid, 1995). Furthermore, the key component to organizational success begins with people, so recruitment is the starting point for improving staff effectiveness.

RECRUITMENT AND SELECTION: IMPROVING ORGANIZATIONAL PERFORMANCE

Effective recruitment and selection ensures that people, the most importance resource, are available to meet the organization's workload. Unlike component orders, or bank overdraft limits that can be altered according to demand, people take time to recruit, induct and train. This is one of the contributory reasons why organizations that downsize too severely in leaner times tend to do poorly when the economy improves. They simply do not have enough people resources to respond to increasing demand, so customers take their business elsewhere. The strategic planning of HR should be about reaching the correct staffing levels. There should be sufficient people to maintain a responsive organization that can cope with new opportunities, but not a top-heavy bureaucracy that is slow to respond to change.

Recruitment and selection is a specialist activity. Managers should therefore receive in-house training, attend an external course or study the HR options on a management degree. Making mistakes in recruitment and selection can mean an uncomfortable experience for both the misplaced employee and their organization. According to one UK survey (Industrial Relations Services, 1997), organizations employing more than 25 employees have an average staff turnover of 20 per cent. This figure may fluctuate considerably from one sector to another and in different organizations. However, if the cost of advertising, interviewing, induction, training and loss of productivity whilst a person in settling into a new job were also considered, the total cost of each replacement employee is considerable (see Welbourne and Andrews, 1996).

● THE RECRUITMENT AND SELECTION PROCESS

1 Where do the vacancies exist?
2 How many more people are required to meet current and planned levels of organizational activity?
3 Is the vacancy a new position, a replacement for someone who has been promoted, temporary cover or a full-time replacement for someone who has moved to another organization?
4 Has a job description been prepared? Is it up-to-date with current requirements? This should include a review of the job requirements and responsibilities.
5 What are the essential and desirable attributes, experience and skills?
6 How are applicants to be found? By advertising internally or externally?
7 Would it be helpful to include external expertise, such as a specialist recruitment consultancy?
8 Which method or combination of selection methods are most appropriate to the vacancy – application form, CV, telephone interview, face-to-face interviews, references, psychometric testing?
9 Does the organization have access to legal advice on recruitment and selection?
10 What is the timescale for the search and selection process?

Situation-specific Solutions

Although it might be simple to assume that there is a best practice, it is difficult to support such a prescriptive approach. Instead, it is more useful to consider fitness for purpose and situation-specific factors. The methodological alternatives can then be considered and applied where they are most appropriate. The only inflexible factor in recruitment and selection is compliance to national and international legislation, for which professional legal advice should in all cases be sought. The majority of HR professionals are not qualified lawyers, so it would be prudent to invite an independent legal adviser to validate recruitment policies and procedures.

Selection Methods

The recruitment and selection methodology is influenced, as with so much in organizational behaviour, by the management style and culture (Judge and Cable, 1997). For example, an entrepreneurial organization that is seeking rapid expansion may place more emphasis on attitudes such as a positive, independent personality. Conversely, a more conservative bureaucracy might prefer compliant people who conform to established procedures (see Smither et al., 1993). The HR specialist should therefore investigate what is required and then select the tools of recruitment that are most appropriate to the task.

By selecting the most effective approach and combination of tools for the particular recruitment assignment, the opportunities for successful recruitment are improved. Listed below are the most commonly used search and selection tools.

- *Publishing the vacancy internally:* The job should be published internally so those existing employees have an opportunity to apply. Sometimes the most suitable person is already in the organization. S/he may be full time, part time or working as a consultant.

- *Publishing the vacancy externally:* It is important to form a general impression of the kinds of people who could be interested in the vacancy. Select the media that the target groups are likely to use and that fits into the agreed budget of expenditure for the particular vacancy. This can include newspapers, national and local, the organization's webpages, radio and television, trade and professional journals. It is important to investigate which specific advertising media is most relevant to the vacancy (see Mason and Belt, 1986).

- *Headhunting:* As the term implies, specific persons are sought out and approached. Care should be taken to ensure that other interested persons are not disadvantaged. Professional legal advice should be sought on issues pertaining to equal opportunities.

- *External consultancy:* It may be appropriate and more cost- and time-effective to brief a specialist recruitment consultancy to search and select candidates for the final short list. There are general recruitment consultancies and ones that specialize in specific areas, such as law, sales and marketing, finance, HR, computing, engineering.

- *The curriculum vitae (usually referred to as a CV):* This is often the first stage of selection, although some organizations may use a brief telephone interview before asking applicants to send in their CVs. The CV offers applicants the opportunity to express their attitudes, knowledge and skills in their own way. This provides the prospective employer with an indication of how well, or not, the applicant is able to present him or herself on paper and give an account of how their unique set of abilities relates to the advertised vacancy. Overall, the CV is a well-tried and commonly accepted method, which is used in conjunction with other selection tools. However, for unskilled jobs, the CV may be unnecessary and even act as a barrier to entry. If literacy and written communications are not key vacancy criteria, it is unnecessary to use CVs as a selection method.

- *Application forms:* The alternative to a CV is the application form. If large numbers of applicants are anticipated for lower level or routine jobs, an application form may be a way of managing the HR workload. The application form also has the potential to provide more standardized data, in that it dictates what specific information is to be included. The use of application forms is more commonly found in the bureaucratic management cultures such as the public sector. The advantage is that it standardizes, while the disadvantage is that human beings are not easily categorized (see Saks et al., 1995).

- *Online application forms:* These may discriminate in favour of those applicants who have personal internet access. For example, undergraduates from less financially prosperous families may need to rely on public and university access alone.

- *Telephone interviews:* This method is particularly useful for vetting applicants for jobs that entail high levels of telephone contact, such as some types of market research, customer services and call centre roles. The telephone interview may also be used as a preliminary selection stage where successfully candidates are then invited to submit a CV or attend a face-to-face interview. This method enables the recruiter to conduct a lot of interviews in a short space of time and provides the applicant with an opportunity to sell their application to the recruiter.

- *Work-based tests:* There is probably no better way of finding out whether a candidate is able to do a job than by getting them to actually do it. While the advantages are obvious, it can also be a time-consuming method and one that is not practical in all situations. Some job roles, such as management, can be difficult to evaluate in a test situation. However, there are many jobs and key elements of jobs, such as presentation skills in university lecturing, where this method could make a valuable contribution to the selection process.

- *Psychometric testing:* This method can be a used as a supplement to other selection methodologies. Each candidate is tested and their performance compared to selected norms. The extent to which the tests are valid and reliable is dependent on the quality of the test design and the skills of the person who interprets the results. The use of tests can be a useful supplement to other methodologies, however organizations should not be tempted to become overly reliant on tests. Some managers may seek to justify selection decisions by the test results, or become predisposed towards a candidate who performs well in the tests. According to Maund (2001, p. 153), there has been a tendency among certain organizations and commentators to seek a pseudo-scientific veneer for recruitment and selection. It is also important to understand that actual work performance has more to do with motivation, determination and persistence, so the 'norm candidates' selected by the tests may not necessarily become the most successful employees.

- *Personality tests:* This type of test, which may also be included as part of assessment and evaluation days, attempts to select people with the kind of personality characteristics that the organization believes to be important *(see teamwork in Chapter 3)*. The interaction of humans and their ability to cooperate towards mutually agreed goals requires many interactive attitudes and skills. The value of personality assessment may be in encouraging self-awareness and development. This would be more useful later during employee development as part of a team-building process (see

Belbin, 1993, 2000). There are numerous types of tests, each claiming to deliver some predicative data. Given that this is a highly skilled area, it is important to select a consultancy firm with a solid track record of performance in administering tests. The recruiters should also consider the tests as one element of a process of selection. The pitfalls are attempting to create a 'clone culture' where they may actually be successful in employing too many like-minded people *(see groupthink in Chapter 3)*.

- *The assessment centre:* This approach utilizes a range of selection tools. In addition to any or all of the above mentioned methods, role plays, team exercises and social interaction observations may be included. The advantage of the assessment centre is that by employing a fuller range of methods over a longer period of time, from a day to a weekend and sometimes longer, a broader picture can emerge of each participating applicant. It should be noted, however, that the applicants are still doing exercises in an artificial environment. For example, in team exercises, the essential element of good teamwork, mutual cooperation, could be eroded where members know that in reality they are not a team at all, but a group of individuals competing for a job. Candidates can have varying reactions to their experiences of assessment centres (Fletcher, 1991). The assessment centre can be a useful tool, although it is clearly likely to be relatively expensive and time-consuming.

- *References:* The reference is one of the most commonly used documents in selection. During the time I have worked as a manager, recruitment consultant and lecturer, I have rarely seen a really bad reference. Although most organizations use this selection method, many managers would admit that since the applicant selects the referees, they are hardly likely to use someone who dislikes them. Conversely, a less than scrupulous manager might be tempted to give an overly supportive reference to a mediocre employee who s/he wants to get rid of or a cooler one to an indispensable member of staff. Furthermore, within British law, both the applicant and the prospective employer may have legal redress against a referee if they can prove that the document was materially untrue. In all cases, remember that the reference is a subjective assessment of past performance in a different situation. The more time that has elapsed between the events that shaped the reference and the present day, the less useful it is as a selection indicator. For example, character references are more useful from someone who is familiar with a person's recent behaviour and abilities, than several years ago. People change over time, as may the referee's impressions.

Summary of Search and Selection Methodologies

It is important to select the correct media to reach potential applicants. Effective advertising will provide a better choice of applicants. The selection methodology employed should be tailored to the vacancy. The more highly valued the role, the more it is worth investing time and resources – select in haste and repent at leisure. It is much easier to employ someone than to dismiss him or her.

The HR specialist should consider the fitness for purpose of the selected methodology. Practical issues such as the time available to recruit staff and cost also need to be taken into consideration. In the majority of situations, a combination of methods such as CV, interviews, work sample and references would suffice. However, more tools may be found to be appropriate in particular organizational situations.

The weight given to a particular element of the selection process also requires consideration. The evidence gathered from current sources and those aspects which pertain directly to the vacancy are particularly useful. Conversely, although the past is relevant, the assumption that it can accurately predict future potential can be problematic. For example, Winston Churchill's school record was poor and would hardly recommend him as a world leader. Richard Branson, entrepreneur and chairman of Virgin, did not go to university, but that clearly did not prevent him becoming a successful businessman. It is therefore inadvisable to make too many assumptions about a person based on their school, university or past employment record. However, these methodologies can be useful in conjunction with others so that a broader picture of the candidate can emerge.

● AKS IN JOB DESIGN AND ANALYSIS

In modern organizations, working practices are less static than they were in times past. More demanding expectations in both private and public sectors have replaced the days when customers would accept the same product. Sir John Harvey-Jones (1995, p. 81), a well-known business consultant and former chairman of ICI, has observed that, in his experience, the world of business never remains static. If this is the case, then job descriptions also require regular updating because what people do in organizations needs to respond to the changing environment.

Although this might sound like common sense, sometimes sense is not that common is organizations. According to Peters (1994, p. 69), many employees work within overly narrow job descriptions *(the role of organizational culture and its influence on behavioural patterns is discussed in Chapter 2)*.

Modern academic analysis and research indicates that a more flexible model of job design is helpful. For example, McKenna and Beech (1995, p. 96) found that traditional job descriptions are being replaced with a more flexible approach. The focus in job descriptions may be moving more towards abilities and skills rather than the traditional list of job responsibilities.

One model that offers a more flexible alternative to the traditional job analysis and design is AKS (attitudes, knowledge, skills (Figure 7.1). This approach structures the analysis and job design on the most recent job requirement and required personal attributes. So how does the theory work in practice? Below are descriptions of the AKS stages.

Attitudes **Knowledge** **Skills**

Figure 7.1 Job analysis and design

Attitudes

Although it may be easier and more quantifiable to concentrate on the quantitative aspects of the recruitment process, most managers recognize that attitudes can be a decisive factor in employee performance. For example, a HR associate might be selected because they can demonstrate knowledge, such as the successful completion of a HR degree, and skills, by successful participation in a recruitment and selection workshop activity. However, a person's attitude to a job can make all the difference as to whether they do really well or just adequately. The reason that attitudes are sometimes left out may be because they are difficult to quantity. For example, I have found it interesting to ask students which attitudes they think a university lecturer should display. Although the content has varied from group to group and year to year, some items such as a sense of humour and willingness to listen have appeared regularly on their lists. These kinds of attitudes can translate into positive attitudes towards students and interpersonal relations.

Knowledge

The easiest area of an applicant's attributes to assess is that of knowledge. Given that knowledge is often associated with the acquisition of qualifications and former experiences, it is a relatively simple task to ask applicants to provide evidence of their course grades and work experience. However, a display of technical knowledge should not automatically be regarded as evidence, in itself, of the ability to perform a job role successfully. While a person might be well qualified and have succeeded in a similar role elsewhere, it is important to consider whether s/he will be able to transfer successfully to another organization structure and culture *(organization structure/culture is discussed in Chapter 2)*.

Skills

Attitudes and knowledge are supported by the skills. According to Reid and Barrington (2000, p. 59), the development of skills is important because if our learning focuses only on attitudes and knowledge, then our behaviour may not necessarily change (). The workplace is an excellent environment in which employees can develop skills by actually doing the job and hopefully learning from their experiences. It is for this reason that experiential learning can be a particularly valuable element of university courses. For example, the skills involved in recruitment can be developed by groups of student's actively role-playing the recruitment processes.

In Chapter 2 the importance of understanding an organization's culture and structure was discussed and the influence this has on management decisions. One of the most crucial decisions managers can make is who to employ and who to promote. An organization is its people, so employment selection is at the centre of any strategic decision. Unfortunately, many managers do not receive the training and development required to make effective selection decisions. Hence, while a person may comply with internal and external protocols, this does not necessarily enable them to make sound selection decisions. Furthermore, it is relevant to consider how decisions are arrived at and the extent to which the selected person is actually able to do the job required.

The selection process should focus on the kinds of attitudes, knowledge and skills the selected person will need to be successful in the job. Managers should also challenge their own preconceptions. For example, when I was lecturing in central London, I was bemused to learn from my students that some stores required temporary Christmas staff to have already attained a good honours degree to be considered for a job selling chocolates or gloves. Why? Surely good interpersonal and communication skills would be more appropriate for a temporary sales role? Any selection criteria should be thoroughly examined with regard to its appropriateness. Keep asking the question why is this important? Is that element of knowledge really essential to the effectiveness of the specific job tasks?

HRM IN ACTION

THE RECRUITMENT ASSIGNMENT

This HRM in action study is based on real recruitment and selection situations I completed whilst working in consultancy.

ORGANIZATIONAL PROFILE

● A successful, city-based consultancy

● Highly profitable

● Well-educated staff

● Accustomed to advising other organizations on staffing matters and performance

● Image-conscious management

● Prestigious offices

● High-profile client portfolio

JOB PROFILE FOR VACANCY IN ESTABLISHED MARKET

- Retain portfolio of business within an established market sector
- Continue long-standing client relationships
- Promote repeat business opportunities
- Ability to learn technical details to service client requirements
- Interpersonal communication skills
- Presentation skills

JOB PROFILE FOR VACANCY IN NEW MARKET

- Market services in a new business sector
- Make contacts and create new client relationships
- Build a new and profitable and expanding business portfolio
- Promote the organization's profile in a new market sector
- Find new business opportunities
- Ability to learn the technical details of client's market sector
- Interpersonal communication skills
- Presentation skills

 Read the two job roles above and consider what the differences are in the kinds of attitudes, knowledge and skills a person would require for an existing client base and developing a new market.

First job profile: Existing clients

Attitudes		Knowledge		Skills	
key areas	desirable	key areas	desirable	key areas	desirable

Second job profile: New client development

Attitudes		Knowledge		Skills	
key areas	desirable	key areas	desirable	key areas	desirable

Evaluate and justify why you have selected certain AKS as essential and other as desirable.

In the real-life situation, I was able to recommend several young people (mid-twenties) who had many of the personal qualities required. Some of the successful applicants lacked the specific consultancy experience the client had asked for. However, it was decided that that the successful candidates could be developed in consultancy skills. It is interesting to note that good presentation skills at interview played a significant role in the appointments *(for presentation and communication skills, see Chapter 12)*. The successful applicants were also, interestingly, not always those who had the closest match to the client's job specifications, nor did they all have a degree. However, they were all able to fit into the organization's culture and management style.

The real-life outcome of the second, new business position was particularly interesting. The person who I eventually recommended had no consultancy experience, no relevant technical knowledge and, initially, no interest in changing career! What the person did have were the right kinds of attitudes and interpersonal skills, knowledge of the market sector and presentational skills to do the job.

The key tasks were therefore to:

● Provide the applicant with sufficient information to decide whether or not to consider making a career change.

● Brief the client organization of the potential added value this person could bring to their business.

● Enable both client and applicant to be flexible in their discussions

The applicant was eventually offered the position on a high salary and generous benefits package. Ironically, it is unlikely that s/he would have been selected if the client's original job description had been adhered to. Ultimately it is a matter for each person responsible for recruitment to decide what kinds of attitudes, knowledge and skills are essential or non-essential to the selection process, which leads us to the discussion areas, noted below.

DISCUSSION AREAS

1 How much influence do you believe organizational culture has on selection decisions? Discuss your thoughts as a small group or seminar activity.

2 Consider the relevance to the job roles discussed above and grade the following elements. Give each a mark out of 7 where 7 is essential and 0 represents unnecessary. Use only whole numbers. Hence you have to make a clear decision either way.

- Ability to work with little supervision   _____

- A driving licence   _____

- Communication skills   _____

- Determination to achieve positive results _____

- Effective time management   _____

- Entrepreneurial characteristics   _____

- Intelligence   _____

- Interpersonal skills   _____

- Professional dress style   _____

- Previous experience   _____

- Qualifications   _____

- Score highly in psychometric tests   _____

● DESIGNING A RECRUITMENT AND SELECTION STRATEGY

The design of a recruitment and selection strategy depends on the organizational context, that is, recruiters should consider the kind of environment they are working in and the influences exerted by the organization's structure and culture. For example, the characteristics required for a HR manager in a highly bureaucratic sector may be entirely different from the kinds of attitudes, knowledge and skills needed for someone appointed to a new entrepreneurial enterprise, although some of the core areas of knowledge and skills may be similar. Recruitment and selection is situation-specific. An integrated approach to recruitment and selection therefore recognizes the need to offer flexibility, not prescription, in the design of recruitment strategies.

An integrated approach to recruitment and selection may include:

● The practical involvement of HR staff, or specialist external advisers, in the strategic planning of recruitment and selection policies.

● Recognition of the organization's culture and, as necessary, a re-evaluation of recruitment and selection policies where they are more a part of 'tradition' than modern practice which meets the organization's current needs.

● Use of external providers such as recruitment consultancies, legal advice.

● Input from external advisers including business schools and professional bodies such as the CIPD.

● Involvement of experienced professionals who have decided to work part time, such as men or women electing to invest more time with their family, or those who have decided to retire from full-time working but who have many years experience to offer.

● An evaluation of the current job role.

● A decision as to the most appropriate selection and recruitment approach.

PRACTISING HRM

NEW GRADUATE AKS

Either: Select an organization and make up a job vacancy, such as human resources associate, marketing assistant or IT assistant (choosing a specific job role will make it easier to compile a profile).

Or: Select a job vacancy from a newspaper or professional magazine.

Then:

Compile a list of the attitudes, knowledge and skills for the vacancy, which a new graduate might apply for. Create two columns for each area, one for whatever is essential and another for the non-essential, but desirable items.

● UNDERSTANDING CVs

One of the most frequent requests I receive from professionals and students is how to improve the layout of their CVs. In a competitive job market, a well-organized CV can make a considerable difference as to whether someone secures a work placement or a permanent job after graduating.

So what constitutes a 'sound' professional CV? This is a challenging question because every person is unique and there are so many different potential employers that it would be difficult to defend any single format for all circumstances. The CV is, however, often the first impression a prospective employer gets of an applicant, so it is important for both applicants and employers to understand how to interpret CV information effectively. In a practical sense, the objectives of the applicant and recruiter should be similar, namely to recognize those aspects of attitudes, knowledge and skills which are most relevant to the job vacancy.

Recently, the chief executive of a voluntary organization asked me to advise him on how to redesign of his CV because he believed that a more refined document would be more likely to help in his future career development. I have been interested in the voluntary sector for sometime and was happy to help him in redeveloping his CV. He told me that a commercial consultancy specializing in counselling senior management had also offered to help him develop his CV, but for a fee of £3000. The very fact that there are consultancies advertising their services in designing CVs for experienced managers highlights the fact that preparing a CV can be a daunting task. Yet even with the help of a consultant, it is still up to applicants to recognize which areas they want to move into and what personal attributes, knowledge and skills they have, or need to acquire, to help them achieve their ambitions.

Some organizations elect to avoid receiving any CVs by requiring potential applicants to complete an application form, either in paper or electronic format from their websites. The decision has to be a matter of fitness for purpose, although a CV is likely to provide a better insight into the applicant than an application form. Alternatively, it can be argued that an application form can be computer scanned for key words, such as honours degree or any other prescribed criteria. In such cases, the recruitment process is predestined by the initial selection criteria and may permit less flexibility. Some of the world's leading entrepreneurs would probably have been filtered out by such electronic systems, which use standard 'qualifications' as criteria because of their lack of conventional qualification and career profiles. The use of CVs places the onus on the applicant to ensure that the information provided is correctly presented, so it is important to invest some time preparing a CV of key information, dates and qualifications before you start setting out the document.

A CV is not just an historical document chronicling everything a person has ever done from birth to the present date. It is a document designed to provide a truthful account of those key achievements that are most relevant to a particular potential employer. From the applicant's perspective, the objective of a CV is to generate sufficient interest to prompt an interview invitation. The value of what is selected for inclusion should therefore be carefully thought about. It is easier to provide too much irrelevant information than to produce an interesting CV that will get you to interviews. Do remember that first impressions can count for a lot if the employer has a large pile of applications, so the first page is particularly important. Some busy managers may get a junior assistant to filter the incoming CVs, so key data has to be clear and easily accessible.

Indeed, some managers may argue that if a graduate cannot present, or lacks the skills to prepare, such an important document about him/her self, a prospective employer may legitimately question the applicant's ability to undertake broader challenges in the workplace.

Example of CV Layout

The section headings below provide a standard format. The new graduate will also find it useful to follow the format when applying for positions either for a work placement, or full-time or part-time employment.

CURRICULUM VITAE

Page 1
> Name
> Address
> Telephone
> Email
> Date of birth
> Marital status (optional)
> Nationality (optional)
> Religion (optional)
> Driving licence
> Higher education
> University
> Dates
> (Full time/part time)
> School
> Dates
> Prizes/special responsibilities
> Languages
> Career and skills summary

Page 2 (and subsequent pages if necessary)
> Current position
> Type of work
> Date to present
> Type of business
> Position/s
> Work experience prior to (date)
> Interests

The first page of the CV is most likely to warm or cool interest, so it is prudent to offer the key points pertaining to the job on this page. Indeed, it may be likened to a good executive summary in a management report. The first page provides applicants with an opportunity to highlight their key skills in relation to the job they have applied for. For example, one of my students was applying to the BBC to work as journalist. When she bought her CV in, I noticed that she had placed her experiences working in South America as a charity aid worker in a general interests section on the second page. Instead, I recommended that she move the information to the front page and highlight what she had learnt from the experience. The skills she had gained in working abroad in a difficult environment could have some relevance to the kinds of challenges a successful broadcast journalist might encounter.

The inexperienced applicant may simply set out a set of positive assertions, such as: 'I am an excellent team player' or 'I always work very conscientiously'. These kinds of statements tell an employer that this is *the way the applicant wants to be perceived*, but provide no evidence as to what he/she has done to substantiate such claims. Writing about the preparation of CVs, Stanton (1996, p. 227) noted that the applicant should try to justify statements and opinions and provide evidence to support any assertions. Hence, a graduate could note a teamwork project as evidence of working with other people, accepting responsibility (shared grades) and coordinating work to meet a specific deadline.

The experienced professional applicant can present key experiences in the summary section. For example:

- The successful design and implementation of a team-building skills programme for (name organization)
- Planning the training programme for X number of fast-track graduate trainees
- Up-to-date knowledge of current thinking in management, education, voluntary sector, health (whichever area the applicant operates in) through professional training/postgraduate course at the university of X.

Exercise 7.1

PREPARE YOUR OWN CV

I have lost count of the number of senior executives, managers and students who have asked me to help them improve their CV. Whilst fashion regarding layout does change over time, the reality is that you are unlikely to get a second chance to be short listed for a job, so making a positive impression with your application is important. You may have achieved really interesting things, but a prospective employer will only know about them if you include them in your CV.

Write a new CV for yourself using the guidelines above (this is particularly useful for students who are required to do a work placement as part of their degree course).

INTERVIEWING PROCEDURES

The most frequently used method of recruitment is the interview. A few sensible preparations can make this a more productive activity for all those involved (see Herriot and Rothwell, 1981; Rynes and Miller, 1983; Smither et al., 1993; Goltz and Giannantonio, 1995).

1   The room selected should be comfortable. It is not conducive to effective recruitment if the room is too small or poorly ventilated.
2   The telephone should be redirected so that there are no unnecessary interruptions.

3　Avoid asking leading questions, or questions which already contain the answer: 'What we are looking for is a real team player. How do you feel about working in a team?

4　Closed questions tend to produce simple yes or no answers.

5　Using open questions encourages interviewees to expand on their replies: Open questions are those which begin with: what, where, how, when, who, which, why.

For example:

- *What* do you most like about working at … ?
- *Where* do you see yourself in two years time?
- *How* useful have you found the work placement in preparing you for full-time employment?
- *When* did first decide you wanted to become a HR specialist?
- *Who* do you regard as the most effective team player in your department? Why?
- *Which* part of your degree course did you find most relevant to your current job?
- *Why* did you choose this organization for your work placement?

6　The interviewers should prepare a plan of questions they want to ask which relate to the attitudes, knowledge and skills that the particular job role requires. The wording of the questions must be fair to all applicants and framed so that they avoid any discrimination towards, disability, ethnic background, gender, race, religion or sexual orientation. Legal advice should be sought through professional associations and in-house or external legal input.

● STEREOTYPING: HALO OR HORNS?

Stereotyping is a psychological process used by humans to assist in the categorisation of the complex world of information that surrounds us (see Devine, 1989; Hilton and Von Hippel, 1996). One of the challenges for people involved in recruitment is the unconscious influence that stereotyping can have on their decision making, more commonly described as the 'halo or horns' syndrome. Stereotyping can prevent recruiters from evaluating the person before them fairly because they allow a stereotype to condition their choices, irrespective of any new information being presented. In this respect, it is important to design an AKS for the vacancy and avoid codifying stereotyping into the model. Hence, each 'essential' quality needs to be critically evaluated from the perspective of whether candidates with this characteristic or qualification are more likely to be successful in actually completing the job functions than someone who does not have the qualification or characteristic.

Desk Note:　You Never Get A Second Chance to Make A Good First Impression

Think about the time it takes you to form an impression of a new person you have met. When I ask students about how long it took them to form a judgement, the time frames they offer are usually measured in seconds. This is because humans use a form of categorization of impressions based on past experiences to make judgements about the people they meet.

Management is not so much a science as a situation-specific art form, with all the emotional uncertainties and conflicts that art rather than science exposes.

This is because we cannot separate all that we are as emotional human beings from the workplace. Indeed, attempts to become mechanistic in managerial approaches can also create difficulties; we cannot have a rule for every eventuality and it may be counterproductive to try.

HRM IN ACTION

FIRST IMPRESSIONS

The following HRM in Action study is based on research with several organizations in the private, public and voluntary sectors. The key elements of managerial behaviour and social interaction were formed from the common themes that emerged from the primary research.

The senior management of an organization were delighted to have Mark join them. Mark had a successful track record in management and was respected by his previous employer, who wrote an affirming reference for him. Mark was also impressed by the senior management at the organization and was looking forward to starting work with them. Indeed, he even visited the offices during his holiday period to make sure everything was in place for when he started the new job role. This was regarded by some of Mark's new colleagues as unusual, in as much as it was so enthusiastic. They wondered if Mark was trying too hard to impress them.

The first indication that Mark gained that all was not quite as positive as he had expected was when he met one of the next level down of management. Mark's first impression was that this person was polite but sceptical. This surprised him because he had been so well received by the senior management. However, it later became apparent that several of his new colleagues held a poor opinion of the organization's senior management and were consequently critical of anyone they introduced to the organization. In other words, the fact that the senior management had employed Mark predisposed some of his colleagues to be less than cooperative with him.

Mark had been on a team-building course with a previous employer prior to joining the organization and knew that if he was to succeed in his new job he needed to win his colleagues' confidence. Unfortunately, it seemed that whenever things went well, his colleagues assumed that it was their efforts that supported the successes. Whenever something went wrong, they absolved themselves of any responsibility and attributed the problem to his lack of competence. In fact, Mark was the best-qualified and experienced person in his management level, although none of his colleagues would have admitted as much.

To counterbalance the negativity he was experiencing, Mark made a particular effort to be social and interactive with his colleagues. For example, he would reorganize his schedule to have lunch with colleagues. Also, in an attempt to stimulate a more cooperative atmosphere, Mark would involve colleagues in decision making, although he often felt ill at ease in their company. For example, his colleagues would often boost of how experienced they were as managers. However, he also noticed that contrary to his colleagues' high opinion of themselves, they were actually just average to poor at managing their divisions, as evidenced by the organization's declining market share which had not been addressed for several years and was now becoming critical.

Despite his best efforts to win his colleagues' confidence, he felt that they were still being unfriendly and uncooperative. Also, while Mark made an effort to include them in decisions, he noticed that they were critical of his decisions and did not reciprocate by asking his opinion on their areas of responsibility. In fact, Mark's colleagues attributed his behaviour as indecisiveness, confirming their original impressions that he was not suitable to do work at their level. Conversely, if Mark did not consult with his colleagues about a decision, they would criticize him for not being a team player.

After a few weeks in the job, Mark discovered that the previous person in his post had asked for a transfer to another part of the organization.

As a result of these negative experiences, Mark decided to meet with members of the senior management team and discuss some of the problems he was encountering. The senior management acknowledged that there were long-term problems with the group of managers Mark was working with and that they had hoped he could have changed the culture and management style within the group. Mark explained, not unreasonably, that most of them were on the same level as him and some were actually senior, so he had no authority and little in the way of influence to alter the group's behaviour. Following the meeting, a rumour went round the organization that the senior management were thinking about promoting Mark over his entire management group. As a result, the group's behaviour, if anything, deteriorated and became even more resentful of senior management and Mark. He now felt that he could achieve little on his own and felt pressured by both the aspirations of senior management and the negativity of his colleagues.

Despite the difficulties and discomfort Mark was experiencing, the areas of business for which he was responsible had improved, even though Mark's market analysis indicated that the organization's competitors were becoming predatorily active. He shared this information with his colleagues who dismissed his analysis. He also observed that in his experience the senior management eventually take direct action if divisional managers continually resist change. His comments, although well intentioned, further alienated his colleagues. They were much more concerned with the internal squabbles with the senior management. In fact Mark was now routinely ignored by most of his management colleagues. After all, he did not seem to be as friendly as he had been when he first joined the organization. Nevertheless, the organization's market share was declining, just as Mark's analysis had predicted and the organization was beginning to gain a reputation with external stakeholders as something of a lame duck; an organization incapable of responding to new market opportunities and competition.

After several months of what Mark described to his friends (all outside the organization) as the 'charm offensive', he decided to change tactics by ignoring his colleagues and getting on with doing his job. He rationalized that if they were unwilling to be part of the solution, there was little point in investing much more time with them. Mark's colleagues also noticed the change in his behaviour. This confirmed their first impressions that Mark was not a person to be trusted and that he had never fitted in with the 'right way' of doing things. He just isn't 'one of us' was their general consensus. However, the problems they were experiencing in the divisions they managed were becoming more acute. The senior management had also decided that since the introduction of a more positive person had apparently failed to change the culture, they would now advertise for a more adversarial director with direct control over all the divisions, with a brief to 'restructure' the underperforming parts of the organization and make redundancies among the management group.

Fortunately for Mark, the difficulties he had encountered working for the organization had considerably improved his management profile. He also had a much better understanding of the complexity of managerial work and that management research and models could help but not provide perfect solutions to workplace situations. He recalled reading somewhere that:

> Management is not so much a science as situation-specific art form, with all the emotional uncertainties and conflicts that art rather than science exposes.

He also realized that what he had learnt at the organization had prepared him to take the next step in management. Given all the problems the organization was now experiencing, Mark began to think it was time to find a new job elsewhere.

QUESTIONS

1 Why do you think Mark's colleagues were predisposed to distrust him?

2 Our first impressions can be formed by preconceived stereotypes. Why are first impressions so important?

3 Do you think people easily change their first impressions when new information becomes available or reinforce their original decision?

4 The last person to hold Mark's management position had asked to be transferred. Should the senior management have discussed this with Mark at his interview?

5 How realistic was the senior management's aspiration that Mark could change the culture and management style of his colleagues?

6 Why do you think Mark's colleagues ignored his market analysis?

7 What are the potential dangers to organizations becoming too intro-spectively focused?

8 What do you think Mark had learnt about the complexity of manage-ment? Why would this help him to get a new management job?

9 What do you think the future business prospects of this organization are likely to be?

10 Do you think changing management style and culture is difficult and if so, why?

11 When we are interacting with and managing people, why is manage-ment more like a situation-specific art form than a science?

● CAN ROCKET SCIENCE GRADUATES MAKE EFFECTIVE MANAGERS?

New HR and business graduates may encounter a common stereotype, which sustains a notion that graduates from certain universities are better, irrespec-tive of the course they have studied. The rationale used to defend this kind of stereotyping is that it creates a barrier to entry and a method of filtering the number of applications. Alternatively, the stereotype may hold that graduates from university A are more intelligent than students from university B. However, is the location of study as relevant or useful a criterion as the course studied? Sometimes this assessment of worth is based on the attended univer-sity's ranking, based on research excellence (a valuable activity in its own right), although, ironically, it could also indicate a lecturing staff that are under more pressure to spend time on their research profiles than working with students.

If it were true that the course studied was irrelevant, then perhaps a business graduate might reasonably be given the job of a surgeon? This is, of course, ridiculous, as no one would risk the lives of patients with an untrained person, no matter how intelligent they were or which university they had attended. The purpose of the illustration is simply to emphasize that management is a profession with its own skills sets. Conversely, this is not to suggest that, for example, a 'rocket science' graduate cannot be developed into an effective manager by attending a suitable postgraduate management programme.

It is worth noting that qualifications should not alone form the basis for selection, which is another form of stereotyping. For example, there are many older experienced managers who have learned the art of management through experiential practice. Although it has become fashionable for new graduates to go directly onto postgraduate degrees, it also worth considering the enriching quality of post-experiential degrees, where all the students already have several years' workplace experience and can thereby link new knowledge acquisition to post-experiential skills.

Exercise 7.2

INTERVIEWING SKILLS

Using the AKS and the CV you prepared for the previous activities, organize short interview role plays. At least one member of each team should sit out of the interview observing and making notes to feed back to the group at the end of the role play.

 CHAPTER SUMMARY

The recruitment and selection process can be a challenging area for even the most experienced of managers. After reading and completing the activities in this chapter, you should now be in a position to understand the recruitment and selection process and be more confident about your own abilities to apply for work placements or a permanent job.

The overall theme of this book is to consider HR as an integrated part of organizations. The design of recruitment and selection strategy has therefore focused on where HR input can become more a part of the whole and not a function apart. Paradoxically, in an environment where the HR team may be quite small, this can sometimes mean recognizing the need to include expertise from outside the organization.

One of the key challenges in successful recruitment is to gain the knowledge and skills to conduct interviews. The effective use of interviews is a valuable skill for any manager and as such the role plays at the end of this chapter should provide a practical forum for personal development and further discussion.

REFERENCES

Belbin, R. M. (1993) *Team Roles at Work*. Butterworth-Heinemann: London.

Belbin, R. M. (2000) *Beyond the Team*. Butterworth-Heinemann: London.

Devine, P. G. (1989) Stereotypes and Prejudice: Their Automatic and Controlled Components. *Journal of Personality and Social Psychology*, **56**.

Fletcher, C. (1991) Candidates Reactions to Assessment Centres and their Outcomes: A longitudinal Study. *Journal of Occupational Psychology*, **64**.

Goltz, S. M. and Giannantonio, C. M. (1995) Recruiter Friendliness and Attraction to the Job: The Mediating Role of Inferences about the Organization. *Journal of Vocational Behaviour*.

Harvey-Jones, J. (1995) *All Together Now*. London: Manderin.

Herriot, C. and Rothwell, P. (1981) Organizational Choice and Decision Theory: Effects of Employers Literature and Selection Interview. *Journal of Occupational Psychology*.

Hilton, J. L. and Von Hippel, W. (1996) Stereotypes. *Annual Review of Psychology*, **47**.

Huselid, M. (1995) The Impact of Human Resource Management Practices on Turnover, Productivity, and Corporate Financial Performance. *Academy of Management Journal*.

Industrial Relations Services (1997) The State of Selection 2: Developments in Basic Methods. *Employee Development Bulletin*, **85**.

Judge, T. A and Cable, D. M. (1997) Applicant Personality, Organizational Culture, and Organizational Attraction. *Personnel Psychology*.

Mason, N. A. and Belt, J. A. (1986) Effectiveness of Specificity in Recruitment Advertising. *Journal of Management*.

Maund, L. (2001) *Introduction to Human Resource Management: Theory and Practice*. Basingstoke: Palgrave – now Palgrave Macmillan.

McKenna, E. and Beech, N. (1995) *The Essence of Human Resource Management*. London: Prentice Hall.

Peters, T. (1994) *The Tom Peters Seminar: Crazy Times Call for Crazy Organizations*. London: Macmillan – now Palgrave Macmillan.

Reid, M. A. and Barrington, H. (2000) *Training Interventions. Promoting Learning Opportunities* (6th edn). London: CIPD.

Rynes, S. L. and Miller, H. E. (1983) Recruiter and Job Influences on Candidates for Employment. *Journal of Applied Psychology*.

Saks, A. M., Leck, J. D. and Saunders, D. M. (1995) Effects of Application Blanks and Employment Equity on Applicant Reactions and Job Pursuit Intentions. *Journal of Organizational Behavior*.

Smither, J. W., Reilly, R. R., Millsap, R. E., Pearlman, K. and Stoffey, R. W. (1993) Applicant Reactions To Selection Procedures. *Personnel Psychology*.

Stanton, N. (1996) *Mastering Communications* (3rd edn). Basingstoke: Macmillan – now Palgrave Macmillan.

Welbourne, T. M. and Andrews, A. O. (1996) Predicting Performance of Initial Public Offering Firms. Should Human Resource Management be in the Equation? *Academy of Management Journal*.

PERSONAL NOTES ON CHAPTER 7

Notes for seminars

_____

_____

_____

_____

_____

_____

_____

_____

_____

_____

_____

_____

_____

_____

_____

_____

_____

_____

_____

_____

_____

_____

_____

_____

_____

_____

_____

_____

_____

_____

NOTES ON CHAPTER 7 *CONTINUED*

Notes for revision/reminders

_____

_____

_____

_____

_____

_____

_____

_____

_____

_____

_____

_____

_____

_____

_____

_____

_____

_____

_____

_____

_____

_____

_____

_____

_____

_____

_____

_____

_____

_____

_____

_____

_____

Appraisals: Paperchase or Motivational Discussion?

Learning outcomes

After reading and completing the activities in this chapter, you should be able to:

1 Critically evaluate the purpose of appraisals in organizations.

2 Discuss and comment on what areas of AKS should be appraised.

3 Understand and be able to avoid the pitfalls that organizations can encounter when using appraisals.

4 Appreciate the role of HR-trained professionals in developing appraisals within organizations.

5 Design a practical appraisal system based on AKS (individual or group activity).

6 Evaluate your own confidence and competence.

7 Role play an appraisal and provide critical evaluations appraisal interviews (group activity).

INTRODUCTION

In this chapter you will learn about the effective and motivational use of appraisal interviews. The content and design of the materials that follow reflect the particularly practical, applied nature of the subject, so there is even more emphasis on activities for seminars and personal learning. This experiential approach provides the opportunity to develop knowledge and skills of the applied and interpersonal nature of appraisal interviews.

If you have had work experience and or interviewed people in organizations, it is likely that you will have some mixed impressions about the value of appraisals. Used correctly, appraisals can motivate employees and help them towards achieving goals. Used incorrectly, appraisals demotivate people and become a meaningless bureaucratic process that wastes organizational resources. It is much easier to achieve a negative outcome with an appraisal than a positive one. This is because what one person regards as 'constructive feedback' can easily be heard as negative criticism by the recipient. Therefore, if an appraisal interview is to be used, careful consideration should be given to the outcomes. Otherwise, appraisal can easily become a costly method for demotivating the workforce, which would be completely counterproductive.

The chapter will therefore ask you to evaluate the purpose and strategic role of appraisals and guide you towards designing situation-specific appraisal schemes that can add value to organizational performance.

WHAT IS APPRAISAL FOR?

To begin with, it is important to establish the purpose of the appraisal. The appraisal is a potentially a controversial HR tool that some organizations use to validate decisions of pay, promotions and status. So it is relevant to reflect on what appraisals should be used for.

The appraisal interview may be used a to evaluate a range of attitudes, knowledge and skills, although clearly the wider the range of objectives set, the more likely the possibilities for conflicts and misunderstandings. Problems with appraisal may also arise when it is used to 'achieve' too many different and sometimes contradictory aims.

Too Many Appraisal Objects?

For example, a set of conflicting appraisal objectives might include the following:

- Assess and award a comparative grade for performance
- Analyse training and development needs
- Set performance objectives
- Assess salary rewards
- Approve individual performance-related pay plans
- Encourage and motivate team working
- Motivate individuals
- Provide a channel for communication
- Provide coaching and counselling
- Identify potential for career development
- Link individual performance objectives to those of the organization
- Gather information to assist HR planning
- Listen and assess individual preferences for personal development
- Select candidates for promotion
- Comply with externally or internally imposed regulations

How Can an Appraisal Demotivate People?

Appraisals can all too easily demotivate people. Select sets of appraisal aims from those provided in the list above and think about how you might feel if you were being interviewed. Are there conflicting aims? For example, if you knew that the appraisal would decide your level of competence and that would decide if you received a pay rise, how honest might you be about your weaknesses (areas for personal development)?

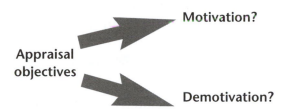

Figure 8.1 Appraisals: Paperchase or motivational discussion?

Before managers ask their people to undertake an appraisal, the objectives should be clearly defined and agreed. Unless both staff and their managers agree with the aims and objectives, then an interview may actually do more harm than good, in that it could demotivate and disaffect otherwise content employees.

What can be done if the organization's external regulator demands appraisals be conducted? It is usually the imposed varieties of appraisal that meet with the most negative reactions. The external, off-the-shelf nature of the design means that they are unlikely to be sufficiently flexible to respond to situation-specific requirements. However, most regulators should be sensible enough to allow local managers the flexibility to design a situation-specific format that meets local needs and preferences within the broader prescribed policy. If employees, volunteers or external providers are involved in the process, the appraisal could become a motivating and beneficial experience. It really makes no sense to impose an appraisal system where the net results are negative (see Schein, 1978; Johnson, 1998; Audit Commission, 2002; Yih-Tong Sun and Scott, 2003).

● PLANNING A SUCCESSFUL APPRAISAL

It is helpful to begin by thinking about what the appraisal is for. What are the likely outcomes? How will people feel after the appraisal? Will the appraisal improve staff, management, worker or volunteer relationships? Sometimes appraisal is misused as a tool to justify the distribution of pay awards. Remember that the only people who are likely to be content with such a procedure are those who are happy with their award. There are more effective and equitable HR approaches to rewarding people *(see Chapter 10, for performance and rewards)*. HR should therefore look at the larger strategic picture of performance, motivation and the influence any intervention, such as appraisals, might have on those longer term objectives. The context of the organization should be considered before the appraisal procedure is designed. For example, volunteers may be appraised, although the objectives and motivations are likely to be different to paid employees in the private sector (see Butler and Wilson, 1990; Osborne, 1996). According to research by Schweiger and Sumners (1994, p. 3), an appraisal should be designed and administered in a manner that focuses on the coaching aspect of evaluations. They found that this approach to appraisal would improve performance more rapidly and increase employee productivity. It is therefore helpful to establish the appraisal plan and design a system that integrates into the wider strategic plans and objectives of the organization. This is also in harmony with the organizationally, situation-specific philosophy of new integrated HR practices.

Pre-appraisal Planning

- Consult with employees and volunteers. What do they want from their appraisal process?
- Be clear about the objectives
- Keep the objectives simple and specific
- Avoid conflicting objectives
- Too many objectives can result in the appraisals achieving none satisfactorily
- Consult with employee representatives, including professional bodies and trade unions
- Consult with the organization's legal advisers.

And remember that appraisals which lack clear objectives can soon become:

- A meaningless ritual
- A form-filling exercise
- Disliked by managers and staff
- Demotivating for everyone involved.

● APPRAISAL METHODOLOGIES

There are many appraisal methods and even more variants. The most appropriate approach will depend on the purposes selected and other local considerations such as time availability, preferences and organizational structure culture. The notion that there may be a best practice somewhere that everyone ought to copy is best avoided. Although organizations can learn from each other, the design and methodology of an appraisal should reflect local situation-specific requirements, interests and needs *(for understanding organizational structure and culture, see Chapter 2)* (see Cederblom and Lounsbury, 1980; Burgoyne, 1988; Amarantunga and Baldry, 2002; Audit Commission, 2003; Kennerley and Neely, 2003).

The list below provides an overview of the more common appraisal methodologies.

Method 1: Appraisal by Immediate Supervisor

In the simplest of appraisal methods, the immediate manager conducts the appraisal and passes a report to the next management level and the HR team. The information then provides a springboard for initiating actions based on the appraisal's objectives. The interviewee is more of a reactive participant in so much as s/he has to respond to the information presented at the appraisal.

Advantages

It is a simple system and less time-consuming than other methods. Providing the objectives are agreed with the interviewee prior to the meeting, the simple system can offer a useful springboard for progressing agreed objectives. The interviewers are all likely to require training by an internal or external HR professional, consultancy or university business school, thereby improving HR knowledge and skills.

Disadvantages

What if the employee and immediate manager do not share or agree on the objectives? The record of the meeting may be predominantly the manager's interpretation of events. Will the interviewee regard this approach as a fair assessment?

Method 2: Self-assessment Appraisal

This approach enables each person to evaluate his or her own performance prior to the appraisal meeting. Clearly, it can be more time-consuming than method 1; however, there is an opportunity for a two-way discussion. The interviewee is able to become more of an active participant.

Advantages

The interview is based on two perspectives, manager and worker, so that both parties bring materials to the meeting to discuss. This creates more opportunity for mutual reflection. The interviewers are all likely to require training by an internal or external HR professional, consultancy or university business school, thereby improving HR knowledge and skills.

Disadvantages

What if the two assessments are very different? What if the employee or worker and immediate manager cannot agree with the outcomes?

Method 3: Peer Appraisal

This approach involves the person's work colleagues providing assessments, based on the appraisal criteria selected. The people we work with generally have an opinion as to our performance.

Advantages

Used non-judgementally, as a team working developmental tool, it can help colleagues to understand each other better and thereby improve effectiveness and cooperation. The interviewers are all likely to require training by an internal or external HR professional, consultancy or university business school, thereby improving HR knowledge and skills.

Disadvantages
It involves more work for colleagues. It can degenerate into a popularity contest. The most effective workers are not always the most popular.

Method 4: Customer Appraisal

This approach involves internal or external customers. So, for example, internal departments assessing the performance of the HR team may use it. Alternatively, the customer could be the clients a person works with, or any other stakeholders with whom the interviewee has regular contact.

Advantages
This approach draws from a much larger sample of inputs than those previously discussed. A wider strategic picture of a person in context may emerge. The interviewers are all likely to require training by an internal or external HR professional, consultancy or university business school, thereby improving HR knowledge and skills.

Disadvantages:
It is a time-consuming project. What are the achievable outcomes that would justify the time and expenditure? Because so many people are involved, it may be difficult to provide feedback that reflects the depth and breadth of the comments received. Who will provide the feedback? How does the interviewer interpret the feedback materials?

Method 5: Upward Appraisal

The employees or workers review their own manager. A person's managerial style and competence can be exposed by the opinions of those who work for him or her. This can be useful in circumstances where there is high staff turnover. Is it the job they are leaving, or the manager?

Advantages
It can encourage people to feel that their views on how the organization is managed are valued. The manager can learn about how he or she is perceived by his or her team. The interviewers are all likely to require training by an internal or external HR professional, consultancy or university business school, thereby improving HR knowledge and skills.

Disadvantages
The method can suffer from unhelpful and hurtful criticism of the manager. The most 'popular' manager might not necessarily be the most effective. The feedback has to be confidential otherwise employees might fear that negative remarks may have repercussions later. What is the intended outcome to justify the process? Will the manager be more or less motivated after the appraisal?

Method 6: 360° Appraisal

Many people are involved in the appraisal from every direction, hence the 360° description. Thus, a whole range of diverse inputs may be included, from immediate subordinates, colleagues, senior management, customers and other stakeholders.

Advantages
The method may produce a wide-reaching and comprehensive picture of a person in their overall organizational and stakeholder context. The interviewers are all likely to require training by an internal or external HR professional, consultancy or university business school, thereby improving HR knowledge and skills.

Disadvantages
There may be a lack of trust or rivalries between colleagues that may render peer evaluation impractical and even problematic. It is likely to be a costly and time-consuming process. Eventually, the feedback has to be delivered in a conventional interview. Who will be selected to interpret the material and present it? Can any anticipated outcomes or benefits of a complex 360° appraisal be justified in terms of the time invested?

Method 7: Appraisal by External Assessment Centre or Consultancy

The organization may decide to outsource part or all of the appraisal procedure to an external provider. External consultancies and university business schools can provide a diverse range of alternative appraisal methods. These can include appraisal by psychological evaluation, role play and outward-bound activities to name just a few alternatives. The discipline of situation-specific design should still be applied and, again, what are the intended outcomes?

Advantages
The process is taken out of house, so employees and workers are not distracted from their primary roles or relinquish their time conducting appraisals. The external provider should design a situation-specific programme.

Disadvantages
The external provider may attempt to sell their off-the-shelf programme. There is going to be an investment cost in using an external provider, although this needs to be regarded in the context that using internal staff also incurs costs in time and lost opportunity. (People have to stop doing their primary jobs to conduct appraisal interviews.) Nevertheless, a strategic HR decision should be made as to how situation-specific the external provider's service is and the value in terms of outcomes.

Method 8: Appraisal by Mentor

This approach may use an independent third party from within the organization, or expert from outside organization (this could be a consultant, a manager from an external organization, a university business school).

Advantages

The mentor is usually selected by consultation, so the interviewee is more likely to feel that the mentor is an 'honest broker' in as much as the person selected is not in their immediate management or departmental team. Some further HR research work may be required prior to the appraisals.

Disadvantages

There is likely to be a consultation investment for the mentor's time and involvement. The mentor may not be as familiar with the organization's internal structure and culture as someone inside the organization.

Summary of Commonly Used Appraisal Methods

The area of appraisal can be a contentious HR issue. Although it can be designed as a motivating and developmental process if managed correctly, it is easier to do more harm to motivation than good. If it is linked to rewards, pay or promotion, the developmental qualities are likely to be lost as people contend for the most favourable package (see Cederblom and Lounsbury, 1980; Halachmi, 2002; Prajogo and Sohal, 2003).

HRM IN ACTION

WHAT IS THE PURPOSE OF APPRAISALS?

I used the case study methodology as described by Yin (1994) for the research below. The case study is particularly helpful for HR investigations because the work can focus on a specific area within the organization. There are, of course, many other useful research methods *(for research methods in HR, see Chapter 11)*. The following studies focused on employee attitudes regarding appraisals and why they can become disaffected by imposed appraisal procedures.

The two short case studies illustrate some of the problems managers I have interviewed encountered in the design and implementation of appraisals. Essentially, they are both concerned with what an appraisal should be used for in organizations.

THE FIRST ATTEMPT

A manager from a major international company told me that his organization had had two completely different appraisal systems in one year. The first appraisal method was internally designed and focused on identifying each employee's areas of strength and weakness. Interestingly, the manager reported that after the employees' weaknesses were identified, there were no prearranged provisions for follow-up personal development and training. This left some staff feeling demotivated because they had been told of weaknesses in their knowledge and skills base, but not given support to improve their performance. He thought that the appraisal procedure had consequently disaffected employees. It was also reported that there had been some negative criticisms by appraisal interviewers that had diminished some employee's confidence and even led to a diminution of competence.

The managers interviewed observed that the appraisal process was a costly investment of employee time and resources. It was really not worthwhile if the outcome was a reduction in performance and poorer management and employee relationships. It was commented that managers didn't need an appraisal procedure to be rude and or demotivate their teams. A simple insult could be just as effective for that 'purpose' as the appraisals had been!

THE SECOND ATTEMPT

An external consultancy firm was brought in to introduce an alternative appraisal method that the company adopted. This system required every employee to sit a set of tests on areas such as literacy and analytical skills. The consultancy advice that followed recommended that employees focus on building on their areas of strength. Again, no specific follow-up training programme as to how people could develop their 'strengths' was put in place.

There was evidence of contradictory messages with the two approaches. In the first appraisal method, the company sought out areas of weakness for the employee to address, while the second encouraged people to concentrate on their areas of strength. Employees reported feeling confused about what was expected of them. The managers I interviewed questioned which of these approaches might be the most beneficial, focusing on weaknesses or building strengths? They regarded the lack of training support and development as a key omission.

DISCUSSION QUESTIONS

1   Why do you think the appraisal procedures were unsuccessful?

2   The managers appeared to have no clear understanding of the appraisal's objectives. Why would this make it more likely to fail?

3   Why is it important to put a follow-up training and development budget in place before beginning appraisal interviews?

4   Why do you think appraisal interviewers should receive training?

HRM IN ACTION

SURPRISE, YOUR JOB HAS CHANGED!

This HRM in Action is derived from a small research study I conducted into appraisals outcomes.

A manager, who was working in computer software development within a major city business, told me of his concerns regarding a conflict of work priorities. During an appraisal, he was advised that his job role was to be changed. This was a complete surprise and occurred without any prior discussion or consultation. The new role meant that in addition to his current responsibilities for software design development, he would also have a general management responsibility. His concern was that the software design and management roles were very different and if the design function was the priority, he should be given the time to concentrate on it. Although he accepted the need for people to have multiple roles, he did not think the appraisal was the best place to announce a change of job function. Furthermore, there was no supporting training or mentoring to help him to achieve the new dual role.

DISCUSSION QUESTIONS

1   What are the potential difficulties with announcing unexpected changes at an appraisal interview?

2   Why is it important to allow interviewees the opportunity to express their career development preferences rather than impose changes?

3   Discuss in what ways a mentor can be useful in post-appraisal, management development?

APPRAISAL: IT'S PERSONAL

One of the key issues of appraisal is to recognize the requirement of fitness for purpose, so one size does not fit all. The HR team should design appraisal formats in close consultation with the people involved towards agreed objectives (see Franco and Bourne, 2003). The one-size-fits-all approach to appraisals cannot reflect the necessarily person-specific nature of an appraisal interview. HR should recognize that people doing different jobs, even if they are in the same department, are likely to have different attitudes, knowledge, and skills profiles. Furthermore, the AKS for an experienced person who has done a job for several years is likely to be different from someone who has just begun the same job role. Clearly, the organization should not expect as much from someone who has been in a job for a short period of time as the more experienced worker. Although it may be bureaucratically expedient to require every-body to follow exactly the same procedure, people are likely to be less comfort-able with a generic format. Is HR about people, or enforcing procedure? I hope you are thinking people.

So What Do You Think of Appraisals?

Are appraisals about management control? Is appraisal a one-way process where managers evaluate subordinates? It is certainly evident that some organizations and regulators have a preference towards control rather than participation (see Raaum, 1998; Bittici et al., 2000).

An experienced executive on a postgraduate course told me that:

> The appraisal process is seen by many as a waste of time. The theory and reasoning behind the policy is excellent but the implementation and development of the process is sorely lacking. Management are sent on a two-day course and are then expected to perform effective appraisals of all their staff, without any continuing help or training.

It is interesting that this person actually received a two-day training course and still felt ill prepared for the task of conducting appraisal interviews. Many people are expected to succeed with absolutely no training. Although training is helpful, it cannot compensate for lack of consultation and agreed objectives. If there is the least suspicion that the appraisal process is just a bureaucratic paper chase, do not be surprised if the results are negative. No one likes having his or her time wasted. The fieldwork conducted by Barlow (1989, p. 505) also found similar attitudes, whereby managers indicated that they found appraisals less useful than personal knowledge and judgement.

Furthermore, appraisals are likely to raise expectations, so plans should be in place to deliver improvements before the appraisals take place. It is better to undersell the importance of appraisal, then overdeliver in staff development, rather than to oversell the appraisals, then underdeliver on improvements, precip-itating demotivation.

THE AKS APPRAISAL MODEL (ATTITUDES, KNOWLEDGE AND SKILLS)

In Chapter 6 we reviewed recruitment and selection. If an appraisal interview is being planned, then the job description can be a good place to begin when constructing the framework. The original attitudes, knowledge and skills for which the person was originally selected may form the starting point for the appraisal design. It is also possible, indeed likely, that the job role and person have developed so the recruitment criteria may be out of date, even after a few months. The framework is similar to the selection process. Begin by agreeing what the key attitudes, knowledge and skills are with the person to be appraised. These can be subdivided into key areas and desirable ones, as shown below.

AKS Appraisals Framework

Attitudes		Knowledge		Skills	
key areas	desirable	key areas	desirable	key areas	desirable

PRACTISING HRM

DESIGNING AN AKS APPRAISAL FOR A LECTURER

Many of the postgraduate and undergraduate students I've worked with particularly enjoy this 'role reversal' exercise, designing an AKS appraisal form for a lecturer, from a student's perspective. I have found it interesting to review the differences between what the consumers think is important and what the providers select.

DISCUSSION QUESTIONS

1 Why do you think different stakeholders may have differing priorities?

2 If there are differences, is anyone's selection more important?

3 Do you think employers should also include those criteria that are selected by their stakeholders?

4 What is the purpose of appraisal?

5 Who do you think benefits most from appraisal?

6 Who do you think should benefit most from an appraisal?

● THE CONFIDENCE AND COMPETENCE MODEL

Our confidence and competence to perform effectively can be influenced by many factors such as personal circumstances, social, health and life–work balance. Each of us comes into contact with other people and how those interactions work can help or hinder our and their success.

Desk Note: It worth remembering that:
Encouragement costs the giver nothing … It can enrich the receiver immeasurably.

In my management and teaching experience, most people respond positively to encouragement. I have also observed that people in the workplace usually respond negatively to managers who resort to sarcasm, insults or negative criticism. Indeed such behaviour should not be accepted in any organization. It follows that providing opportunities for personal development and nurturing improvements in self-worth are not only good for people, but can improve organizational performance too. A longitudinal study by Axtell and Parker (2003, pp. 113–31) indicated that membership of an active improvement group and personal development could influence confidence in performing proactive, interpersonal tasks. We work more effectively if we have a better self-image. The appraisal interview is therefore an ideal opportunity to help build on the positive aspects of a person's attitudes, knowledge and skills. The model below is provided to help you evaluate your personal perception of confidence and competence (Figure 8.2).

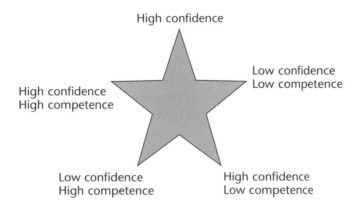

Figure 8.2 Confidence and competence model

High Confidence

A person who does not appreciate the nature or complexity of management may express high confidence in what they believe to be a less than challenging set of attitudes, knowledge and skills. The person's competence is not listed at this point because it has yet to be tested. A common example of this position is someone who has enjoyed success in a functional role, which could be any task where the primary function is about doing, rather than directing the work of others. Indeed, the more functionally successful a person has been, the higher their confidence is likely to be. This can include numerous roles including computer programmer, salesperson, accountant or lawyer. In each case, when a person is moved to take on more responsibility, a period of development is necessary, particularly if the new responsibilities include managing and leading a team which is different from the functional 'doing' role to which the person is accustomed.

Those who are new to the workplace, such as younger graduates, should also take care not to misunderstand the significant differences between resolving business case studies and role plays in the safe environment of a seminar group, to the challenge of making decisions in real time inside an organization. Although vocational business courses provide an excellent foundation for organizational life, they cannot supply someone who has little or no work experience with all the attitudes, knowledge and skills they will need in a lifelong career. Instead, first-degree business courses may be viewed as a starting point of a lifelong learning process, which can include further formal education, professional development as well as experiential learning.

An example of experiential learning is where an experienced manager delegates some tasks to an aspiring young employee precisely to build up their confidence and experience. This experience is a valuable first step in preparing someone for future promotion.

Low Confidence, Low Competence

If an employee is promoted into a managerial or new position of responsibility too quickly, they may feel overwhelmed by their new job role. Any initial bravado or confidence can evaporate quickly in the heat of workplace pressures. In this scenario, the newly promoted employee is likely to display low confidence and low competence because, unless sufficient support is provided, s/he is likely to make a more than average number of errors and misjudgements, which in turn dampens their confidence. This is like the proverbial swimming 'instructor' who throws the novice into the deep end of the pool. It such circumstances, it really is sink or swim. This approach is likely to be inefficient because the inexperienced manager or employee will doubtless make many mistakes and without adequate guidance it is by no means certain that they will gain the attitudes, knowledge and skills required to be successful.

High Confidence, Low Competence

Most people are capable to learning from their mistakes and gaining some competence through the attrition of experience and by seeking out professional development. However, there are those employees and managers who appear to continue having the same experiences without developing their own attitudes, knowledge and skills. One of the areas where high confidence and low competence is most likely to be evident to HR professionals is where managers continue making errors in staff recruitment, or fail to induct and develop employees, resulting in higher than usual staff turnover. In such situations, the manager tends to disassociate his/her actions from the consequences, so it appears that the new employees 'fail to meet expectations', the high staff turnover in his/her department has nothing to do with poor motivation, and projects fail to deliver because of the team's poor performance rather than his/her lack of leadership skills.

Low Confidence, High Competence

Workers who return to employment after a career break or people moving into a new sector are likely to bring a wealth of experience to their new organizations.

However, entering a new situation can be disconcerting, so such people may display low confidence. In higher education, I have noticed that some mature students can be found in this category. Providing sufficient encouragement and recognition is given, such people can perform very well, hence they have high competence. Mature returnees may (although certainly not in all cases) require some additional training in the use of new information technologies. The knowledge and skills such employees can bring to an organization is worth the small additional investment in training to build up confidence.

High Confidence, High Competence

High confidence, high competence refers to accomplished managers and professionals who can achieve high standards of performance and are sufficiently confident to understand the importance of continuous professional development for both themselves and the people with whom they work.

My research with recruitment consultancies indicated that confidence and competence did not automatically ensure selection to senior organizational positions. This may be because a significant part of career success also relates to cultural behavioural norms and organizational politics. Hence, it is also possible that senior managers may lack the confidence to select the most capable person for a job precisely because their high level of ability might lead them to challenge the status quo that top management may wish to preserve. Nevertheless, there are clear advantages in personal professional integrity and self-worth by aiming to be the best that you can be in any given job role. The values portrayed by confident, competent employees are likely to increase employability and are more likely to result in new job opportunities. In an employment environment where no one organization can realistically guarantee long-term employment, the only real security is employability. It is therefore worthwhile investing in personal professional development, irrespective of whether it produces immediate progression in a current organization.

Exercise 8.1

CONFIDENCE AND COMPETENCE

Read the descriptors for the confidence and competence model. Think about a specific work situation you are, or have been, involved in, to answer the self-assessment questionnaire. The context of your answers can also be based on a course of study you are currently following. There are no right or wrong answers to the questions. Instead use them to reflect on the extent to which you feel confident and competent to undertake the work you are involved in.

If you are working in a team, it may be useful to have a discussion about your results with your colleagues. Please do not be judgemental. The aim is to encourage others in developing self-confidence and competence.

1	Strongly disagree	5	Slightly agree
2	Moderately disagree	6	Moderately agree
3	Slightly disagree	7	Strongly agree
4	Neither agree nor disagree		

1   I am always confident that I will be successful in whatever work I do.

   1   2   3   4   5   6   7

2   I am very good at the work I am currently involved in.

   1   2   3   4   5   6   7

3   If someone is finding their work difficult I am usually able to help them.

   1   2   3   4   5   6   7

4   I have received a lot of personal support to help me to improve my work performance.

   1   2   3   4   5   6   7

5   It is rarely the case that someone finds I have made a significant error in the work I am responsible for.

   1   2   3   4   5   6   7

6   I have to check my work several times to correct earlier mistakes.

   1   2   3   4   5   6   7

7   I do not think I am naturally very good at the work I am currently required to do.

   1   2   3   4   5   6   7

8   I enjoy working on my own more than working with other people.

   1   2   3   4   5   6   7

9   I felt more confident doing my previous job or course.

   1   2   3   4   5   6   7

10   The work I have been given is too difficult.

   1   2   3   4   5   6   7

ROLE PLAY AN APPRAISAL INTERVIEW

It is now time to try to convert critical evaluation and personal reflections into a real appraisal format. This exercise provides an experience of appraisal design and the opportunity to evaluate critically the key factors involved in appraisal implementation.

Using the AKS framework, design an appraisal for:

A management student on your course

Or

An HR associate in your organization

Or

Your own job

AKS Appraisals Framework

Attitudes		Knowledge		Skills	
key areas	desirable	key areas	desirable	key areas	desirable

Designing the appraisal can be an individual or team task. However, to get the most from the appraisal interview, form teams of three, the interviewer, the interviewee and an observer.

Afterwards, the observer can feed back to the team on how effective the appraisal interview was.

Observer's brief:

Make notes on the following:

- How positive was the interviewer?
- Where was the interview conducted? Was the environment conducive to discussion or was it too public? Were there interruptions by outsiders, the telephone or passers by?
- Did the interviewer and interviewee agree?
- If there were disagreements, how did the interviewer handle the situation?
- Was the overall outcome of the appraisal likely to increase or decrease the interviewee's motivation?

● CHAPTER SUMMARY

As with so many aspects of HR, appraisals may be interpreted differently by individual organizations. However, this is in harmony with a view of HR as a situation-specific service. Although appraisals may be used for all kinds of supervisory reasons the key issue should be whether employee, worker or volunteer motivation is improved or lessened by the appraisal process. If appraisal is designed as a motivating and developmental process, it can be a useful aid to employee development. However, appraisals that aspire to achieve too many objectives can do more harm than good to motivation levels. Commentary that may sound like constructive criticism to the interviewer may be interpreted as negative feedback by the interviewee. Hence, appraisals with many conflicting objectives are likely to fail. An appraisal that is linked to rewards, pay and promotion is less likely to achieve developmental aims as interviewees contend for the most favourable package. Issues such as discipline and pay should not be dealt with in appraisals. Instead, separate and specific meetings should be arranged to deal with such matters.

● REFERENCES

Amarantunga, D. and Baldry, D. (2002) Moving from Performance Measurement to Performance Management. *Facilities*, **20**(5/6).

Audit Commission (2002) *Targets in the Public Sector*. London: Audit Commission.

Audit Commission (2003) *Acting on Facts: Using Performance Measurement to Improve Local Authority Services*. London: Audit Commission.

Axtell, C. M. and Parker, S. K. (2003) Promoting Role Breadth Self-efficacy Through Involvement, Work Redesign and Training. *Human Relations*, **56**(1).

Barlow, G. (1989) Deficiencies and the Perpetuation of Power. Latent Functions in Management Appraisal. *Journal of Management Studies*, **26**.

Bittici, U. S., Turner, T. and Begemann, C. (2000) Dynamics of Performance Measurement Systems. *International Journal of Operations and Production Management*, **20**(6).

Burgoyne, J. (1988) Management Development for the Individual and for the Organisation. *Personnel Management*, June.

Butler, R. J. and Wilson, D. C. (1990) *Managing Voluntary and Non-profit Organisations. Strategy and Structure*. London: Routledge.

Cederblom, D. and Lounsbury, J. W. (1980) An Investigation of The User Acceptance of Peer Evaluation. *Personnel Psychology*, **33**.

Franco, M. and Bourne, M. (2003) Factors that Play a Role in 'Managing Through Measures'. *Management Decision*, **41**(8).

Halachmi, A. (2002) Performance Measurement: A Look at Some Possible Dysfunctions. *Work Study*, **51**(4/5).

Johnson, A. (1998) Performance Monitoring and Policy-making: Making Effective Use of Evaluation Strategies. *Total Quality Management*, **9**(2/3).

Kennerley, M. and Neely, A. (2003) Measuring Performance in a Changing Business Environment. *International Journal of Operations and Production Management*, **23**(2).

Osborne, S. (ed.) (1996) *Managing in the Voluntary Sector: A Handbook for Managers in Charitable and Non-profit Organisations*. London: Thomson International Business Press.

Prajogo, D. I. and Sohal, A. S. (2003) The Relationship Between TQM Practices, Quality Performance, and Innovation Performance: An Empirical Examination. *International Journal of Quality and Reliability Management*, **20**(8).

Raaum, R. B. (1998) Control and Controls: Is There a Difference? *The Government Accountants Journal*, **47**(1): 10–12.

Schein, E. H. (1978) *Career Dynamics: Matching Individual and Organisational Needs*. Massachusetts: Addison-Wesley.

Schweiger, I. and Sumners, G. E. (1994) Optimizing the Value of Performance Appraisals. *Managerial Auditing Journal*, **9**(8).

Yih-Tong Sun, P. and Scott, J. L. (2003) Towards Better Qualitative Performance Measurement in Organizations. *The Learning Organisation*, **10**(5).

Yin, R. K. (1994) *Case Study Research* (2nd edn). London: Sage.

PERSONAL NOTES ON CHAPTER 8

Notes for seminars

_____

_____

_____

_____

_____

_____

_____

_____

_____

_____

_____

_____

_____

_____

_____

_____

_____

_____

_____

_____

_____

NOTES ON CHAPTER 8 *CONTINUED*

Notes for revision/reminders

_____

_____

_____

_____

_____

_____

_____

_____

_____

_____

_____

_____

_____

_____

_____

_____

_____

_____

_____

_____

_____

_____

_____

_____

_____

_____

_____

_____

_____

_____

_____

Chapter 9

Integrated Employee Development

Learning outcomes

After reading and completing the activities in this chapter, you should be able to:

1 Appreciate the value of employee development in improving organizational performance.
2 Evaluate the application of differing methodologies in employee development.
3 Understand and apply the employee development star.
4 Recognize the key stages of employee development and apply the employee development star.
5 Apply the competence and confidence model to employee development.
6 Understand the role of HR-trained professionals in developing an integrated organizational plan for employee development.
7 Appreciate why some organizations underinvest in employee development and the case for advocating greater investment.
8 Recognize the value of experiential learning.
9 Present a case (individual or group presentation) on the value and place of employee development in modern organizations.

● INTRODUCTION

Employee development is an essential and arguably continuous organizational endeavour. The case for this kind of investment does however need to be made by HR professionals to colleagues who may have a number of other projects demanding investment of resources. It is important for the HR specialist to be equipped to provide recommendations regarding the management of an organization's most valuable asset, people. Irrespective of whether employees are full time, part time or volunteers in the not-for-profit sector, they can achieve more, become more fulfilled, if they are nurtured and encouraged in the work for which they are responsible. Whilst organizations normally know the costs of items such as buildings and equipment, the energies of people can be squandered on demotivating and uninteresting tasks that may do little or nothing to achieve the organization's key objectives *(planning is discussed in Chapter 11)*. Moreover, potentially valuable ideas and developments may be lost unless the organization recognizes the value of its people and the contributions they can make.

⬤ DOES TRAINING AND INVESTMENT IN PEOPLE REALLY WORK?

The question managers are likely to be asking HR professionals, is does training and investment in people really work? In plain balance sheet terms, is training a cost or an investment? The evidence from research is encouraging, linking effective training to improved performance. According to Savery and Luks (2004, pp. 119–23), in a four-year study, the Australian government collected data on approximately 10,000 registered SMEs conducting business. The evidence indicated correlations between training investment and productivity. However, detractors could argue that correlations do not necessarily prove causality. To illustrate the point, if researchers studied students who spend lots of time reading, they might find a correlation between hours spent reading and improved coursework results, so correlation could be established but causality could be more difficult to quantify. I have known some students who have read so much material that they became confused, conversely, others are able to scan read material quickly to a gain an impression of the key points. Returning to the workplace, how much training is necessary to produce improved productivity? It is a difficult question because it is probably the wrong question to ask! Although an exact measured link between people development and performance is difficult to quantify, humans behaviours – self-worth, motivation, commitment, enthusiasm – undoubtedly make a major contribution to workplace performance. While these qualities are difficult to measure, few managers would argue that they have no influence on work performance. In studying people and what they do for organizations, it is not always the quantifiable, but the qualitative that can make the difference.

The value placed on employee development has been found to vary considerably from one organization to another and according to national culture. For example, British companies spend 0.15 per cent of their turnover on training. In Japan, France and Germany, it is between 1 and 2 per cent (Hutton, 1995, p. 187). People working for the public or charity sectors should not assume that these concerns only apply to the commercial sector. In an environment of league tables for schools and hospitals and where charities have to persuade stakeholders of the efficaciousness of their cause, effective leadership and management are complimentary necessities to sound public service. Indeed, within the not-for-profit sector, it is arguably more important to seek the highest standards of professionalism, given that the purpose of the work is to serve the needs of other people, whether through healthcare, education or charitable activities.

Employee development is therefore a continuous process where employee knowledge and skills are enhanced to meet the new opportunities and challenges that are an inevitable part of organizational life. The HR specialist can provide valuable input by sensitively anticipating developmental needs, providing employee development initiatives which meet both the individual's aspirations and the needs of the organization.

INTEGRATED HR IS FOR SMEs TOO

With the modern integrated HR approach, the HR specialist becomes fully involved in helping managers to achieve their objectives. In practice, this means more than just disseminating information and procedures. The modern HR professional should be able to integrate with the management team helping them with appropriate knowledge and skills, thereby empowering managers to be more effective. This movement has been noted by academics, for example Bratton and Gold (1999, p. 275) argued that human resource development has been moving out of the training departments as organizations increasingly become aware of the value of integrating work with learning.

The integration of HR is particularly useful to SMEs. My research studies and consultancy work with SMEs indicated that, in a significant number of organizations, there was no training department or even on-site HR specialist. Indeed, many SMEs may not have the resources to employ a full-time HR team. So these organizations are dependent on external sources of advice and training. If resources are limited, it is all the more important to invest in activities that add real value to performance. According to research by Kirkbride (2003, pp. 171–80), HR input is sometimes wasted by spending too much time on administrative aspects of the role whilst neglecting some of the more strategic matters. This is interesting because it reflects the old-style personnel management preoccupations with policies and procedures. Whilst procedures are important to the smooth running of any organization, the adage 'less is more' can release valuable staff time to forming strategic plans and investing in the continuous development of employees, workers, volunteers – the people who make things happen in organizations. The outsourcing of HR by SMEs can work more effectively if they have someone to oversee and integrate the external providers with the strategy of their organization. For example, a university business school can provide independent advice and support to SMEs in their local area.

Integrating management development has to be relevant and seen to be useful to the workforce. Utilizing a longitudinal survey methodology, Belling et al. (2004, pp. 234–55) found both perceived barriers and facilitators to the transfer of learning back to the workplace. For management development plans to be successful, employees, workers and volunteers need to understand the value and application of what they are learning; this also applies to students. The pursuit of esoteric intellectualism might be mentally stimulating; however, it is the translation and communication of learning theories into managerial applications that facilitates the transfer of learning into the workplace. The progressive, modern business schools are interacting more with the organizational world of practitioners.

There is a further challenge to any external provider; the content and language of training materials should be situation-specific. So terms such as 'costs minimization', 'administrative compliance' and 'cost benefits analysis' may be not be the best language to convince a hospital doctor, a charity fieldworker, a volunteer or a teacher of the benefits of a development or change programme. It is up to the training provider to demonstrate empathy and understanding: to be part of the solution, not another additional administrative problem.

Asking open questions can help to determine training interests and needs:

● Please describe the key activities you are involved in?
● What do you see as your key training needs?
● How can additional training help with your work?
● What advantages to your own work satisfaction and career is this training likely to have?

Management development has to be designed to meet a person's requirements as well as the organizational aims and objectives. Mighty and Ashton (2003, pp. 14–31) offered the proactive challenge of whether management development is a 'hoax or hero'? Certainly, organizations should expect their developmental plans to deliver benefits. Irrespective of whether the HR input is delivered internally or from an external source, the integrated approach requires the provision of training in recruitment and selection, induction, appraisals, team management, time management, employee motivation, employee development and rewards, linked to the strategic organizational plan. This can include internal courses, external management development via business schools or an appropriate management training organization or consultant. One of the barriers to such initiatives can be that some operational managers may wrongly believe that they do not have enough time to undertake these activities. Indeed, it is quite possible that a manager has reached their position through operational successes and has had little or no specific managerial training. There is considerable value in experiential learning; however, the addition of targeted managerial development initiatives which focus on specific training needs can be beneficial to improving management performance. Understandably, some managers may feel uncomfortable discussing their own training needs and development with an internal HR employee. In such cases it may be worthwhile recommending a business course at a university, or an external mentor or consultant to assist them.

In Chapter 4, the implications of psychological contracts were discussed, regarding employee commitment and loyalty to their organizations. In the modern workplace environment, some employers have chosen to reduce their commitment to providing long-term employment security. The effective manager should recognize that in the absence of a long-term psychological contract *(psychological contracts are discussed in Chapter 4)*, the best inducement for attracting and retaining well-motivated staff is the provision of opportunities for career development that can also enhance longer term employability. While it is inevitable that some of the best people will move to new challenges and career opportunities, they are likely to be more effective and motivated if they are being provided with personal development. Such initiatives may be an encouragement for employees to remain longer with the same employer, who thereby benefits from a more stable workforce. Conversely, the disruption caused by staff turnover in terms of disturbed internal and external relationships can weaken organizational momentum and alienate influential stakeholders. According to Storey and Sisson (1993, p. 183) organizations are beginning to recognize that customers are more likely to form impressions through their interactions with people rather than the quality documentation or publicity statements. This reinforces the case for more investment in employees who are ultimately the people who deliver, or not, on the promises made by the organization's marketing people and quality assurance documentation. This also cautions managers to invest more in developing their people, rather than imposing more and more so-called quality assurance documentation, which may distract and demotivate and consequently reduce the quality of service and productivity.

In the traditional form of personnel management, it was not always recognized as a key function to provide organizations with proactive guidance on the strategic planning of employee development. For example, research by Purcell and Ahlstrand (1994, p. 65) found that management did not always utilize a strategic approach to the development of people, instead a reactive, short-termist approach appeared to be common. However, it is arguable that the role of modern HR-trained specialists should be to give leadership in people management issues inside their organizations. Stephen Covey, interviewed in *People Management* by Stern (2002, p. 38), has asserted that people have to decide to lead and that leadership is a proactive decision to act, not a name on an organizational chart. Such action requires courage and it can be easier to remain silent in organizational cultures that can punish criticism, however true it might be. Hence the organizational clichés are so common, such as 'not rocking the boat', 'go with the flow' 'custom and practice', 'it's always been done that way', 'best left as it is', 's/he is a safe pair of hands'. It takes courage to change and respond to new circumstances. According to Senge et al. (1994, p. 11), the only sustainable source of competitive advantage is an organization's ability to respond and learn quicker than its competition. So change is an inevitable part of management development, including how to implement progress and draw on the experience and knowledge within the organization. Thus, it is people who are the key to success in whatever an organization is aiming to achieve and continuous development requires proactive action.

The organization that is willing to invest in management development will also benefit from their enhanced knowledge and skills (see Mumford, 1993). During the course of researching this book, a few of the senior executives I talked to privately expressed concerns about what they perceive as the danger of developing employees so that they can leave to join their competitors. Of course, it is true that people do move on to seek out new opportunities and challenges. However, is it better to have highly skilled staff working in your organization that others would welcome on their staff, or employees with out-of-date skills who would find it difficult to get another job?

HRM IN ACTION

NOTHING TO DO AT INFORMATION CO.

This HRM in action study is based upon qualitative research interviews *(for research methods see Chapter 11)* with a sample group of employees (fictitious names have been used to protect their identities) in an organization I shall refer to as Information Co.

Robert is a conscientious computer systems designer. When the project he was leading came to a successful completion, he hoped to be given a new and interesting project, which would stretch his abilities and offer an interesting challenge. Instead nothing happened. He was asked to attach himself to a management team, but there seemed to be no specific work to be done.

Peter found himself in a similar situation to Robert and decided that the best option was to 'appear busy' and become involved in several high-profile management action groups, although little action appeared to result from their deliberations. Peter was aware of some dysfunctional team projects as well as problems with both the confidence and even competence of some senior managers and colleagues. He therefore tactfully contacted the HR department and asked for some advice as to how these issues might be addressed. Aware that the situation with the teams and senior managers could be politically difficult for the HR employees, Peter also asked if they might consider talking to an external HR professional for an outsider's view of the situation. This possibility was politely considered and then not acted upon.

Meanwhile, Robert was becoming increasingly disaffected with the organization. He told me that he had nothing of any significance to do. As a successful person with a distinguished employment track record, Robert found the situation frustrating. However, because the organization's performance was falling below top management's expectations, Robert had heard unconfirmed rumours that some employees might be made redundant. Confident that he could find alternative employment when required, he decided to stay with Information Co. in the hope that it might offer him a generous package to leave. This was a potentially risky strategy, but Robert had high confidence in his employability, although more so from his earlier experiences with the organization than for the work he had done recently. In fact it took over a year for the organization to approach Robert about redundancy, but when the package was offered he accepted and left a few weeks later.

Peter felt that the organization had made mistakes in its employee development strategies and was vindicated when performance results continued to be poor, bringing the organization's share price to a new low valuation. Although he was a competent manager, Peter lacked the confidence to challenge the status quo. The redundancies tended to encourage Peter towards caution in his relations with the senior management.

Robert was now unemployed, but with a valuable redundancy package, which was sufficient to maintain his family for several months, he decided to take some time off work. However, within a couple of weeks of leaving Information Co. a old contact telephoned Robert to discuss the possibility of doing some work on an interesting project. This person was now managing a successful consultancy firm and was keen to have Robert's expertise on the team for a new client. While negotiations were in progress, Robert had further offers of work and also sought advice on new avenues for career development. Consequently, he tendered in a much higher priced proposal for the work on the consultancy project. Robert was therefore surprised when the overpriced tender was accepted without hesitation.

The project had an estimated duration of three years and the client had had to pay well above premium rates to attract the high-calibre team the consultancy firm had managed to build for the project. Robert began work on the new development work immediately and occasionally had to visit the client's offices. The client was his old employer, Information Co.

Robert was happy to do the work with his former colleagues in the knowledge that he was now being paid much more, working on an interesting project and free to follow other interests in his spare time. Conversely, Information Co. was now paying a premium rate for the knowledge and skills of someone they had previously made redundant.

DISCUSSION QUESTIONS

1   Why do you think that a lack of interesting work can alienate employees from their organization?

2   Assess the HR department's response to a request for support in management development by Peter.

3   What do you understand by the expression 'politically difficult' for the HR employees to make recommendations to senior managers?

4   In what ways might the HR department have been able to save the organization money by inviting an external HR person to advise them on employee development?

5   Peter is described as more competent than confident. How did this influence the decisions he made?

6   List and discuss the failures in employee development highlighted in the case study.

7   The organization had indirectly re-employed Robert after they had made him redundant. Comment on the issues this raises for senior management development.

PRESENTING EMPLOYEE DEVELOPMENT

Design a ten-minute presentation to deliver to your seminar group (individual or group presentation) on:

Why employee development is important to modern organizations *(presentation skills are discussed in Chapter 12).*

● TO E-LEARN OR NOT TO E-LEARN?

The use of new technology is nothing new. Humans have been employing new implements ever since the first person decided s/he would use a stone. The modern techno-addicts might assert that some management development is pre-techno revolution. Conversely, inadequate staff training can lead to techno resistance. However, the integrated approach to HR encourages situation-specific awareness of fitness for purpose, whereby the best tools are selected for the particular task. It is the management development objectives and learning outcomes that should inform the methodological selection.

E-based HR

The use of web-based distance learning can provide useful HR materials that can be designed to a meet a specific HR requirement. According to Long and Smith (2004, pp. 270–84), modern computer technology can facilitate innovative training methods. Furthermore, the transfer of HR materials out of filing cabinets onto more user-friendly accessible formats is a step in the right direction and is compatible with the model of integrated HR, whereby managers are increasingly responsibility for the local HR matters.

Web-based Programmes in Australia, Hong Kong and Singapore

Liyanage and Poon (2003, pp. 579–602) studied the epistemological, pedagogical and organizational factors impacting on the design and delivery for web-based programmes in Australia, Hong Kong and Singapore and argued for a more pragmatic use of technology management education. Essentially the use of any medium including e-learning can be evaluated on the basis of fitness for purpose and the extent to which it may add value to the management development process.

It is also relevant to note that the underpinning decision making for management development can benefit from the academic rigour in critically evaluating methodology. Evidently, there are many alternative approaches to HR delivery. A business student is usually required to defend his/her selections of primary and secondary tools for their research dissertation. Similarly, effective management development programmes should be based on the best delivery tools for the selected learning outcomes.

E-learning Programmes in the UK

According to Overton's research (2004, p. 17) into 15 UK-based organizations, including IT, financial services, government, telecommunications, manufacturing, retail, consultancy and transport, 60 per cent of e-learning programmes in organizations failed. However, more encouragingly, those programmes that centred on learner's needs and motivations were more successful. Hence, the imposition of e-learning, whether for technological or cost-saving priorities, is less efficacious than a programme built to meet learners' needs, motivations and their situation.

● THE EMPLOYEE DEVELOPMENT STAR

Although most of the organizations I have come into contact with through research and consultancy have different approaches to HR, they share a common desire to employ competent people who can make a contribution to their objectives. What organizations also share are variations in their performance in recruiting and retaining people who match the organizations needs *(recruitment and selection is discussed in Chapter 7)*. The employee development star (Figure 9.1) provides a framework from which practitioners may formulate HRM initiatives appropriate to their specific organizational situation. The five areas are discussed in more detail in the rest of the chapter.

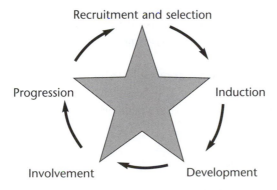

Figure 9.1 Employee development star

● RECRUITMENT AND SELECTION

The key first step in effective employee development is to select the right people. Indeed, the relationship between the individual and the organization actually begins before they are invited to an interview. Potential employees form impressions of what a prospective organization might be like to work for from a multitude of sources, including advertisements, personal experience as a customer, public relations, recommendations (from friends, lecturers, or current employees) and research activity into a particular employment sector. Given that Chapter 6 is dedicated to recruitment and selection, it is sufficient here to acknowledge the importance of considering the work a person will be expected to undertake so that the AKS (attitudes, knowledge and skills) profile meets the current needs of the job role *(see Chapter 7 for recruitment and selection)*. If the position has become available because of the progression to a new role by a current employee, then their input into the essential and desirable AKS will be valuable in helping to form a profile for the vacancy. Some organizations attempt to select a new person who is similar to the pervious incumbent. However, neither similarity nor dissimilarity is particularly relevant in comparison to the suitability for the new job role, which may have changed considerably since the previous person was employed and may therefore require a different AKS.

The salary and rewards package should be benchmarked against other organizations in the sector, as well as job roles available to people with similar experience and qualifications. If the package is not sufficiently attractive, it will be difficult to recruit new staff and without opportunities for improvement employees may leave or become dissatisfied.

Recruitment and Selection Summary

- Prospective employees gain impressions of the organization before they join, so ensure that HR expertise is available to colleagues with responsibility for marketing and customer relations.
- Design a new profile of the AKS for the vacancy. The job may have changed since the last person was employed in the role.
- Be realistic about the qualifications and experience needed to do the job.
- Select someone who meets the essential and most of the desirable requirements set out in the AKS.
- Be honest with interviewees about what the job entails and what they are expected to achieve.
- Benchmark the salary and rewards package.

● INDUCTION

The recruitment and selection process may be likened to a kind of courtship where both prospective employer and employee are presenting their best attributes. Unfortunately the higher the employer's hype, the greater the disillusionment is likely to be once the new employee discovers the reality of their new job. Therefore effective induction really begins at the recruitment stage, by ensuring that applicants are given a realistic report of what is to be expected of them and the opportunities and challenges they are likely to encounter. For example, an experienced HR consultant or lecturer might be tempted to apply for an HR directorship, but quickly become disillusioned if the reality of the role entails more operational bureaucracy than strategic leadership.

Prepare a plan of initial induction including both local and macro familiar-ization with the organization's structures and systems. It is important for new employees to feel comfortable in what can, potentially, be a stressful situation of starting a new job. This can range from extensive and long term, up to a year in some organizations, to a day's induction or less. The key to designing an induc-tion programme is fitness for purpose and the value it has for the new employee. It is also desirable, where possible, to reduce the new employee's workload during the induction period so that they have time to assimilate all the new information they are being given.

Select an approachable and supportive mentor who is not the employee's line manager. A new employee is unlikely to want to ask their new boss a lot of questions, which might indicate a lack of confidence or competence. Again the selection of a mentor is essentially about fitness for purpose. The mentor should be in a position to provide helpful support, advice and encouragement. The person selected may be a more mature manager for whom the mentoring role represents an interesting opportunity to pass on hard-earned managerial experiences. Alternatively, an external person who understands the organiza-tional environment may offer more detached support. This could be semi-retired former employee *(valuing mature employees is discussed in Chapter 6)*, who acts as a consultant to the current management team. The selection of the mentor may be best judged through discussions with the new employee. Clearly there can be many areas of advice from the prosaic, (where is the fifth floor coffee machine?) to the sensitive (which board directors have most influence on budgetary decisions for HR?).

The induction period should be followed up with an evaluation to assess which areas of the induction programme were really helpful and where the system could be developed further. A short questionnaire can provide the HR team with valu-able feedback so that improvements can be made as and where appropriate.

PRACTISING HRM

INDUCTION FEEDBACK QUESTIONNAIRE

1	Strongly disagree	5	Slightly agree
2	Moderately disagree	6	Moderately agree
3	Slightly disagree	7	Strongly agree
4	Neither agree nor disagree		

1 The induction programme met the needs of my job role completely.

    1   2   3   4   5   6   7

2 My mentor was approachable.

    1   2   3   4   5   6   7

3 The induction programme was scheduled over just the right length of time.

    1   2   3   4   5   6   7

4 The induction programme has made a significant contribution to presenting me with a positive impression of this organization.

    1   2   3   4   5   6   7

5 What I have learnt about this organization during induction is very different from what I was told at interview.

    1   2   3   4   5   6   7

6 The induction programme has encouraged me to think I made the right decision in joining this organization.

    1   2   3   4   5   6   7

7 The induction programme needed to be more specifically designed around my job role.

    1   2   3   4   5   6   7

8 I was given sufficient time away from my job tasks to follow all the induction units.

    1   2   3   4   5   6   7

9 I shall continue to be in regular contact with my mentor.

    1   2   3   4   5   6   7

10 My immediate manager has been supportive of my participation in the induction programme.

    1   2   3   4   5   6   7

11 The three main benefits of the induction programme have been:

i)

ii)

iii)

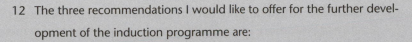

12 The three recommendations I would like to offer for the further development of the induction programme are:

i)

ii)

iii)

From answering the questionnaire, do you sense that your or your respondent's induction experiences are mostly positive, neutral or negative? For example, if your answers to the questions 1–10 are 7, 7, 7, 7, 1, 7, 1, 7, 7 and 7, then you or the respondent are likely to be very satisfied with the induction process because all the most positive answers were selected. Think about any questions you awarded a 4 and consider whether you actually feel more or less positive about that particular aspect of induction. Further qualitative (face-to-face interviews or group discussions) work could be necessary to establish more in-depth personal preferences *(see Chapter 11 for project and research methodology)*.

Induction Plan Summary

- Evaluate the induction needs of new employees and design programmes suitable to their specific job roles.
- Ensure that practical matters – pay, work area, access to relevant work equipment, essential 'hygiene factors' – and any health and safety matters are organized, preferably before the new employee commences.
- Arrange for a discussion with the new employee regarding their mentoring requirements.
- Evaluate the induction process for areas of excellence and development.
- Initiate induction plan changes in response to feedback.

INTEGRATED DEVELOPMENT

Employees, whether part time or full time, or unpaid volunteers in the charity sector, should be offered opportunities for personal development, which enhances their performance in the organization and their own long-term employability and effectiveness.

Effective employee development is a win–win relationship that becomes an integrated part of organizational structure and culture *(see Chapter 2)*. The organization benefits from well-trained people, and the employee gains new knowledge and skills, enhancing their career prospects. An analogy can be drawn from the way sports team members receive regular training. It would be very odd for a coach to buy a new player and expect them to be a top performer without any ongoing training, but unfortunately this does happen in some organizations. Following the sporting analogy further, it is also a flawed argument to say that poorly trained people are less likely to leave for a new job; this management approach would hardly win many championships!

The content of a personal development programme depends on a number of variables, including the person's aspirations and interests as well as the needs of the organization. In this, as in so much of people management, the approach has to be person- and situation-specific. The alternative, mechanistic approach assumes that everyone has identical developmental needs and aspirations and therefore provides the same programme for every member of staff in a set job role. Instead, it is perhaps more useful to champion equity of opportunity and resources. Hence, one employee may wish to have time to follow the CIPD courses, while another may seek development through a postgraduate masters degree. Alternatively, consultancy support may be more relevant, or time provided through a sabbatical leave to advance professional development, research and so forth.

The possibilities for employee development are numerous and varied, so I have provided a list of interventions below as an initial guide. These are organized into development activities and investments.

Developmental Activities:

- Workplace-based, job-focused training by a colleague
- In-house, job-focused training through the HR or training team
- In-house, job-focused training delivered by an external HR specialist
- Externally based, job-focused training through a university business school or consultancy
- Accredited professional course undertaken externally
- College or university courses
- Mentor counselling sessions
- 'Shadowing' a senior colleague for experiential learning
- 'Acting-up' by undertaking a selected range of management responsibilities for managerial experiential learning
- Mentoring junior or less experienced colleagues
- Work placement with another organization to gain experience of different organizational procedures and processes
- Research project – individual or team.

Developmental Investments:

- Payment of fees for professional development
- Time off work to follow a training course of qualification
- Reduced workload during periods of training development
- Day release schemes
- Time allocated for mentoring sessions
- Time allocated for professional development counselling
- Paid sabbatical leave for professional development or research work.
- Unpaid sabbatical leave to pursue personal interests.

A significant number of postgraduate students I meet say that while their employers are sometimes prepared to provide the cost of course fees, they are less willing to ring-fence a time allocation for the addition workload. This can place working students under considerable pressure to maintain a full-time job and study for a postgraduate qualification. It is for this reason that it is important to agree some time for career development as a part of the HR package of employee development. Organizations are the sum total of the attitudes, knowledge and skills their people have, so it's an eminently sound investment to ensure that these valuable human assets are well trained and effectively developed.

When I visit organizations for research or consultancy, it is always interesting to ask employees what they do outside their workplace. There are usually a fair number of people who have significant roles of responsibility outside the organization, including sports team management, school governorships, church leadership and many other responsible civic duties. These kinds of roles require areas of competence, which are easily transferable to workplace situations, such as leadership, planning, team management, financial control, emotional intelligence, communication skills and commitment. However, organizations may miss the talented people they have by failing to recognize the person behind the current job title. Effective employee development should include recognition of what more the person may be able to contribute. Conversely, some people may not wish to move to new roles and this choice should also be respected. They may thereby become valued and respected mentors to new employees by sharing their in-depth experience of their specialist area. The key message for employee development is essentially that it should be regarded as an intrinsic element of employment and not as an optional supplementary.

Development Plan Summary

- Employee development is a win–win relationship for the organization.
- Employee development is an ongoing process.
- The development programme should reflect the aspirations and interests of the employee as well as the needs of the organization.
- Resources, including time, should be allocated to employee development because it is an intrinsic element of employment, not an optional add-on.
- Encourage people to use their talents and become the best they can be.

● DEVELOPMENT BY INVOLVEMENT

Involvement in the shaping of work processes can be both developmental and motivational. It is courteous to consult people about arrangements for their work and it is quite possible that new initiatives can come from those closest to the task. Ian McCartney, the government minister for the Department for Work and Pensions in Britain, has commented that: 'All workers want to be recognized by the company' (cited in seniorsnetwork.co.uk). The involvement of people in the decision-making process can also energize the creative talents of the work teams. A degree of autonomy of operation is also beneficial to encouraging people to become more involved in organizational life. As employees gain experience of the organization, they can make valuable contributions to planning and practice. This can involve all levels of employees. An example of increasing involvement can be the use of 360° appraisals where employees are actively involved in peer and management evaluation.

● DEVELOPMENT THROUGH EXPERIENTIAL LEARNING

One of the key values of encouraging involvement in decision making is the benefit it can have in employee development, whereby people become more engaged in their work and learn through active experience. Experiential learning is also used within academic courses to involve students in the practice of the theoretical concepts they are studying. One of the most obvious examples is the difference between studying the theories of team working and actually working with a team of fellow students on a project. The theory can be delivered in fine theoretical evaluations of models and research. The reality of team working can, as students quickly learn through experience, be more complex and challenging than discussing theoretical models. It is also interesting for both academics and HR specialists to consider the importance of involvement with regard to learning and retention. According to Wind and Main (1998, p. 269) learners can retain and recall approximately 15 per cent of what they hear in a lecture, but their performance dramatically improves when they are proactively involved in their own learning, increasing retention to 80 per cent. The exact percentages are less important than the underpinning messages about learning.

The development process depends on the proactive involvement of the learner in participating in the programme or course. The ACTIVE model below provides a step-by-step reminder, encouraging students and anyone who is interested in their own career development to become an active, rather than passive, learner in both vocational and academic courses and in the workplace.

ACTIVE Learning Model

Ask questions, listen to other viewpoints. Be open to alternative approaches.

Cooperate with your colleagues in teams and projects. Learn from those around you.

Take part in a range of activities, seminars and learning situations. Make your own notes. These help you to assimilate ideas. Do not depend on course or seminar notes alone. Learning is an active process.

Invest in yourself, lifelong learning. Regard personal development as a continuous process.

Vision. What do you want to achieve? Set realistic targets and goals in personal development.

Evaluate new ways of working, be flexible. Change is the one constant factor of organizational life. Be ready to embrace new opportunities.

Involvement Plan Summary

● Quality enhancement teams. These review work processes. Employees evaluate their own work processes and feedback to colleagues and managers.

● New product or service consultative teams. These bring together people

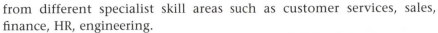

from different specialist skill areas such as customer services, sales, finance, HR, engineering.

- 360° appraisals *(appraisal methods are discussed in Chapter 7).*
- Cross-divisional management teams. These share experience and expertise in areas such as strategic planning, employee development initiatives, employment policies and practices.
- Peer reviews. Colleagues observe each other's work and provide constructive feedback, sharing best practices.
- Section, team or departmental forums, works council consultations and trade union consultations. These can provide ideas and feedback to managers and other teams, sections or departments on how well the organization is functioning.
- Become ACTIVE in your own development.

DEVELOPMENT THROUGH PROGRESSION

Employees are more likely to remain in an organization if there are opportunities for career progression. For some people, progression is perceived as promotion and increases in salary. Another way to view progression is as opportunities to undertake new tasks and challenges. Alternatively, some employees may be content to remain in the same role for many years. It is still important, however, to recognize a person's contribution to the organization. This would be particularly true of the not-for-profit and voluntary sectors, where the volunteer is not being paid so recognition of service is even more important. As with other HR activities, the area of progression is person- and situation-specific, so it is important for employees and volunteers to receive a regular appraisal so that they have an opportunity to discuss their aspirations *(appraisal interviews are discussed in Chapter 8).*

There is a tendency for organizations to promote successful operational workers to managerial positions without much reflection on the large differences between the AKS required for 'doing' roles and those for 'managing'. Furthermore, once a person has been given a new role, it is important for them to receive training and development to ensure a smoother transition into their new task set.

Progression Plan Summary

- Create opportunities for people to use their talents in the organization, rather than moving to elsewhere.
- Encourage people to undertake new tasks and challenges.
- Support newly appointed or promoted staff in their new role with training and development.
- Design support initiatives to respond to individual needs as identified in the confidence and competence model.
- Organizations have a responsibility to be efficient by developing the talents of their people.

- Each person should prepare his or her own progression plan. This could be a useful item for appraisal discussion.
- Employees who are happy to remain in a job role should be encouraged to mentor less experienced or new employees.
- Training should be part of the progression planning, not an afterthought.

HRM IN ACTION

INTERVIEW WITH A SENIOR EXECUTIVE

In this extract from an interview with a company chairperson, I was probing how employees are treated if they perform unexpectedly well and promotions. The consultancy has a long and successful record in recruitment and selection and the chairperson was discussing the actions of a client company, which he asked me to keep anonymous.

Question: Please tell me about a case which you think is relevant to people management [development].

Answer: We placed somebody last year in X and they were not expected to produce any business in the first six months because of long lead times on the business cycle. In the first three months, they produced a quarter of a million pounds worth of sales.

Question: A quarter of a million?

Answer: In the first three months, new business, very, very intelligent person. The manager [of the new employee] left at that time, he was head-hunted to go to another company so the directors decided that they would take somebody from one of their competitors. This scenario went on for six months of talking to a specific applicant who wanted the job then didn't come, wanted the job, didn't come, going back and forward.

The person who we placed, very successful in a short space of time, good management experience, went to the management and asked, Why aren't you giving me the opportunity to apply for this job? He didn't say: I want to apply for it. He said: Why aren't you giving me the opportunity? A different attitude.

He was very direct, he said: I've done it before, I could do this job. The old manager [who recently was head-hunted to another company] had been using this guy to help him. The director said: No we don't want you [for this role], we are going to stick with this other person. They wouldn't give him a trial so subsequently he left.

DISCUSSION QUESTIONS

1   What are the disadvantages of not considering existing personnel for promotions before seeking someone from outside the organization?

2   Do you think it is possible that the senior management wanted to keep the new person in the role where he had proved to be exceptionally successful?

3   Write a list of actions that senior managers can take to encourage and help to retain successful employees, other than promoting them.

● CHAPTER SUMMARY

In this chapter you have been able to evaluate the place and value of employee development in improving organizational performance. Through the application of management modelling in the employee development star, you are now able to identify the key stages of employee development. The self-evaluation exercises and activities should also have provided you with an understanding of your own areas of competence and confidence. The HR-trained professionals should therefore be developing integrated organizational plans that invest in people and organizational performance.

● REFERENCES

Belling, R., James, K. and Ladkin, D. (2004) Back to the Workplace: How Organisations can Improve their Support for Management Learning and Development. *Journal of Management Development*, **23**(3).

Bratton, J. and Gold, J. (1999) *Human Resource Management. Theory and Practice.* Basingstoke: Macmillan – now Palgrave Macmillan.

Hutton, W. (1995) *The State We're In.* London: Jonathan Cape.

Kirkbride P. S. (2003) Management Development: In Search of a New Role? *Journal of Management Development*, **22**(2).

Liyanage, S. and Poon, P. S. (2003) Technology and Innovation Management Learning in the Knowledge Economy: A Techno-managerial Approach. *Journal of Management Development*, **22**(7).

Long, L. K. and Smith, R. D. (2004) The Role of Web-based Distance Learning in HR Development. *Journal of Management Development*, **23**(3).

Mighty, E. J. and Ashton, W. (2003) Management Development: Hoax or Hero? *Journal of Management Development*, **22**(1).

Mumford, A. (1993) *Management Development. Strategies for Action* (2nd edn). London: CIPD.

Overton, L. (2004) Fighting Fit. *E-Learning Age.* Dec 03–Jan 04. Bizmedia.

Purcell, J. and Ahlstrand, B. (1994) *Human Resource Management in the Multi-Divisional Company.* Oxford: Oxford Press.

Savery, L. K. and J. A. Luks (2004) Does Training Influence Outcomes of Organizations? Some Australian Evidence. *Journal of Management Development*, **23**(2).

Senge, P. M., Roberts, C. Ross, R. B. Smith, B. J. and Kleiner, A. (1994) *The Fifth Discipline Fieldbook. Strategies and Tools for Building a Learning Organisation*. London: Nicholas Brealey.

Stern, S. (2002) Flex your HR Muscle. *People Management*, 21 March.

Storey, J. and Sisson, K. (1993) *Managing Human Resources and Industrial Relations*. Buckingham: Open University.

Wind, J. Y. and Main, J. (1998) *Driving Change*. London: Kogan Page.

PERSONAL NOTES ON CHAPTER 9

Notes for seminars

_____

_____

_____

_____

_____

_____

_____

_____

Notes for revision/reminders

_____

_____

_____

_____

_____

_____

_____

_____

_____

_____

_____

_____

_____

_____

_____

Performance and Rewards

Learning outcomes

After reading and completing the activities in this chapter, you should be able to:

1 Appreciate the value of HR specialist input (internal and external) into the evaluation of an organization's reward systems.

2 Recognize the role of HR rewards planning in relation to external factors – PEST analysis.

3 Apply sectoral analysis to the application of HR reward management interventions and strategies.

4 Critically evaluate the use of performance-related pay schemes.

5 Critically evaluate the case for more flexible reward systems.

6 Appreciate the role of rewards strategies in employee development.

7 Evaluate the place in organizations of non-financial rewards such as education and training.

8 Appreciate the differences in HR planning required in rewarding volunteers and the not-for-profit sector.

● **INTRODUCTION**

The subject of rewards is particularly interesting to all of us. People like being rewarded. A child smiles when s/he receives a gift. Our colleagues generally respond positively to encouragement. Yet we are all individuals, preferring and making different life choices. So while a young and ambitious City trader may respond to the opportunity to earn large bonuses, the voluntary worker's efforts receive no pay, although their work may be very rewarding. The first step in evaluating rewards is to consider rewards appropriate to the situational context. In this chapter you will be able to evaluate rewards as person- and situation-specific. It is therefore worthwhile referring to Chapters 1 and 2, where we considered integrated HR and organizational structures and cultures which can have powerful influences on the rewards culture of organizations.

● REWARDS: SITUATION- AND PERSON-SPECIFIC

One of the key themes of this text is to advocate the value of HR professionals adopting an integrated approach to HR management, whether they are acting as internal HR managers or externally as consultants and advisers. This should also include independent consultants, who could be partly retired managers with decades of management knowledge and skills, and university business schools. The independent nature of such consultancy may offer an organization more critically evaluative perspectives on HR and managerial issues *(HR students can build a holistic view of an organization they are studying by combining the PEST analysis presented in this chapter with SMARTA and REACT, which can be found in Chapter 11)*.

With an increasingly diversified workforce *(see Chapter 6)*, including workers who maybe employed, full time, part time, on contract, consultancy, mature returners, women returners, home-based, what each person prefers as a rewards package can vary considerably. The rate of change in the working environment, stimulated by faster communications, new technology and globalization, means that employees also require more training to remain effective in their current job and retain employability for their next job move. Therefore, training and education should be included in the rewards package because it reflects an investment by the employer into the medium- and long-term employability of the worker. However, sometimes employees dislike changes and unless new developments are underpinned by sound employee rewards strategies, managers may encounter resistance to their change plans. If a person identifies a personal benefit in adopting something new, they are more likely to accept the change than someone who does not recognize the need to change. The terms 'change' and 'employee flexibility' are not unassailable icons of organizational progress. From an employee's perspective, new developments and changes can sound like more work for the same rewards. In a competitive market, people who have invested in their employability through education and training are in a better position to find a new job. Employers who reward their people with learning opportunities may both retain and attract more effective staff.

● PEST FOR HR

Externally initiated factors can have a major influence on organizational rewards systems. A useful model for HR and other managers to analyse the environment in which their organization operates is a PEST analysis. Students of HR can also use this model to study an organization as part of their research work. Indeed it is often helpful to critically review external factors before moving on to internal research activities. For example, if the marketplace for employees in a particular sector is competitive, then an organization may have to offer a better package of rewards and incentives to attract and retain staff.

The PEST analysis provides four areas of investigation, political, economic, social and technical. These external factors can lead to internal organizational changes in strategy, structure, working practices and employee relations. This reinforces the proposition that organizations are co-dependents with a variety of other interested parties, often referred to as 'stakeholders', which broadly represent sections of the community, local and international, in which organizations operate. It also follows that HR managers need to be cognisant of these broader contexts when designing policies and strategies for their organizations.

Most organizations can recognize their market competition and adjust their services, products and offerings accordingly. HR specialists can study the marketplace relating to employee availability, training, rewards and working conditions, so that they can advise their organization of appropriate HR initiatives. For example, if their competitors are providing better working conditions, career development, flexible working hours for women and mature returnees, then organizations with less employee-friendly policies may encounter difficulties recruiting and retaining staff. The PEST analysis provides an overview of external factors that may influence the organization's performance and thereby provides helpful indicators for HR management to act upon.

Political

The political background can be interpreted in a broader context to include local and national government policies. Additionally, international laws, treaties and agreements as well as employee contracts and trade union agreements need to be addressed by HR policies. The legal elements of HR are complex and constantly changing in response to legislation, local, national and international, so a legally trained professional should oversee them. However, strategic HR professionals should form the overall policy.

Economic

The economic environment can influence profitability so it is relevant to evaluate the market for the organization's goods or services. Self-evidently, more affluent environments are more likely to benefit most organizations, but not all. For example, debt relief management services may actually do better in weaker economies. It is also interesting to compare and contrast economic performance of different organizations in the same marketplace. If one is outperforming the competition, it can be useful to study what they are doing regarding the recruitment, development and retention of employees.

Social

The social context can be a helpful guide regarding trends, fashions and attitudes to goods or services. From an HR perspective, it is also important to observe employment trends such as women and mature returnees. In the West, the population is ageing, caused by a falling birth rate. This may mean that there are fewer young people to recruit. Additionally, more people may want or need to remain in full- or part-time employment to supplement pension incomes. The workforce is getting older, so it is more important to train and retrain older workers and also train and develop young entrants.

Technological

Technological changes can change job content and the attitudes, knowledge and skills required. In some cases, whole tiers of employees may require retraining. The HR professional will need to design new training initiatives and recruitment strategies to maintain efficiency and performance.

Exercise 10.1

PEST ANALYSIS

Conduct a PEST analysis on an organization you are interested in studying for your coursework or seminar activities.

It is helpful to begin a PEST analysis by thinking about the kind of industry, business or sector that your selected organization is in. Start by thinking about whether it is a for-profit or not-for-profit organization. Once the general sector is established, consider the more specific factors that influence HR activities. If the organization you have selected is not-for-profit (charities, non-governmental organizations, schools, the NHS, aid agencies), then HR planning will need to include the rewards and motivation of staff whose primary motivational drives may not be financial, including unpaid volunteers. It should become evident that although organizations may be placed into a generic sector, each one will have situation-specific requirements, the recurring theme of this text. Explore the sectors' similarities and differences.

The experienced HR manager will be accustomed to analysing their organization's requirements in relation to its market sector and stakeholders. However, I have found that sometimes new HR students can experience difficulties in relating HR analysis to an organization they are studying. Try to think about the connections between the employee relation's policies and how you might respond if you were working for the organization. In reality, the preliminary stages of the process are quite straightforward and the research can produce many interesting insights into an organization's HR requirements. Some HR students may progress to conduct an in-depth PEST analysis if this is appropriate to their interests and course requirements. An overview of the external factors, which can be studied with PEST, combined with more detailed, organization-specific research should yield some interesting findings.

Discussion points

1 What were the key points highlighted by PEST analysis on your chosen organization?

2 How do you think the organization's HR team should respond to the PEST findings?

3 Evaluate how effective PEST has been in providing you or your team with an overview of an organization within its sector.

● WHERE YOUR TREASURE IS

The things we value most are informed by personal priorities. In organizations, the senior executives select the organization's priorities and rewards for those workers who conform and work towards achieving those priorities. For example, in an overly competitive working environment, priorities may lean towards short-term successes over longer term strategies. During 2002, the disadvantages of a preoccupation with short-term profits became evident when Enron, the American power supply company, collapsed and its auditors, Arthur Andersen, were alleged to have illegally shredded relevant documents. Stephen Covey noted that, in the case of Enron, the pressure to achieve short-term successes led people to sell out on their principles and that short-term remedies can create long-term problems (Stern, 2002, p. 37). The strength of consultancy input should be in the independent perspectives the consultant brings to an organiz-ation as a critical observer. Conversely, if the client and consultancy relationship becomes too symbiotic, the role of consultants as critical friends is eroded. It is arguably the duty of the consultant to provide best practice advice to the client, but best practice may not always be what the client wants to hear or, more importantly, wishes to pay for. In such situations, it is the consultant who feels secure in knowing that they will be supported by their chief executive for behaving with integrity who is more likely to resist client pressures to compro-mise. The chief executive has the opportunity to influence what happens in their organization and with clients by selecting appropriate priorities and rewards within their organization. Alternatively, s/he can foster a more competitive, short-term, performance-oriented environment that focuses the rewards proce-dures on profit maximization. In a report by Delves-Broughton (2002), it was observed that the individual performance-related rewards and appraisals used by Enron created a highly competitive environment where achieving results became all important and managers employed a system known as 'rank or yank'. The appraisal system *(see Chapter 8 for appraisals)* was used to 'rank' employee's perform-ance from one to five. The lowest performing 15 per cent of the workers were required to leave. The consultants, who were not directly employed by the company, were undoubtedly in a stronger position to offer constructive criticism of such policies, but this in turn depends upon their management's willingness to risk a client's fee to retain the integrity of their advice. In both organizations, it is arguable that the influence of their 'rewards structure' negatively influenced the quality of employee decision making. A longitudinal field study by Fried et al. (2003, pp. 787–805), of employees in an organization undergoing major restructuring, found a moderating influence of job security and role clarity on employee performance. Job performance increased over time when both role clarity and job security were high. Whilst the modern environment means that change and the rate of change is more pronounced, it should be possible to create the kind of supportive environment where employees and workers can feel secure and that their contributions are valued. 'Thank you' and 'what you do is appreciated' are valuable rewards.

There is a common saying that whatever is being measured, get done. So it follows that those activities that are rewarded gain our attention. Good HR? Not necessarily.

Exercise 10.2

CHOICES

Consider the following examples and discuss the choices facing various professionals when they are set performance targets:

1 If a factory worker is measured on the quantity of units produced, does quality suffer?

2 Does focusing on reducing hospital waiting lists mean the easier to treat, less urgent cases get attention in place of more complex, serious illnesses?

3 If teachers are rewarded on examination results, do schools avoid selecting 'less able' students?

4 When salespeople are targeted on how many new customer accounts they open, does the quality of customer retention and care decline?

During the late twentieth century, a culture of accountability and compliance emerged from the earlier bureaucratic management model (see Henderson and Parsons, 1947). However laudable the aspirations of the quality controllers might be, more regulations may not produce better performances. The constraints of unnecessary bureaucracy often created by government and 'quality agencies' can prevent, or at least discourage, people from taking initiatives outside their prescribed area of work. It may also encourage a 'jobs worth' management culture (a person who constantly points to regulations and claims its more than her/his 'job's worth' to break any rule or guideline). Professor Moss Kanter (1990, p. 144) has observed that an overemphasis on numerical accountability can stifle innovation. The problem is that by targeting rewards to specific items, other activities may be reduced or given less priority. Anyone who has worked in an organization that is being 'quality audited' would probably admit, at least privately and off the record, that much of the organization's real work was overshadowed by the paper chase of self-justifying documentation. It is worth noting that it is perfectly possible to have a policy document for every eventuality, and do little, or conversely to achieve a lot of effective work, with little documentary self-justification (see Kuhl, 1992). The balance between sensible regulatory compliance, rewarding effective work and allowing people to get on with their jobs is a strategically difficult decision. However, it is more likely to be successful if the decision emerges from consent and consensus, than compulsory compliance. Reward systems are intended to direct the efforts of employees, so it is worth reflecting upon what activities will have less attention and time given to them in order to accommodate the additional attention to the selected areas of work *(see time management in Chapter 5)*.

PERFORMANCE PAY

Performance-related pay (PRP) schemes attempted to link organizational reward systems to employee performance. In practice, targeting selected activities to rewards was difficult to achieve with equity (see Kessler and Purcell, 1992; Kohn, 1993; Randle, 1997). PRP relied on conformity of employee motivations regarding rewards that simply may not exist in a diversified workforce *(see Chapter 6 for diversified workforce)*. Moreover, individuals are usually part of a team of people, so individual contributions can be difficult to isolate from the efforts of the wider team and the interaction of people in other departments. For instance, although the salesperson might sign the new customer order and may be rewarded, the credit controller processes the account, the dispatch team organizes delivery and the service department handles customer problems. The use of PRP could therefore be divisive if it rewarded certain employees more than others. The academic research evidence on PRP has indicated that the successful maintenance of performance rewards systems can be problematical and even the most ardent supporters of PRP accept that it can be difficult to manage well (see Swabe, 1989; Geery, 1992; Neale, 1992). The research I conducted within both the private and public sectors also echoed earlier research reservations regarding PRP systems. In particular some public and voluntary sector employees and workers expressed concerns regarding the appropriateness of performance targets within complex services such as education, healthcare and charitable care.

HRM IN ACTION

UNMET EXPECTATIONS

I heard this case about salespeople and expenses claims some years ago from a successful area sales manager. At face value it is easy to dismiss what follows as simply falsification of company documents. However, there are some interesting underlying issues regarding employee relations relating to company policies and actual practices. Read the HRM in Action case and reflect on the pay and rewards issues.

Many years ago it was customary for insurance salesmen to wear dark suits and a bowler hat, which was effectively the uniform for city banking and insurance employees. Therefore, when a young man joined an insurance firm, his manager advised him that he should buy the appropriate attire. The salesman's area included the south coast, so he made appointments to visit his clients in Brighton. As he was walking along the promenade, a gust of sea breeze took hold of his bowler hat and cast it into the sea. Knowing that his new employers insisted that all salesmen wear a bowler hat, he promptly called into a local department store and bought a replacement. Later in the week the salesman duly filled in his expenses claims form, listing his travel expenses and under the 'other items' column he noted a claim for the replacement hat.

A few days later, the area manager telephoned the salesman to advise him that the company would not be able to recompense him for personal clothing and so the cost of the bowler hat had been deleted from his expenses form. This irritated the salesman because the hat was quite expensive and had, after all, been required by the company and lost while on company business. He therefore decided to try to reclaim the cost of the hat again, with a note explaining the circumstances in the hope that his manager would relent and refund the cost of the hat. The salesman was delighted when the manager telephoned him, only to be disappointed when the area manager restated company policy about the cost of the hat.

The following week the area manager was pleased to see that the new salesman's third expenses claim did not include the cost of the hat. In fact, the area manager felt so triumphant in having successfully asserted company policy that he telephoned the young salesman to congratulate him on complying with company policy.

'No bowler hat in your expenses claim this week!', he proclaimed with delight.

'Oh, it's in there, you find it.', replied the young salesman who had sought the advice of some of the more established members of the sales force about how to 'work the system'. His expenses claim form was paid in full that week and the regional manager was also able to uphold company policy regarding the non-reimbursement of claims for lost hats since no specific item for a 'lost hat' was included on the form, although expenses in each of the other columns were all marginally higher.

DISCUSSION QUESTIONS

1   The company expected its salespeople to comply with a particular dress

code. Was it reasonable for the new salesman to require the company to pay for the hat he had lost during the course of his work?

2   The company rules stated that it would not replace employees' property, such as bowler hats, in the event of loss. Evaluate the regional manager's decision not to accept the expenses claim for the hat on the first two attempts by the salesperson.

3   What do you understand by the term 'working the system'?

4   Why do you think the regional manager paid the full expenses claim on the third occasion?

5   What recommendations, if any, would you make regarding the company's policies relating to salespersons' expenses reimbursement?

 ## CAFETERIA SYSTEMS

The term *cafeteria systems* refers to the application of flexible choice to employee benefits. Why? People are individuals and as such have differing needs and requirements. For example, a free crèche facility can be a valuable benefit to people who have young children, although not to those without childcare responsibilities. Although the traditional one-size-fits-all approach to HR may have been more acceptable in the past, the modern diversified workforce requires a more person-centred approach *(see Chapter 6 for the diversified workforce)*. There has also been a continuing tendency for people to change jobs and organizations more often. The old paradigm where a worker joined as an apprentice and stayed until s/he retired related to the old world of bureaucracies. In the modern workplace, worker security is more likely to be found in employability (the knowledge and skills to be able to obtain a new job) rather than staying in one organization (Cooper and Rousseau, 1994). Conversely, organizations need both a changing perspective as well as the stability of longer stay employees who retain the organization's corporate memory. Hence, it is quite likely that any given workplace may contain people who intend to stay for a couple of years, others who plan to remain much longer, career starters, experienced staff, women, men returnees, (returning to work following a career break), part-timers and mature returnees (those who decided to continue working part or full time after the age of retirement). A traditional one-size-fits-all HR benefits package is unlikely to meet the needs of these diverse groups.

The research I conducted into how organizations have responded to the more diversified workforce indicated that while there are some innovative solutions available, some elements of the traditional approach were still prevalent. The interview below illustrates one of the more proactive approaches to cafeteria systems in which both traditional core elements, such as pensions, are fixed while the employee can select other benefits.

HRM IN ACTION

INTERVIEW WITH A SENIOR EXECUTIVE

The following extract is taken from a research interview, which was part of an in-company survey regarding HR activities and inputs. The questions and answers below sought to uncover the attitudes to innovative approaches to employee benefits within the organization.

Question: Have you considered cafeteria benefits?

Answer: We have flexibility within our benefits so people can trade up to a different car by putting more money in even if that car is two levels above [the employees grade entitlement] However, we would struggle if someone said they didn't want a pension plan or a health plan. So we have considered the cafeteria approach, but there are some core benefits, which we would probably demand that employees take. The question is, then, are we being more paternalistic than we need to be?

Question: So would it be possible to have a core package and a flexible part from which employees could select according to their needs?

Answer: What I'm interested in from your research is whether there's a set of benefits which we are ignoring or are there others?

The old approach was work hard; get stock in the company and the stock will be worth something. People have had house extensions paid for by the increased value of their stock [shares in the company which can increase in value, but can also fall in value]. If the stock value falls, people are extending their horizons and looking at the other things the company provides for them, so we need to define, quite precisely, the nature of this employment relationship. We are now using the phrase 'the employee partnership' which is inwardly focused. I am going to brand everything that the HR department does as part of the employee partnership. The thing about the HR function or any internal service organization, it's a bit like the health service, there is infinite demand and it's subject to continuous subjective review. Therefore we need to address it as if everyone is a consumer. There's a drive to get more of a business partnership approach with our HR managers. We are achieving this by bringing in more capable HR managers who have a direct link into a portion of the business. So it's like an account management function.

Question: There is a trend towards organizations having fewer people in the HR function, so that HR is moving from an operational role to a strategic one. Is this the case here?

Answer: We are planning to do exactly that.

DISCUSSION AREAS

1   If an organization does decide to provide a core benefits package, should employees have the right to opt out of it?

2   What do you understand by the term 'cafeteria benefits'?

3   What are the advantages to employees of a flexible benefits package?

4   Why do you think employees are 'looking at the other things the company provides for them', apart from financial incentives?

5   The executive used the term 'employee partnership' to describe the company's new HR innovations. What do you think the difference in emphasis might be with 'employee partnership' compared to the more traditional 'employee relations' approach?

6   What do you think is the difference between an operational HR role and a strategic one?

7   How can having specific 'HR managers who have a direct link into a portion of the business' enable the HR function to be more business-focused and closer to the needs of employees?

The content and design of a cafeteria system should be organization-specific so that those involved can discuss and agree the elements to be included.

The cafeteria benefits package can include:

Salary
Pension
Healthcare: personal and family
Personal insurance: accident and death
Car or car allowances
Subsidized staff lunch and vending machines
Extended holiday entitlement
Extended sick pay allowances
Extended carer time allowance (including partner, elderly parent or children)
Crèche facilities
Flexible working hours
Subsidized travel to work allowance
Free car and bike parking

Concessionary agreements with other companies (discounts on travel, restaurants, clothes, holidays)
Bonuses
Share options
Commission payments

The above list is not intended to be exhaustive and each organization should decide what is appropriate to its particular needs (see McDermott, 1997; Schrage, 2000). So, with so many possible options, can a cafeteria system also be fair, or will some people benefit more than others? The research I conducted indicated that the key to a successful cafeteria system was the initial set-up and preparation. For example, in one highly successful UK recruitment consultancy with offices throughout the UK, the chief executive advised me that all the benefits were available to individual choice. The way it worked was that each employee was given a total 'spend' according to his or her job role. Within that total spend, employees could then decide what to include in their personal benefits package. For example, the chief executive told me that it was possible for people to select a higher salary if they opted out of the company's pension provision, although he also said that he would counsel staff not to take such a short-term approach. However, the choice was there for people to choose between options, up to their personal package limit.

The choice of how to reward employees is key strategic area for any organization (see Lawler, 1990, 1995). Most people hope to enjoy their work, and a benefits package that is tailored to their personal needs is more likely to attract and retain employees than a one-size-fits-all approach.

● REWARDS FOR VOLUNTEERS

In the previous section we looked at strategies for rewarding paid employees. However, rewards are not always about money or paid benefits. The voluntary sector, in common with other sectors, requires situation-specific HR rewards and management strategies. One size or any notional 'best practice' does not fit all organizations (see Davis Smith and Hedley, 1991; Clary et al., 1992; Cnaan and Amrofell, 1994; Davis Smith, 1998; Rochester, 1999; Bowgett et al., 2002; Zimmeck, 2002). The voluntary worker should be rewarded and their efforts recognized. How is this to be achieved with no wages or bonuses? In common with paid workers, the volunteers should have the opportunity to agree tailored packages to meet situation-specific requirements. When I have worked with voluntary sector organizations, I have often been impressed by their ability to use the so-called 'soft' HR elements such as positive feedback and encouragement (see Swinburne, 2001). It is also relevant to remember that all the elements of sound psychological contracts and life–work balance *(see Chapters 4 and 5)* apply to the not-for-profit and voluntary sectors too.

Examples of non-salary rewards include:

● Recognition of good work
● Public praise of successful volunteers by senior leaders and governors

- Choice of next project
- Funding to set up new initiatives
- Overseas assignments
- Training and development
- Funding to attend college courses
- Mentoring
- Flexible working hours
- Healthcare plans
- Childcare support
- Travel expenses.

The above list is not exhaustive. Each voluntary and not-for-profit organization should decide its own approach to attracting and retaining volunteers. However, in the absence of financial rewards, even more care needs to go into the HR initiatives for rewarding voluntary workers. To begin with, it would be valuable to conduct some internal research with existing volunteers regarding their needs and motivations. For example, school governorships are voluntary and unpaid so it is important to offer appropriate travel assistance and encouragement so as not to deter the less prosperous applicants or parents from participating. The alternative is for the governor membership to become too much of a middle-class enclave. It can also be helpful to offer training courses for governors if and where this may be appropriate. These kinds of initiatives provide opportunities for widening participation in citizenship (see Davis Smith and Hedley, 1991).

The voluntary sector provides society with many valuable services and can also enrich the quality of life and experiences of those who serve in the sector. There is also a delicate balance to be evaluated between well-intentioned commitment and the professional delivery of services. If the commercial sector can deliver high standards of efficiency for profit, it is arguably just as important, if not more so, for the voluntary sector to deliver not-for-profit service to its clients. In this respect, HR professionals can assist the sector in designing situation-specific initiatives to enhance the relevant knowledge and skills so that services can be more effective. It should be recognized, however, that the content, style, delivery method and language used should be empathetic to the organization.

Sensitivity to different working environments is valuable because it helps us to tune initiatives in harmony with the needs of a particular organization in its context. One of the misunderstandings of the late twentieth and early twenty-first century has been a tendency by some institutions to seek private sector, for-profit solutions for not-for-profit organizations. Given that the cultures, structures *(see Chapter 2)*, developmental interests *(see Chapter 9)* and the kind of rewards available are likely to be very different, it would be less than remarkable if such projects were less than successful (see Rashid et al., 2003). It is also relevant to consider that the language of profit, performance enhancement, cost minimization and productivity may turn off people who are working for a cause they believe in or serving the community in the public services (see Marsden and Richardson, 1994).

By investing in the developmental elements of rewards, a voluntary organization can encourage volunteers through personal development. For example, for students taking a break from education, the voluntary sector can offer a breadth of experiences and enhance their CVs more than an extended trip abroad, valuable as that might also be. Indeed, many of the larger charities have service abroad so it may be possible to combine travel with a working experience.

⬤ CHAPTER SUMMARY

In this chapter you have reviewed the value of HR in the development and evaluation of organizational reward systems. This included practical research using PEST analysis related to the role of HR in rewards planning. You should also have become aware and more sensitive to the differences in sectors, so that your HR approaches to rewards can be situation-appropriate. Non-financial rewards are valuable elements of the employee reward and developmental strategy. You should now understand the use of rewards systems including performance-related pay and the more flexible, person-centred cafeteria systems and their use and application in rewards management. Furthermore the chapter studied the specific requirements of the not-for-profit sector, rewarding volunteers and not-for-profit, public sector employees.

⬤ REFERENCES

Blyton, P. and Turnbull, P. (eds) (1992) *Reassessing Human Resource Management*. London: Sage.

Bowgett, K., Dickie, K. and Restall, W. (2002) *The Good Practice Guide for Everyone who Works with Volunteers*. London: National Centre for Volunteering.

Clary, G., Snyder, M. and Ridge, R. (1992) Volunteers' Motivations: A Functional Strategy for the Recruitment, Placement and Retention of Volunteers. *Nonprofit Management and Leadership,* **2**(4).

Cnaan, R. and Amrofell, S. (1994) Mapping Volunteer Activity. *Nonprofit and Voluntary Sector Quarterly*, (234).

Cooper, C. L. and Rousseau, D. M. (eds) (1994) *Trends in Organisational Behaviour*. Chichester: John Wiley.

Davis Smith, J. (1998) *The 1997 National Survey of Volunteer Activity*, London: National Centre for Volunteering.

Davis Smith, J. and Hedley, R. (1991) *Volunteering and Society*. London: National Council for Voluntary Organisations.

Delves-Broughton, P. (2002) Enron Cocktail of Cash, Sex, and Fast Living. News.telegraph.co.uk 28 January.

Fried, Y., Slowik, L. H., Shperling, Z., Franz, C. H., Ben-David, A., Avital, N. and Yeverechyahu, U. (2003) The Moderating Effect of Job Security on the Relation Between Role Clarity and Job Performance. A Longitudinal Field Study. *Human Relations*, **56**(7).

Geery, J. F. (1992) Pay Control and Commitment Linking Appraisal and Reward. *Human Resource Management Journal*, **2**(4), pp. 36–54.

Henderson, A. M. and Parsons, T. (1947) *Max Weber. The Theory of Social and Economic Organization*. New York: Oxford University Press.

Kessler, I. and Purcell, J. (1992) Performance Related Pay: Objectives and Applications. *Human Resource Management Journal*, **2**(3).

Kohn, A. (1993) Why Incentive Plans Cannot Work. *Harvard Business Review*, September–October.

Kuhl, J. (1992) A Theory of Self-Regulation: Action Versus State Orientation, Self-Discrimination and Some Applications. *Applied Psychology: An International Review*, **41**.

Lawler, E. E. (1990) *Strategic Pay*. San Francisco CA: Jossey-Bass.

Lawler, E. E. (1995) The New Pay: A Strategic Approach. *Compensation and Benefits Review*, July–August.

Marsden, D. and Richardson, R. (1994) Performing for Pay? The Effects of Merit Pay on Motivation in the Public Sector. *British Journal of Industrial Relations*, **32**(2).

McDermott, D. G. (1997) Case Studies: Gathering Information for the New Age of Compensation. *Compensation and Benefits Review*, **29** March/April.

Moss Kanter, R. (1990) *The Change Masters. Corporate Entrepreneurs at Work*. London: Unwin.

Neale, F. (ed.) (1992) *The Handbook of Performance Management*. London: CIPD.

Randle, K. (1997) Rewarding Failure: Operating A Performance-Related Pay System in Pharmaceutical Research. *Personnel Review*, **26**(3).

Rashid M. Z. A., Sambasivan, M. and Johari, J. (2003) The Influence of Corporate Culture and Organisational Commitment on Performance. *Journal of Management Development*, **22**(8).

Rochester, C. (1999) One Size Does Not Fit All: Four Models of Volunteering in Small Voluntary Organisations. *Voluntary Action*, **1**(2).

Schrage, M. (2000) Cafeteria Benefits? Ha! You Deserve a Richer Banquet. *Fortune*, 3 April.

Stern, S. (2002) Flex Your HR Muscle. *People Management*, 21 March.

Swabe, A. I. R. (1989) Performance Related Pay: A Case Study. *Employee Relations*.

Swinburne, R. A. (2001) How to Use Feedback to Improve Performance. *People Management, **7***(11).

Zimmeck, M. (2002) *The Right Stuff: Approaches to Volunteer Management*. London: Institute for Volunteering Research.

PERSONAL NOTES ON CHAPTER 10

Notes for seminars

NOTES ON CHAPTER 10 *CONTINUED*

Notes for revision/reminders

_____

_____

_____

_____

_____

_____

_____

_____

_____

_____

_____

_____

_____

_____

_____

_____

_____

_____

_____

_____

_____

_____

_____

_____

_____

_____

_____

_____

_____

_____

_____

_____

_____

_____

Chapter 11

Human Resources Audits and Planning

Learning outcomes

After reading and completing the activities in this chapter, you should be able to:

1 Recognize the importance of HR planning.

2 Understand the value of auditing HR activities in relation to planning new HR interventions.

3 Evaluate the appropriate use of a variety of HR research methods.

4 Appreciate the significance and application of critical evaluative organizational studies.

5 Understand and apply the REACT system to HR planning.

6 Understand and apply the SMARTA system to HR planning.

7 Design an HR audit (individual or group activity) to conduct both primary and secondary research into an organization's HR planning and implementation.

8 Apply business research to identify HR issues in organizations.

INTRODUCTION

Auditing and evaluating existing management strategies can be one of the most interesting and valuable elements of any business course. For HR students, it can be a vehicle to get out of the seminar room and into real organizations to listen to what people have to say about their organizations. Live research can be surprising, even shocking. Learning just how different the perceptions of senior management, operational managers and employees can be about the same organization often breathes life into the theories and models that students have learnt in college or university. This is because the ability to discern differences between what organizations proclaim in their publicity and their actual behaviour is an important part of developing critically evaluative skills. Auditing and evaluating organizations can also be fun if teams of students work together on a research assignment. In this chapter you will learn how to organize an HR research project.

Can Planning HR Be Interesting?

HR planning can be interesting, if there are clear objectives to be achieved and the management team recognizes the value and relevance of planning HR and then putting new initiatives to work. Within this chapter you will find materials to help you work through some of the theoretical and practical aspects of HR planning. There is a new planning model, REACT, and an updated version of the SMARTA approach. The HR audit approach integrates HR into the organization so that it can be more effective at designing and delivering initiatives that really add value to the organization it serves.

In studying this chapter, you will be encouraged to consider a variety of approaches to evaluating HR in an organization and how to prepare an HR audit *(the structure and presentation of business reports is discussed in Chapter 12)*. These activities have both practical and academic learning outcomes because they provide a platform from which to reflect on the actual practice, with reference to relevant academic literature (see Harrison, 1987).

● HR AUDITING AND PLANNING

In common with other functional managers, HR professionals are accountable to their colleagues and should be able to explain the basis for HR investment decisions. It is for this reason that it can be helpful to describe planning in terms of an audit of HR requirements. The word 'audit' is usually associated with accounting professionals because it accurately describes an investigation, which is, hopefully, impartial, comprehensive and has financial implications. HR can also be presented and recognized as an investment in organizational performance. Otherwise, why bother? I cannot think of any business or organization leader who would want to spend money for no appreciable advantage! HR auditing and planning can also be an exciting and rewarding activity for both HR professionals and students studying organizational activities. In essence, it is about uncovering what HR improvements are required and then setting in motion HR initiatives which address those needs. Effective planning can lead to more efficient organizations and better performance, so investing time in an HR audit is an important step in the planning process (Figure 11.1).

Figure 11.1 Auditing and planning HR

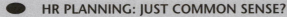

● HR PLANNING: JUST COMMON SENSE?

It certainly makes good sense to apply academically rigorous standards of research study to evaluating organizational performance. However, 'sense' is not always common in organizations and sometimes managers have to work hard at streaming innovative practices through their organizations. Following a series of meetings with one London project manager, he telephoned to let me know that his implementation of team-based work and empowering employees *(see Chapter 3, team working and Chapter 6, motivating a diversified workforce)* had been so successful that the directors had asked him to apply the same innovative 'techniques' across the organization.

The model he applied was:

> The process is *not* the goal
> Behaviour is *not* the goal
> Ownership *is* the goal (team working)
> It is not process that matters, it's outcomes

It is always encouraging to find examples of effective HR management – HRM in action. Ownership usually stems from good HR policies that have grown upward, in consultation, rather than being forced on workers (see Argandona, 2001). However, good practice tends to be noteworthy because significant numbers of modern organizations are still focusing on processes, compliance and targets. In the pursuit of improving performance, it is easy to forget that it is not processes that matter, but outcomes. However, within certain environments, a negative blame culture can arise because managerial behaviour is under public scrutiny and it is perhaps understandable if some organizations submit to the notion that it is 'better' to be seen to be following the processes than to risk take and be innovative.

However, in matters of management, there are usually alternative perspectives. Hence, in defence of the value of process management, it is arguable that a team of students who have learnt a lot about working together ought to be rewarded for their efforts (the process of learning), even if the 'outcome', their management report, is not necessarily excellent. These dual objectives can be achieved if the course validation allows. Returning to the world of HR and work, positive behaviour should be recognized, although this should be addressed in the wider acknowledgement of workers and HR rewards strategies *(see Chapter 10)*. This is a different simple adherence to process because it acknowledges effort and learning. Also in support of process adherence and in harmony with an underpinning philosophy of integrated HR, policy and practice are situation-specific. So there are some workplace situations that require adherence to procedures. Individuals do not give the law to flexibility or innovation and at a day-to-day level computer programme commands are inflexible – unless you press the right button, it will not work. It is a matter of appropriateness to purpose. Sense, then, can become more common when it is supported by useful, practical academic consultancy and research.

Linking HR Planning to Organizational Objectives

HR planning should be linked to whatever the organization defines as its key performance objectives. It is also important to recognize that key objectives are likely to differ considerably from one organization to another, so HR audits should be designed to meet the requirements of the particular organization, rather than a one-size-fits-all approach (a framework for HR audits is provided later in this chapter). For example, the management in one commercial sector company may have highlighted increasing market share as the main priority, while managers in a different company may focus on new product innovations. Alternatively, a not-for-profit or public sector organization may concentrate on how many people their services are helping, while another might be concentrating on restructuring the interaction between the employed staff and the volunteers. It therefore follows that the HR audits are situation-specific and need to focus on agreed key areas, so that the resources available can be put to best use. Hence, the need for integrating the individual's knowledge and skills with the needs of the organization (see Argyris, 1990).

● RESEARCH: FIND THE REALITY INSIDE THE RHETORIC

Uncovering the truth, or at least more of what organizations really do, can be exciting and challenging. It is worth noting that critical evaluation is non-judgemental. For example, if an organization is overburdened by overly restrictive or complex compliance procedures, it is quite possible that the gap between policies and practices could be considerable. Employees may learn to pay lip service to overly restrictive systems so that they can get on with their work. However, it is much better to have procedures that can be seen to be useful in practice. This applies to any sector, although the public sector tends to be more prone to overbureaucratization. Hence, it is possible that an HR audit may indicate that the procedures are the problem and the non-compliance is part of the solution – that is the fascination of research, the outcomes can be startling, even controversial.

Unexpected outcomes can also be found in the private sector. In a project conducted by a team of undergraduates with a multinational organization, the respondents advised them that the HR team were a manipulative arm of senior management! I checked the findings in an interview with one of the company's vice-presidents and the results of the initial student work stimulated a major survey of staff and a subsequent rethink of HR policies. So as well as achieving a good coursework grade, effective applied research can make a real difference to organizations researched: a win–win relationship of mutual advantage.

HR: Part of the Solution

Desk Note:　　HR has to be and be seen to be a part of the solution: not a part of the problem.

It is interesting to note that people from a diverse spectrum of organizational experiences tend to ask similar questions about the place and role of HR planning. For example, experienced managers on MBA courses have asked me to justify HR initiatives in terms of value for money and the financial bottom line. Alternatively, students on an MSc in voluntary action management have questioned me on whether businesslike planning is compatible with the 'higher motives' of people whose objectives are to help others rather than 'just make money'. Some others have argued that people will just get on with whatever needs doing, so where does HR fit in? It is important to recognize such concerns in your current and future workplace and be able to address them. So, in the case of the business sector, it is perfectly reasonable for colleagues to expect a return on their HR investment. HR managers need to appreciate that their activities are not an end in itself, but rather a means to an end.

Focusing on Outcomes Not Inputs

The effectiveness of any HR plan and subsequent initiatives will be measured by the outcomes in terms of whatever goals the organization has set itself. This means that if a team of employees have received effective development, they should be better equipped to do their work. For example, if sales and marketing staff have received training in interpersonal skills, communication, presentations and negotiating, then the outcome should be better customer relations and retention, which should translate into increased profits. It is perfectly reasonable for their sales manager to judge HR initiatives on outcomes, rather than the quality of the process, the HR training. Conversely, it has to be recognized that it can be difficult to prove a linear correlation between employee development and performance. For example, in a highly competitive market sector, it may be difficult to make significant improvements in market share, no matter how well trained employees are. It is quite possible that staff require developmental input just to retain the organization's share in its environment.

HR in the Voluntary Sector

In the voluntary sector as with the commercial sector, HR managers can present their recommendations for staff development, based on HR audit research, linking it to the aims and objectives of the organization. However, HR professionals need to be sensitive to the language, culture and values of the charity and not-for-profit organization *(see Chapter 2 for discussion of HR in context)*. Some traditional-style volunteers (including younger as well as older volunteers) may cling a culture of well-intentioned amateurism, so it is important for HR to be and be seen to be a part of their solutions. Of course there is always a valuable place for unpaid volunteers who give up their leisure time to work for the good of others. It should not, however, be acceptable for 'workers', paid or unpaid in the voluntary sector, to be well intentioned but inefficient. Indeed, if corporations can work efficiently to make money for their investors, it is surely at least as important for voluntary organizations to work effectively for the causes they serve. HR is about getting the best performance from people and it is people who run organizations, whatever the goals may be. If you are advising a charity, a service which I have tried to deliver free of charge whenever practical (the university work culture has become more 'business-oriented'), it is relevant to encourage volunteers to work towards giving of their best to the work they undertake.

Fail to Plan – Plan to Fail!

Planning management research takes time and usually more time than many students plan for. I have recently been reading Morrell and Capparell's (2001) book *Shackleton's Way*. According to their account of Shackleton's expeditions, the heroic early twentieth-century explorer planned his expedition with meticulous care so that there would be sufficient supplies and equipment for his expedition to Antarctica *(reference to Shackleton can be found in Chapter 3)*.

In the twenty-first century, the organizational environment can be just as unpredictable as the uncharted landscape that Shackleton's team faced in their expedition to Antarctica. The ability to plan a project, work together, implement the plan and then make adjustments to the work in progress is a valuable management skill. Start learning to plan and prepare on your first degree course. The habits you learn will benefit your career and help you to be potentially more successful.

● AKS: HR RESEARCH AND PLANNING

It is worth mentioning that the attitudes, knowledge and skills to initiate and successfully implement HR management strategies take time and patience. Even when the plan is sound and the objectives are clear, colleagues can still resist change, or simply not enjoy working with each other. The tendency of twentieth-century management theories was to operate at the level of rationality. However, humans are emotional as well as rational. When I interviewed a senior project manager regarding the main issues influencing the achievement of successful projects, he responded with 'ownership'. In other words, for a project to succeed, it is important to gain the proactive involvement of colleagues.

HR initiatives should encourage inclusiveness, so that people can feel they own the process rather than have it imposed on them. Even then, HR management is more likely to be a situation-specific art form than a science. We are working with people, with all their richness of diversity, thoughts and differences. One size does not fit all. This why many modern courses in HR require students to plan a research study on an organization, either in the form of primary research or the critical evaluation of case study materials. Indeed, the ability to critically evaluate organizational activity is a valuable transferable skill for any business student. Unless a manager can effectively evaluate the existing situation, it is unlikely that s/he will be in a position to recommend effective new initiatives. Therefore time spent investigating the current status of an organization's strengths and areas for development can also make it easier to target new initiatives to where they will be most effective. If the study can be organized to include team-working activity, so much the better. Working with other people is the one constant part of organizational life, so practising this valuable set of attitudes, knowledge and skills in a supervised learning situation is an asset to any management course.

Research and planning can actually reduce costs in two ways: by ensuring that new HR investments are directed where they are most needed and that money and time are not wasted on areas which are not a priority. In a competitive funding environment, HR professionals have to recognize that any recommendation for strategic HR initiatives has to bid effectively for organizational resources. This means that a professional HR person who can support his or her request for funding with sound primary research is much more likely to be able to convince colleagues of his or her proposal's investment merit.

HRM IN ACTION

OWNERSHIP

Please read the following management evaluation. It was sent to me by Will Porter (a senior IT project manager), following several meetings and discussions on HR and management performance.

Mike,

I thought I should send you a quote …

So here goes:

When an organization sets out to improve, people will recognize the need to improve both process and behaviour. The problem is how do you achieve this? Quite often, the need to make a change comes at a time of crisis. People are too busy trying to do the job, and have little time to talk about change, yet alone implement it. So how do you break the cycle? I believe it is a big mistake to launch a program with stated goals of process improvement or behaviour change. These can be perceived as patronizing, or disconnected from reality, with an overhanging fear of the 'process police' getting ready to pounce. I have found that you can introduce both process improvement and a change in behaviour by focusing on ownership. First of all be clear on what you aim to achieve and why (this must be a business imperative to have teeth!). However, very early on identify key stakeholders and ensure they agree there is a need and impetus for change. The big question of 'how' is then discussed. The key to success will be good facilitation, drawing out the good ideas, and bringing them to the fore. These ideas for change will have come from those affected. They will therefore be 'their' ideas. They will own them. The ideas can be tested to see how well they contribute to achieving what you aim to achieve, and will help validate whether or not this is correct. Ownership then continues as the team (which you should now be) work out how these ideas can be implemented. Actions can be identified, and assigned (owned). This should not take much time. The ideas should already be ripe within those contributing. It is your job just to bring them out. If things are taking too long, do you have the right people, or are you doing it the right way? Beware of getting it wrong, as the second time around is much harder!

With ownership established from the beginning you gain the following:

1) Buy-in from those involved. The ideas are their ideas.

2) Peer pressure from other owners. If they are delivering their actions, others must as well. This assumes the methods of facilitation include suitable team building.

3) Accountability for achieving the agreed aims. The ideas are not your ideas; they are the ideas of those participating. If the idea does not achieve the agreed aims, it will be clear who is responsible. This is further incentive for those involved to make the ideas work.

4) The ideas and methods of implementation will improve on their own over time. Given the clear accountability described above, those responsible for delivering the agreed aims must be given enough leeway (ownership) to evolve the ideas and methods of implementation.

All of the above must be underpinned by appropriate methods of communication and management. Standard project management practice already provides a good enough definition of how this achieved.

That's it Mike. It's very long. Feel free to edit, but if you do so, please let me know what you propose.

Good luck with the book.

Will

QUESTIONS FOR DISCUSSION

1   Why do you think the writer regards 'ownership' as so important?

2   Who or what are the 'process police'? Why do you think some organizations may appear to emphasize process over worker or employee ownership of projects or change?

3   Why do you think regarding changes and new plans that 'the second time around is much harder'?

4   What does this case study suggest about the value of team working and involving people in decisions?

5   Evaluate the role of HR input in developing the teams and managers' knowledge and skills in facilitating meetings *(see Chapter 12)*.

APPLIED CASE STUDY RESEARCH

Preparing a case study research project can be helpful in developing your management evaluation skills. It can also be valuable to the participating organizations in that the resulting documents can provide insights into their organizational behaviours. A concise case study of between 3000 and 4500 words can provide a useful vehicle for a useful research study (see Eisenhardt, 1989; Fergin et al., 1991; Yin, 1994a; Zikmund, 1994; Churchill, 1995; Saunders et al., 1997). The case study approach also suits individual or small teams researching organizations and writing reports on HR performance.

It has become increasingly common for business courses to require students to conduct a research investigation into a selected organization as part of their HR pathway studies. This activity has many advantages for addressing the application of theoretical knowledge to a practical situation. There can also be advantages regarding personal career development. I have also known students to obtain either a valuable business reference or even a full-time job after graduation through their contact with an organization that was initiated by an HR audit study. Participating organizations also benefit from having access to business school consultancy, particularly if they develop an ongoing relationship with a university. This can help managers to evaluate the potential value of any new initiatives with independent research. Indeed, some SMEs may have no HR-trained specialist staff, so the assistance of external consultancy could be particularly valuable.

The process of HR planning begins with a review of the current position, which should encompass a range of viewpoints, including senior managers, supervisors and staff. In smaller organizations, it may be possible to discuss matters with every member of staff. For example, if there were just 10–15 employees, it would be more effective to include everyone in the research.

The HR audit is a tool for identifying:

1   What needs doing most
2   When and where would investment be best applied
3   How the HR initiatives should be delivered
4   Who would most benefit from immediate assistance.

The actual structure and focus of any given HR research project will be shaped by whatever learning objectives a course leader has had validated for their particular course. Given that team-working skills *(teamwork is discussed in Chapter 3)* are such an integral part of modern organizational life, it can be helpful, where assessment criteria allow, to organize the HR audit investigation as a team activity, rather than as an individual project. This will also depend on the learning objectives and validation of a particular course. Alternatively, it is possible for one student to complete a successful HR project. Indeed, when I teach postgraduate courses such as the MA in HR, the MBA or voluntary action management MSc, the coursework reports are individual rather than group assessments. In such circumstances, students sometimes prefer to work in teams and conduct research into each other's organizations or discuss their research with their peers, but produce individual reports to comply with the validation requirements. This has the added benefit of presenting each student's organization with an external report conducted by an experienced professional from outside his or her organization.

● HOW TO REACT AND GET SMARTA

For the purposes of HR research and planning, I have designed a new model, REACT, which you first saw in Chapter 2. I have also adapted one which has been around for sometime, SMARTA. These two models offer a complementary choice of perspectives on HR activity. With REACT, the whole cycle, from research to implementation, is set out in easy to use stages for the HR student or professional, whereas operational managers who have had the diagnostic and planning recommendations completed by an outside consultant or HR professional might find SMARTA more appropriate.

To begin, lets look at the REACT approach:

Research: Conduct an HR audit of the organization to establish the current position and where HR investment is most likely to yield the most productivity benefits.

Evaluate: Examine the results from the audit and consider what most needs doing, when and where investment would be best applied, how the HR initiatives should be delivered and who would most benefit from immediate assistance.

Action: People expect to see concrete actions and new initiatives in response to the research and evaluation. Make recommendations and get the new initiatives implemented as soon as possible. Consider whether the initiatives can be delivered internally, or if a business school or consultant may be better able to produce the outcomes required.

Control: Monitor the progress and adapt the new HR initiatives as and where necessary. Even the best-laid plans need fine-tuning. Be prepared to respond flexibly to people's needs. Remember, it really is results that count, if HR is to justify its place in the organization. So focus on outcomes, not processes.

Time: Set realistic, time-bound objectives so that colleagues can be kept informed of progress. Staff morale can be boosted by recognition, so praise improvements and successes throughout the process, not just at the end.

SMARTA: Working Smart, Not Hard

Once an overall HR plan has been established, it is the responsibility of the operational managers to ensure that it is implemented and progressed. There is a lot to commend good planning, but it is of no value unless those plans are successfully implemented. Review consultancy and training initiatives in the short, medium and long term to assess the prolonged benefits of the initiative. The HR professional or operational manager has to focus on outcomes, not processes. In other words, the research, planning and preparation should produce improved outcomes, otherwise the processes, however skilfully conducted, have failed. The SMARTA system does not include the research and planning stages. Instead, it proceeds directly to the implementation of the specific objectives and moves through the managerial implementation beginning with specific objectives.

Specific: Clearly state objectives and actions so that colleagues are not confused about what is expected of them. Clarity of purpose will encourage commitment to the aims and objectives of the HR initiative.

Measurable: It can be difficult to measure individual HR initiatives, but colleagues should be made aware of the outcomes, such as better recruitment, improved retention of staff, more profitable sales performance, better time management, employee morale and so forth. Individual and organizational needs have to be met and performance improved.

Achievable: The new initiatives should be accomplished within the budgets and resources available to the organization. Can the initiative be delivered internally, or would it be more effective to use an external resource?

Realistic: Consider the influencing factors facing participants such as organizational culture and structure (see Deal and Kennedy, 1982; Watson, 1994). For example, is it realistic to have three or four key workers out on a training and development day in a small enterprise? Set realistic targets for outcomes. It can be demotivational to have unrealistic aims.

Time: Set practical, time-bound objectives. Staff morale can be boosted by recognition, so praise improvements and successes throughout the process, not just at the end.

Agreed: It is much better to consult to obtain acceptance before the new initiatives begin so that colleagues understand and accept responsibility for their part in making it a success. Listen and respond to constructive feedback.

⬤ **EVALUATING HR RESEARCH METHODS**

The following sections provide a step-by-step guide to conducting a research project. The methodology can be used by students for business management projects and by managers researching their organizations.

Selecting the Right Research Tools

Whether the research project is an HR audit in a small organization or a comprehensive study of a multinational corporation, it is helpful to begin by evaluating the aims of the research and the tools which will be most effective in carrying it out. It is also helpful to think in terms of fitness for purpose and how doable a research audit is. Hence, a large quantitative study (questionnaires) may be useful for a well-funded commercial research project, but is it realistic or necessary for a group of students to use such a large tool to do an HR audit? To use a simple analogy, if someone said they intended to mow a football field with a hover mower, one would question how effective their selected 'tool' would be in achieving the job. Conversely, a tractor and trailer would be overdoing it for a domestic garden! Translating the analogy back to research methods, it would probably be more appropriate to use a large sample, quantitative approach to investigate the whole of a large multinational and a case study approach for a more concise HR audit.

The key consideration in the assessment of methodological instruments has to be the extent to which any particular approach would best serve the requirements of the HR audit. It can be helpful to consider HR research design with reference to three simple criteria:

- The extent to which it can achieve the aims of the research project (fitness for purpose)
- The practical implications and limitations of using the method within the potential host organizations (doable)
- Can the HR audit be carried out within the time allocated (doable)?

The Documents File Search

The second step in setting up an HR audit is to think about collecting a documents file on your selected organization. This will help to establish a profile of who they are and their organizational style and structure. Do not be put off if the organization does not have any or all of these documents. Smaller organizations may not have many formal documents and some large ones may be reluctant to give external researchers access to their internal papers for reasons of commercial sensitivity. If you try and fail to obtain documents, keep a record of this for your project. In the early stages of HR research, it is often a matter of pursuing several lines of enquiry to find out which produces the best results.

It is helpful to gain access to and information about an organization from:

- HR documents
- Mission statement
- Publicity literature
- Website.

Websites are readily accessible to students and sometimes have a lot of useful information about the organization being studied. Additionally, if it is a large organization, there is likely to be a substantial amount of press and business literature material. The documents file is helpful in establishing the espoused standards of the organization and how it is perceived in the wider community.

Observational Research: Do They Do What They Say?

Many undergraduate students have jobs to help to pay their way through university. While the primary purpose of working is clearly pragmatic, it is usually not too long before students begin exploring the differences between the modern HR practices they are learning and some of what is actually happening in their part-time workplaces. It is also fair to say that many employers are conscientious and effective in managing HR, yet there is usually enough of a gap between the organization's espoused HR aspirations and actual practice for students to observe the practical challenges of implementing HR policies in the workplace.

If you have a part-time job, it may be possible to conduct some observational research. In Gill and Johnson (1991, p. 143) it is argued that observational studies can follow the idiosyncrasies of people working which is at the centre of research matters. Hence, observational research can provide valuable materials regarding actual HR practice as opposed to espoused policies. To use the American analogy, do people: Walk the walk as well as talk the talk? While methodologies such as questionnaires can produce statistical data on a variety of subjects, they depend on the honesty of the respondents. For example, when members of the public are interviewed about their voting intentions, prior to a general election, some may say that they are willing to pay more taxes to improve education and health funding because they believe it is the 'right' thing to say, but then go into the ballot box and vote for the party offering the lowest taxes. Observational research puts to researcher, metaphorically, in the ballot box. Whatever an employee says, or the company documents claim, the actual test of their authenticity is what employees actually do.

Another approach to observational studies that the employed student may find interesting is that of participant observation. As the term suggests, rather than avoiding involvement, the researcher actively seeks to become involved in the work of the organization. Whether as a participant or non-participatory observer ,the inclusion of observational research is likely to yield some useful materials for an HR audit.

It should be noted that the use of observation as part of an HR study depends upon permissions being granted. Also, it has to be recognized that the very act of observation may actually influence behaviour. However, elements of observable social behaviour, casual banter or remarks may be valuable in assessing what employees really think of HR and the extent to which they practise what they proclaim. Indeed, the sociologist Albrow (1997, p. 3) has observed that the reality of organizational life is not to be found in the boardroom or balance sheet but in the way people behave, their interactions, aspirations and social patterns. Using observational research as one part of an HR audit can therefore be a useful tool for gathering information on actual practices in a workplace.

Interviews

The key to a successful HR audit is to collect honest responses from the respondents about the current condition and value of HR activities, as they perceive them. Think about which approach is more likely to encourage respondents to offer their true thoughts and feelings within the particular organization being studied. One possibility is the semi-structured interview schedule. This method is sufficiently flexible to allow the researchers to ask supplementary questions and probe answers.

Ask open questions which begin with the words: what, how, when, why, where, and who. This kind of approach has been described by Phillips and Pugh (1994, pp. 46–7) as intelligence gathering. It enables the researchers to probe and follow up ideas made by the interviewees. According to Bell (1993, p. 91), an interviewer can use follow-up questions to probe responses and investigate motives and feelings. For example, the tone of the voice and facial expressions can provide information that a written response may conceal. This view is also ascribed to by Yin (1994b, p. 57) who has observed that as an interviewee recounts an incident, a good listener can capture the moods and context of the interviewee's perceptions. It is those interviewee perceptions of their organizational world, and the role HR plays in it, which can form an effective HR audit. The interview allows the researcher to critically evaluate responses and make comparisons between the statements made by the various respondents. Walker (1985, p. 157) recommended that interviewers should follow up on any discrepancies that emerge between the statements made by people and between what they say and what they do and between the organization's policies and actual practices.

An unstructured interview can provide more flexibility. Conversely, a structured interview has many more specific questions and in some cases the interview is effectively controlled by the interviewer, but it does constrain the opportunities to develop lines of enquiry by supplementary questioning which could encourage the respondents to express their views and feelings more openly. So, if an interview schedule is organized in a highly structured format, the respondents have less opportunity to articulate their insights or impressions. Alternatively, a less structured approach can be followed while still ensuring that specific question areas are included.

Questionnaires

There are occasions when it is useful to gather information from a larger group of people for the audit. For example, subject to permission being granted, questionnaires can be sent to employees throughout a large organization. The information collected from the larger questionnaire study can then be compared and contrasted with the responses gathered from the interviews. Although the questionnaire method lacks of the advantages of the individual interview, it does have the potential to gather more material from a broader spectrum of respondents.

Remember that the researchers are not present when respondents answer the questionnaires. Make the questions easy to follow and design the format so that you can analyse the results later. Provide user-friendly scales of choice so that the respondents can simply tick the most appropriate answer. Make sure the selections do not overlap to avoid confusion as to which section to tick, and do use a full-scale range. Sometimes students assume they know the answer and miss some of the range. Instead, let the respondents provide the evidence.

For example: What age are you?

16–21
22–30
31–40
41–50
51–60
61–65
66 plus

The age breaks are clear and unambiguous and do not overlap so someone is either in the 16–21 bracket or the 22–30. These are not, of course, universal age breaks. It is quite likely that different age breaks may be appropriate in the organization you are studying. However, the important point is to ensure that a full range is available and that the sections do not overlap. For example, if one of the purposes of the HR audit is to investigate whether managers are actively employing mature workers, then the age range question could contribute a valuable element of evidence, providing the scale includes the age of retirement and beyond.

Focus Group Interviews

The focus group interview offers the opportunity to interview a group of colleagues and ask them to give their impressions of HR from a team or departmental perspective. In this case it is important, subject to permissions being granted, to tape-record the meeting, as it will be difficult to note down the many insights, comments and interactions which a group of several people are likely to produce. On the plus side, colleagues may encourage each other to comment, whilst the disadvantage is the obvious lack of confidentiality for individuals (see Morgan and Kruger, 1998). Getting approval for and setting up a focus group entails a lot of planning. HR and other department managers are usually busy people so it is important to be available to meet them when they are willing and available.

Diary of Events

Another possibility worth considering is to ask a group of staff to complete a diary of significant events and activities during a specific time frame. This provides an overview of the kind of work people are doing as opposed to what may be set out in their job descriptions. This is particularly useful when considering what new HR training initiatives would best fit within the work that staff are actually doing as opposed to what is stated in their job description *(change is discussed in Chapter 4)*.

However, the commitment of the diarists is crucial to the success of this method. It can be work well if the HR audit is being conducted by an 'insider' such as a student working part time who has a working relationship with the diarists. If the research is being conducted in an organization where there are no established relationships, then obviously it will be more difficult to gain commitment to this method. Bell (1993, p. 102) has also cautioned that this method can be time-consuming and even irritating to people who are already busy doing their jobs. It is worth remembering that for every new activity HR or management ask staff to do, something else will have less time invested into it.

PILOTING RESEARCH METHODOLOGY

It is worthwhile discussing your research methodology with the tutorial staff at your college or university. The scrutiny of an experienced academic can really help to refine the HR audit research approach to the particular learning outcomes of your course. However, it also has to be acknowledged that the best-laid plans can still go adrift and it is as well to recognize that the work may have to be adapted in the negotiations with the organization being studied. Certainly, it is good practice to ask a course tutor to critically review the research model before the primary research work begins and offer advice as the project proceeds.

It is also helpful to 'pilot' the research tools with an HR professional who is not employed by the organization being studied. Whether this is doable depends on the contacts the HR audit team has available.

RELIABILITY, VALIDITY AND TRIANGULATION

The methodologies selected for the HR audit should provide a balanced mix of research tools whereby a greater measure of triangulation can be achieved. This simply means ensuring that the research has been seen from more than one perspective. It does not mean that you have to use all the research methods! A valid research model should be able to demonstrate that the methods selected measure what they are designed to measure. Hence the approach adopted can be selected on the basis of its compatibility and suitability to the HR research being conducted.

For a primarily qualitative HR audit (interviews, focus groups, diaries, observation), Gill and Johnson (1991, p. 151) have asserted that triangulation has a more limited role. Furthermore qualitative research can be completed successfully by using observation, interviews and documentary evidence. It is therefore helpful to include interviews with both senior staff and other employees, together with a review of any relevant company documents such as mission statements and HR documents pertaining to the research area. Internal validity can be strengthened by the replication of particular research methods, hence, interviewing and reinterviewing the same participant. Try to arrange observational sessions on different days and then compare and contrast the outcomes. A summary of the research interviews can also be sent to the senior managers with whom they have been conducted. This provides them with the opportunity to comment on their own observations. Any feedback which the senior managers might offer regarding the HR audit would itself provide another source of valuable research material.

● THE HR LITERATURE REVIEW

Reviewing HR literature and journals is essential. It will enable the HR auditors to compare research and recommended approaches and models with what they have found in their study. There is safety in many counsellors so do look at a variety of sources and compare and contrast ideas and approaches. The ability to critically evaluate how effective HR activities are being managed is made a lot easier when it can be compared with the approaches advocated in the published HR literature. Beware of anonymous items of 'business wisdom' on the internet. It is better to use materials from published textbooks, journals and the quality press.

● ETHICS IN RESEARCH PROJECTS

Given the nature of an HR audit, the project must be conducted in an ethically rigorous manner. Each university will have a set of guidelines for students conducting research. One general example, which is available on the web, is the BSA (British Sociological Association guidelines which can be downloaded from www.britsoc.org.uk).

The guidelines offered by the BSA include the following:

- As far as possible research should be based on the freely given, informed consent of those studied.
- The research participants should be made aware of their right to refuse participation whenever and for whatever reason they wish.
- Research participants should understand the extent to which they are afforded anonymity and confidentiality. They should also be able to reject the use of data-gathering devices such as tape recorders and video cameras.

The method of recording the interviews has to be subject to approval with interviewees. All respondents should be asked if they are willing to have their interviews recorded or if they prefer note taking. This is both sound ethics and helpful in obtaining a richer quality of qualitative research material. One of the main objectives in using interviews is to obtain deeper observations and comments and reflections by asking more probing questions about what the person thinks of HR in their organization. This, however, requires respondents to feel sufficiently relaxed to share their feelings and attitudes candidly. Powney and Watts (1987, p. 27) argue that the use of recording equipment might detract from the desired atmosphere, asserting that paper and pen is less intrusive than tape recorders or video cameras. Furthermore, some potential respondents may reject being tape-recorded but accept conventional notes. In the many HR studies I have conducted, it has been interesting to note that even when an interviewee agrees to being recorded, their body language relaxes when the tape reaches the end. Indeed, sometimes the most frank and sincere observations have been offered when the tape was not running. Writing on the area of research ethics, Kervin (1992, pp. 450–1) has asserted that there are three particular ethical issues to be considered: informed consent, confidentiality and anonymity, and contact effects:

- *Informed consent:* highlights the need to inform respondents of the purpose of the research and respect their right to refuse to answer questions or have their comments recorded on tape or video.
- *Confidentiality and anonymity:* ensure that the information collected should not be available to unauthorized persons.
- *Contact effects:* the researcher should not unnecessarily invade the respondent's privacy or cause anxiety in probing matters which may be distressing. We have a responsibility to people before research.

If practical, it can be useful to produce a consent form to give respondents, an example of which is shown below.

RESEARCH CONSENT FORM

CONSENT FORM FOR HR RESEARCH CONDUCTED BY . . . . student/s at . . . .

Thank you for agreeing to take part in this HR audit.

The research title is . . . .

Your consent to participate in this research is appreciated. As a research participant, you should be aware of your rights to:

1　Refuse participation whenever and for whatever reason you wish.
2　Withdraw from participating at any time.
3　Refuse to answer any question or complete all or parts of a questionnaire.
4　Have your anonymity maintained, if you so request.
5　Decide to retain anonymity regarding part or all of any responses you provide.
6　Be able to reject the use of data-gathering devices such as tape recorders and video cameras.

Signed by Researcher/s: . . . .

Signed by Respondent: . . . .

Date: . . . .

Exercise 11.1

HR IS OK HERE, ISN'T IT?

A business student was asked to make a study of HR planning. S/he knew that primary research would be required so she contacted the head office of the organization where s/he was working part time and made arrangements to interview the HR manager. However, because the hand-in date for the course-work was several weeks away and s/he was doing the project alone, there was no peer pressure to make a start on the work. Unfortunately, the lack of progress also meant that the student felt too embarrassed to attend the workshops on HR auditing which the course tutor had provided.

However, the student was confident about the assignment because s/he had attended some lectures on general research methods for another business management unit, vaguely recalling something about qualitative and quantitative approaches, but not the key details. For example, one of his questions asked:

'As you know, strategic HR is absolutely essential to modern successful organizations. Please tell me how many months or years you spend on staff consultation for major change programmes.'

1 year and over	A
1 year	B
9 months – 1 year	C
6 months – 9 months	D
3 months – 6 months	E
3 months	F

As the hand-in date for the project drew closer, s/he decided it was time to do some interviews with the HR manager and her assistant. The HR team noticed that the student was somewhat less than well prepared for the meeting, but were keen to help out with the project. Given that the questions were so specific, it was easy to give the kinds of answers the student was looking for without the need to qualify their responses. For example, they answered the above question with D, 6–9 months. After the student had left, the assistant asked the HR manager why she had given that answer? The reality was that no formal consultations had taken place. The HR manager replied: 'We did talk to a few people informally and it took around three months to set the policies in place. I wasn't sure whether to select E 3–6 months, or D 6–9 months, so I opted for D because it took us around six months to complete the compulsory redundancies'.

Discussion questions

1 What were the main mistakes the student made in planning the research?

2 Why do you think the research failed to obtain more accurate material about what was really happening in the organization?

3 In what way, if any, might the project have been more likely to succeed had the student been working in a team?

● EFFECTIVE RECOMMENDATIONS

The process of investigating HR is likely to raise interest among staff and expectations as to what will happen next. When I am supervising postgraduate managers who intend to use their coursework reports inside their organizations, I emphasize the importance of preparing a set of effective recommendations shown in Figure 11.2.

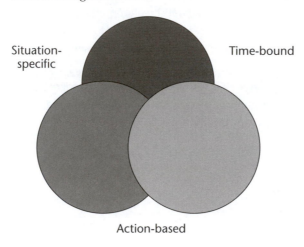

Figure 11.2 Effective recommendations

The audit recommendations should be designed to be feasible and applicable to the organization being studied. There is no point recommending initiatives if they have no resources, financial or personnel, with which to implement them (unless the recommendations are to employ new people, if finances allow). The recommendations should be deliverable in an agreed time frame, otherwise the report may be so much critical evaluation without any practical outcomes. The recommendations should also centre on concrete actions (doable).

● ACT

The purpose of an HR audit is to provide an assessment of where HR investment and input is necessary. Once the audit is complete and the recommendations have been accepted, a plan of action should be put in place to translate the audit recommendations into positive actions. The ACT model stands for action, control and time and these are expanded on below.

Action

Employees, workers and volunteers will expect to see concrete actions and new initiatives in response to the research and evaluation. Make doable recommendations and get the new initiatives implemented as soon as possible. Consider whether the initiatives can be delivered internally, or if a business school or consultant may be more able to help produce the outcomes required.

Situation-specific solutions

Effective HR audits deliver a set of recommendations which the organization can use. For example, in a large company, it may be both desirable and practical to invest in a postgraduate course in HR for employees who are promoted to senior management posts. Alternatively, in another organization a set of short management courses may be more appropriate. Modern organizations do not always have a full range of HR experts on their payroll. Even those with a substantial HR department might like to consider introducing some external expertise to assist with the delivery of training and development initiatives. Recommendations should take account of the organization's culture and structure, so that although they may be challenging, the style and content is empathetic to the organizational environment they serve.

Time-bound solutions

A recommendation is strengthened if it can be seen to be achievable within a specific time frame. The HR audit recommendations therefore need to be set in reasonable timescales for implementation. For example, if it is recommended that managers improve their interview skills, then the recommendation should be clear as to how and by when the training should be implemented.

An HR audit that lacks time-bound recommendations may excite temporary interest, but fail to stimulate real progress as the day-to-day pressures of work distract managers from the aspirations of the report. It is therefore desirable to offer clear guidance as to what should be done and by when it should have been achieved.

Action-based solutions

The recommendations should focus on actions, rather than aspirations. For example, most managers would agree that staff motivation should be encouraged, but what actions are recommended for achieving higher levels of motivation? By setting specific aims, the HR professional can focus management attention on the key actions.

Example of recommendation:

> It is recommended that the heads of department undertake a short course (two days) to improve their performance in interviewing techniques. The training should be supervised by HR qualified staff or external consultants and completed within four months following the publication of this HR audit report.

Control

Monitor the progress and adapt the new HR initiatives as and where necessary. Even the best-laid plans need fine-tuning. Be prepared to respond flexibly to people's needs. Remember it really is results that count if HR is to justify its place in the organization. So focus on outcomes, not processes.

It may be necessary to modify the programme in response to unforeseen developments. An effective HR professional will also focus on what is being achieved. It is not enough for the development programme to be delivered successfully; it has to deliver results in terms of organizational performance.

Time

Set realistic, time-bound objectives so that colleagues can be kept informed of progress. Staff morale can be boosted by recognition, so praise improvements and successes throughout the process, not just at the end.

Providing feedback of progress encourages staff that they are involved in an ongoing process of professional development. Praising progress also rewards participants and encourages staff to continue with whatever development plan they are working with.

PRACTISING HRM

ORGANIZATIONAL AUDIT

Choose two subjects from the chapter titles at the front of this book. Select an organization you are interested in and write a management report critically evaluating what influence, if any, your chosen subjects have had on that organization's HR performance *(details on management report writing are contained in Chapter 12)*.

● CHAPTER SUMMARY

HR planning is an important step in improving organizational performance. The use of tools such as REACT and SMARTA provide practical frameworks for analysing progress with a step-by-step system. The HR audit design outlined in this chapter can assist a management team and students of HR to produce a more objective report, based on tools that have been refined in the academically rigorous environment of social science research. As such, the results are likely to offer a more reliable source of information than less formal organizational research. The HR student is therefore better able to analyse human resources issues. HR managers who receive an audit report will be in a better position to make informed decisions regarding their recommendations for improving staff performance.

● REFERENCES

Albrow, M. (1997) *Do Organisations Have Feelings?* London: Routledge.

Argandona, A. (2001) Managing and Acting 'Beyond the Call of Duty'. *Business Ethics: A Euoropean Review,* **10**(4).

Argyris, C. (1990) *Integrating the Individual and the Organization.* London: Transaction.

Bell, J. (1993) *Doing your Research Project.* Milton Keynes: Open University.

British Sociological Association's *Statement of Ethical Practice.* www.britsoc.org.uk.

Churchill, Jr, G. A. (1995) *Marketing Research. Methodological Foundations* (6th edn). Fort Worth. Dryden Press.

Deal, T. E. and Kennedy, A. A. (1982) *Corporate Cultures. The Rites and Rituals of Corporate Life.* Wokingham: Addison Wesley.

Eisenhardt, K. M. (1989) Building Theories For Case Study Research. *Academy of Management Review,* **14**(4).

Fergin, J. R., Orum, A. M. and Sjoberg, G. (eds) (1991) *A Case For The Case Study.* Chapel Hill: University of North Carolina Press.

Gill, J. and Johnson, P. (1991) *Research Methods For Managers.* London: Paul Chapman.

Harrison, M. I. (1987) *Diagnosing Organizations.* Newbury Park, CA. Sage.

Kervin, J. B. (1992) *Methods For Business Research.* New York: HarperCollins.

Morgan, D. L. and Kruger, R. A. (1998) *The Focus Group Kit.* London: Sage.

Morrell, M. and Capparell, S. (2001) *Shackleton's Way.* London: Nicholas Brearley.

Phillips, M. and Pugh, D. S. (1994) *How to Get a PhD* (2nd edn). Buckingham: OU.

Powney, J. and Watts, M. (1987) *Interviewing in Educational Research.* London: Routledge & Keegan Paul.

Saunders, M., Lewis, P. and Thornhill, A. (1997) *Research Methods for Business Students.* London: Pitman.

Walker, R. (ed.) (1985) *Applied Qualitative Research.* Aldershot: Gower.

Watson, T. J. (1994) *In Search of Management. Culture, Chaos and Control in Managerial Work.* London: Routledge.

Yin, R. K. (1994a) *Applications of Case Study Research.* Newbury Park, CA. Sage.

Yin, R. K. (1994b) *Case Study Research* (2nd edn). London: Sage.

Zikmund, W.G. (1994) *Business Research Methods* (4th edn). Fort Worth. Dryden Press.

PERSONAL NOTES ON CHAPTER 11

Notes for seminars

_____

_____

_____

_____

_____

_____

_____

_____

_____

Notes for revision/reminders

_____

_____

_____

_____

_____

_____

_____

_____

_____

_____

_____

_____

_____

_____

_____

_____

_____

_____

_____

Chapter 12

Communications and Presentations

Learning outcomes

After reading and completing the activities in this chapter, you should be able to:

1 Understand the role the HR specialist has in marketing HR initiatives within organizations.

2 Write effective business communications.

3 Organize and manage more productive meetings.

4 Apply the REACT system to facilitating meetings.

5 Conduct an effective business presentation (individual or group activity).

6 Recognize the importance of interpersonal communications in organizational performance.

7 Design an effective HR presentation.

8 Critically reflect on your interpersonal skills in managing and working within teams.

● INTRODUCTION

However good our plans and proposals may be, they need to be communicated effectively to achieve results. As an undergraduate or postgraduate, you will be keen to gain excellent grades on your business course and get on in your future career. Whilst it is fair to say that good communications cannot deliver poor materials, poor personal communication skills can weaken the influence of good quality materials. In this chapter you will learn how to design effective written and presentational communications.

Professional organizations, academics and writers may provide guidance materials, but it is ultimately up to people to communicate the message inside their organizations. Highlighting the need for HR professionals to be more proactive in persuading management colleagues of the need for people development,

Alberg (2002, p. 23) has asserted that the CIPD has done its best to give HR professionals the information required supporting their case. It is therefore worth emphasizing that one of the key roles of HR-trained professionals is to communicate the importance of investment in employees to their management colleagues, both the senior team and those in first line roles such as team leaders and supervisors (see Bedward et al., 1997). In an environment where the communication of information has become faster and often central to efficient organizational performance, the modern professional manager needs to be able to communicate effectively with his/her team. This applies irrespective of whether it is a commercial company (has to produce profits), the public sector (has to deliver efficient services) or a charity (which cannot help anyone unless it can attract volunteers and donations).

Modern HR has also become more of a strategic management role than an operational one *(the changing roles and responsibilities of HR professionals are discussed in Chapter 2).*

Functional managers who lead teams *(team management is discussed in Chapter 3)* will also find it helpful to develop their communication skills. This means that non-HR specialist students as well as specialists can enhance their management communication performance. Communicating HR messages effectively is part of all managers' job roles where they are responsible for improving performance via people, which really includes all team leaders and supervisory personnel *(employee relations is discussed in Chapter 4).*

● COMMUNICATION: WHOSE PRIORITIES COME FIRST?

Think about your priorities. What is at the top of your communications list? Is it your own needs, your agenda, your plans and proposals? Then do not be surprised if other people are disinclined to listen to you. Do many of your communications begin with: 'I want', 'I need', 'I think'? When you offer a new initiative or proposal at work, do you consider the advantages to the other people involved first or is it your own position, career, security that comes first?

I   We   You?

Or

You   We   I?

It can be interesting to listen to the priorities people employ in their verbal and written communications. If a speaker's focus of importance usually begins with their own interests, it can communicate less empathy with those around them. For example, '*I want* to have the appraisals completed by January because *I am* being monitored by *my boss* to pass a quality audit, so *we must* get them done as soon as possible and *you have to* submit your evaluations to me by Friday because that fits *my agenda*' sounds very self-centred *(appraisals are discussed in Chapter 8)*.

An alternative approach could be: 'Are there any issues about your work *that you would like* to raise with me? If so *we can get together* as soon as it is convenient *to you* for an appraisal, to discuss if there is anything *I can do to help you*.'

In the first example, it is evident that the manager is much more concerned with fulfilling an appraisal process than listening to employee's needs. This kind of enforced 'quality assurance' alienates staff and has the opposite outcomes intended by its initiators. The indication that the manager is under pressure to complete the appraisal process may be due to internal or external forces to meet 'quality standards' regarding employee monitoring. Nevertheless, it is the second approach that is more likely to produce more positive responses from employees because the manager centres the request on the employee's needs rather than a demand to meet her/his needs.

Effective communications (see Stanton, 1996) are particularly relevant because modern HR managers may be required to 'sell' the HR portfolio of services to colleagues in other functions within the business, which might have the right to elect to buy in a external services, such as recruitment search or training. Hence, functional managers can use their budgetary discretion to select those services which are most appropriate to their requirements. In the public sector, within UK schools, the principal and governors can choose whether or not to buy in the services of their local authority's HR team. In the private sector, an HR department can be organized as a separate cost centre where, similar to the local authority team, they have to secure work on a competitive basis with external providers *(the changing roles and responsibilities of HR professionals is discussed in Chapter 2)*. The role of HR people has therefore changed dramatically with the movement to outsource service functions so that organizations, both public and private, can concentrate on their 'core activities'. These changes have consequently placed much greater emphasis on the need for HR professionals to be effective communicators (see Covey, 1999).

CUSTOMER SERVICE: UNDERSELL – OVERDELIVER

In an ideal world, organizations would produce services or products and deliver them with faultless perfection. However, in the real world, such faultless performance can be difficult to achieve. This is not an excuse for poor workmanship or service. The simplest way to reduce customer dissatisfaction is to drive quality throughout every part of an organization. The beginning of better customer satisfaction is therefore more likely to be achieved through improvements in organizational performance than any amount of advertising and publicity. Communication is, of course, important yet most advertising and public relations consultants would probably agree that their best efforts are unlikely to sell a bad product or service more than once to any potential customer. Moreover, it is possible that if there is a significant gap between the publicity and the actual product, then the customer may be all the more annoyed when things go wrong because their expectations were raised, thus fuelling disappointment if the product or service is unsatisfactory. While the tendency for advertisers might be to oversell, it may actually be better for long-term customer relations to slightly undersell and overdeliver service.

The need to be customer sensitive applies to all sectors, public, private, not-for-profit and voluntary. Thus, whatever activity an organization is engaged in, it needs the approval of those people it serves, whether retail shoppers or the donors giving to a charity fund. Palmer and Hoe (1997, p. 47) found that for every customer who complains, nearly fifty have a poor impression of the organization. Even more alarming for organizations is the finding that as few as just one in seven customers actually make a complaint. So, there is no room for complacency in caring for our customers, whether internal or external.

Most happy customers are unlikely to say much when the services they receive are OK. For example, I doubt many people would spend their lunch break telling all their colleagues that their computer worked perfectly all morning. Alternatively, if the machine had crashed, lost valuable information and the support services provider was slow and inefficient, it is likely that the tale of woe is would be told and retold. Such negative publicity can easily lead to a supplier being delisted if the problems remain unresolved. The reality is that an organization's reputation with its customers and potential customers can be damaged if complaints are not resolved promptly. HR is a service provider so the people with whom the HR professional interacts are customers, whether internal or external. In the modern organizational environment, HR has to market its services (see Nieto, 2002).

⬤ COMMUNICATING THE HR MESSAGE

The concept of mission statements was not the creation of modern writers or managers, but came from the traditional use of mottos for military regiments and family hierarchies. It is also interesting to note that mottos were and indeed still are generally short and purposeful. For example, the family motto of the Antarctic explorer Sir Ernest Shackleton was *Fortitudine Vincimus* (By Endurance We Conquer) (Morrell and Capparell, 2001, p. 2). It is noteworthy that Sir Ernest chose to name the ship he purchased for one of his expeditions *Endurance,* to convey the message of the mission to Antarctica. The modern mission statement became popular in organizations during the 1980s and is associated with the trend to change organizational cultures. By the late twentieth century, many organizations felt impelled to say something positive about their mission and publish the document in their publicity. Unlike mottos, the mission statement has tended to evolve into an all-encompassing document asserting the many and varied aims and aspirations of a particular organization.

The aspirations expressed in mission statements and common assertions have to be converted into concrete actions if they are to transcend the rhetorical. The phrase 'people are our greatest asset' may have become common in HR mission statements but that does not always mean it has also become part of the actual management behaviour (Nieto, 2002, p. 31). There has also been a growing recognition that customers learn more from dealing with an organization's staff than through formal statements (Storey and Sisson, 1993, p. 183). For all the potential criticisms of the mission statement, it is encouraging to see organizations trying to set out an agenda of principles and then work towards applying them. For example, The Royal Dutch Shell Group set out some general business principles for the guidance and conduct of its business. These included profitability, investment, integrity, politics (obey the law, non-partisan), health, safety and the environment, community, competition (fairness), communication (openness with stakeholders (see Broadhurst, 2000, p. 95). It is interesting to find *integrity* and *communication* listed – perhaps the company recognized the importance of being honest and communicating effectively with stakeholders. However, there may be tensions and challenges for HR people who work on making such broad public proclamations a reality and Broadhurst (2000, p. 96) correctly observed that while Shell has been a prototype firm representing a trend towards increasing responsibility, there are also critics who dismiss such efforts as public relations. Time will certainly expose whether the critics are correct or if the organization proves able to convert mission aspirations into HR reality. It may also be arguable that organizations should make fewer public assertions until they are sure they can deliver on them. Perhaps a case for underselling and overdelivering is appropriate. Alternatively, making a bold statement and then working towards achieving it can communicate a purposeful goal.

The research by Garrett (1992, pp. 21–6) on the Virgin organization indicated that Branson gives priority to HR issues such as staff retention, believing that too many organizations offer insufficient employment security. In this case, it is not so much what Virgin tells its stakeholders about their values in a mission statement, but the way senior management behaves which is being used to convey values and the wider HR mission. While senior management behaviour alone does not necessarily indicate the condition of core values throughout their organization, they can provide example, leadership and incentives for other employees to behave similarly (see Goffee and Jones, 2000).

WRITING AN HR REPORT

The style, content and structure of written communications should be designed to serve the needs and interests of the reader. Obvious? One of the most frequent questions undergraduates and postgraduates ask me is how to write an academic report, rather than a management report. The academic paper is underpinned by references to both primary and secondary research, whilst a management report usually draws from the primary research based on the organization and its environment. Of course there are many different ways to write a report. Effective communication is about meeting the particular audience's needs. So, different academic journals require different styles and emphasis, as do different professional magazines. However, redesigning our writing style to serve different audiences requires thought and a little effort.

One senior manager told me that he asks potential new graduate trainees a simple question: 'How would you set out a management report?' The best answer should be: *who is the report for?'* Why is this point important? The prospective audience should influence the content, style and range of what the report will contain. For example, a report outlining the need for new training initiative could highlight the cost-saving implications for the finance director, the improvements in staff performance to the projects managers and the ongoing HR support to the trainees (see Aragón-Sánchez et al., 2003)

It has become usual, particularly for postgraduate study and specialist HR courses, to ask students to prepare a report including primary and secondary research on an organization, as part of the assessment procedure *(see Chapter 11 for a report activity)*. Each university and college will have set particular guidelines and students should always refer and comply with whatever regulations apply to their course. Several leading universities in the UK, Europe and the USA are using this model, so it can provide a helpful framework upon which to construct an HR study *(see Chapter 11 for HR research design recommendations)*.

An academic report will usually have all the sections listed below:

● *Executive summary:* The purpose of this section is to briefly outline the report. Ideally divide this into three paragraphs setting out:
  – What the report set out to investigate
  – Briefly – the methodology used
  – The main conclusions.

  The executive summary is the first item the reader is likely to review. Take care to write something that would encourage the reader to think the report will be interesting. A report does not get a second chance to make a good first impression.

● *Contents page:* This provides a simple guide to the contents of the report.

● *Acknowledgements:* It is polite to acknowledge organizations, individuals and academic staff for their contributions and advice in the preparation of the report.

● *Introduction:* Outline of the organization. Area of study and research methodology.

● *The literature review:* It is helpful to select headings or themes that link to the primary research. If you use the same subsections for the three key sections – literature review, findings and analysis – it encourages focus.

● *Findings:* The primary research results, such as information from interviews, observation studies or questionnaires. Note that assignment word restrictions may require a critical evaluation of what to include in this section.

● *Analysis and discussion:* This includes references to literature and compares and contrasts the practices found in the primary research with theory, models and case studies as discussed in the literature review.

● *Conclusions:* A summary of the main results. No new material should be introduced in this section.

- *Recommendations:* These should be specific to the organization, time-bound and achievable with the organization's resources and culture.

- *References:* cited from published works rather than generic lecture notes. It should just include those texts directly used or referred to in the report. It should not be just a long book list.

- *Appendices:* These provide additional background such as examples of interview schedules, questionnaires (blank copies only) and other relevant material if available such as mission statements, letters to organization.

It can be helpful to type in each of the above headings into a file so that future materials can be correctly allocated as and when required. For example, you may find an interesting reference and type it into the literature section in readiness to use later.

The report structure can, of course, be modified to meet situation-specific requirements. Recently, I was commissioned to prepare a HR study report for a charity. The brief was to analyse the organization's current HR status and the background study indicated that some of the management committee required convincing of the value of HR. The report they received consequently had a larger section on research methodology, less of an introductory overview and references to literature were sparingly used to support the situation-specific analysis. In common with most reports, the executive summary and recommendations were key elements.

If it is consistent with the learning outcomes of your degree validation, it can be helpful to adopt what might be described as a 'prac-academic' approach, wherein the research benefits from the rigours of academic discipline, but is designed to produce some practical outcomes for the organizations who take part in the work, hence a report that is both *practical* and *academic*.

It can also combine some of the rigour of academic methodology with practical applications to produce studies that retain academic integrity and deliver the practicality of consultancy reports. However, the point highlights the challenges and difficulties of preparing reports that meet the requirements of the client or readers. My own students have enjoyed this approach and some have so impressed their organizations that they have been offered HR or management positions after graduation.

If the study is to be conducted by a team of students, it can also be useful to include a reflective review of the learning experience. The HR report provides an opportunity for the team to make a reflective statement about the team's learning experiences whilst carrying out the report. Include a personal reflective summary of your learning outcomes through working as a member of a team.

MEETINGS: WHAT'S THE POINT?

Meetings can be called for any number of reasons, political – social, compliance requirements and, sometimes, a genuine exchange of ideas. It is useful to review the reasons that meetings are called in an organization before attempting to streamline the process. Torrington et al. (2002, p. 121) have also observed that modern HR specialists may have to chair meetings for staff selection, management and many more. The extent to which HR people are called on to attend management meetings will depend on the type of organization as well as its structure and management culture *(for structure and culture see Chapter 2)*. The integrated HR model tends to place HR personnel into the key strategic decision-making roles in organizations. This tends to mean more meetings with a wider diversity of colleagues. Adopting a structured model to guide the meeting process can assist efficiency and reduce time being wasted as colleagues drift onto either non-agenda items or use up too much time on individual items.

Facilitated Meetings Guide: REACT

To facilitate meetings successfully, the facilitator needs to be able to REACT to the needs of the participants.

Research   Research issues that are important to the participants. What do the people coming to the meeting want to discuss? Circulate a request for agenda items in advance of the meeting.

Empathy   Make every effort to understand colleagues' viewpoints. Listen to the opinions and ideas expressed.

Actively   Encourage the participation of quieter people and the less confident. Their silence does not necessarily indicate either agreement with the general flow of discussion or that they have nothing to contribute, it may just be shyness or diffidence to take part in the discussion.

Control   Stay calm, endeavour to ensure fairness to all opinion groups. Try not to let the most vocal dominate the discussion.

Time   Agree a time to *begin* and *end* the meeting. Provide regular breaks for tea, coffee and so on. *Do not allow* the meeting to overrun. This creates a more professional atmosphere and encourages focus. Colleagues usually have other important activities scheduled.

How long is the time allocated? Do not be tempted to include too much information. The nervous or inexperienced presenter sometimes takes comfort in having large amounts of material and then simply ends up reading their script. This approach simply does not produce an interesting or persuasive presentation. The skill in presenting is in selecting the materials that are most relevant, rather than to try and include everything. Do not overrun the allocated time. It is much better to complete your presentation within the time and that should also include the time allocated to taking and answering questions.

● WHY PRESENTATION SKILLS MATTER

Few activities or assessments seem to be able to strike fear into the heart of business students like a presentation. I have seen grown men and women with senior management jobs become nervous over this relatively simple activity. At a time when the HR role in organizations is becoming more strategic *(see Chapter 2)*, you are more likely to be called upon to make a presentations. So it is important to be able to communicate the HR message to colleagues effectively.

Presentations are more than the delivery of information. If all you want to do is give out information, it would be easier, although less effective, to send an email or put the material on a website. The skill of presenting is in generating interest, not downloading information on an audience. Why? The attention and retention levels of an audience can vary considerably according to how interested they are in what they are hearing and seeing. If the audience feels involved, engaged, they become active listeners rather than just passive observers. Dull presentations produce bored observers who are likely to remember little of the presentation content. Presentations are successful if they communicate successfully. It is not whether the presenter has delivered materials, but whether the audience has understood the presentation. Remember to design your presentations around the needs and interests of the audience, not your own.

The research conducted by Albert Mehrabian (cited in Egan, 1994, p. 95) on how we receive messages found that:

Verbal (words only) accounted for	7%
Vocal (tone of voice) accounted for	38%
Non-verbal (expression) accounted for	55%

Whilst the exact division of percentages may vary in experimentation, the trends in the importance that humans place on non-verbal communication is still revealing (see Morris, 1978, 1994; Hayes, 1991; Hunt and Baruch, 2003).

The research evidence of the past 40 years indicates that how we say something is more important that the words alone. Anyone who has received a hollow greeting from a store assistant whose boss has demanded s/he 'greet' every customer can recognize the difference between genuine friendliness and a forced smile. It is therefore useful to remember to have eye contact with the audience. Do not be tempted to just read notes from the screen (this can cause the presenter to turn away from the audience). Try to learn some or all of the materials so that you can concentrate on communicating rather than reading the materials.

Presentations: Asking the Right Questions

The following questions can help to establish the content of the presentation:

Who for?   Who is going to be in the audience? Business colleagues, clients, academics? Remember it is important to design a message that is relevant to the particular audience.

Achieve what?	What do you want to achieve by making this presentation? Persuade others to support your viewpoint? Increase awareness of HR issues? Gain funding? Obtain a job promotion? Get a top assessment grade?
Why should they listen?	Why are people attending this meeting, seminar, presentation? Why are they coming to listen to *you*?
Expectations?	What do they expect from you? Are they hoping to hear an in-depth detailed analysis or an overview of the subject matter? It is always helpful to put yourself in the place of the audience when thinking about how to design your presentation. Put bluntly, *why* should they listen to you? What's in it for them?
Special interests?	What is the audience most interested to hear about?
Amuse?	What is likely to amuse and engage them?
Vocabulary?	What language is likely to offend or alienate members of this audience? Remember, the use of appropriate language is important. So, for example, whilst the directors of an international company may respond favourably to a presentation about strategic planning and auditing HR performance, these terms may not be as well received by a group of charity fieldworkers who have just returned from working in a famine zone. Always consider the interests and the terms that are appropriate to your audience.
Relevant examples	Are you examples up to date? Regularly updating materials will make your presentations interesting for both you and the audience.

Collecting Presentational Materials

The following items provide a simple guide to collecting information which can make presentations more interesting:

1   Topical news reports
2   Relevant publications and journals
3   Recent research papers
4   Your own research
5   Textbooks
6   Company financial reports

7   Quotations from literature
8   Anecdotes and stories
9   Interviews with staff and managers
10 Interviews with clients and users

Handouts

If there is a lot of general background information, it is more useful to hand this to the audience in the form of an information pack after the presentational session. However, the professional presenter should be aware that most managers do not have time to read a long briefing document so it is *still* more effective to discuss an outline of the most important issues during the presentation.

⬤ THE INTRO PRESENTATION SYSTEM

Many students have told me that the most difficult part of a presentation is getting started. Below is a recommended introduction plan that can help to get your presentation off to a sound start, I call it the INTRO system:

⬤ INterest

Aim to gain the audience's interest from the outset. How this is achieved depends on the audience. Refer to your earlier work on who the audience are and what their expectations are. You never get a second presentational chance to start with a good impression. Plan the introductory statements carefully. It is important to start off with a bang, gaining their attention right from the beginning.

⬤ Time

It is not only polite, but also practical to give the audience some indication of the length of the presentation. Declaring the intended duration also indicates your level of preparation and ability to work within a specified time frame. It makes the presenter look professional and may encourage the audience to be more attentive in the knowledge that what they are about to hear is likely to be concise and relevant. Include any time allocated for questions and answers in the time.

⬤ Range

Explain the range and depth the presentation will contain. For example, are they going to hear about all aspects of management development in the organization or an overview followed by a more in-depth evaluation of one department?

⬤ Objectives

The benefits of declaring your objectives are that it informs the audience about why you are doing the presentation and focuses you or your team on the key objectives so that you or they are less likely to stray from the main subject.

Practise, Practise, Practise

Once the presentation materials are complete, there are three more things you or your team need to do to ensure it runs smoothly: practise, practise and, yes, more practise. This is particularly important for team presentations because it takes practice to coordinate the speakers.

GROUP ACTIVITY

WORKING TOGETHER

One of the key factors in developing successful team presentations is the ability to work together. Wherever possible I encourage students to think about the application of theories and models to role-play situations, discussions and activities. While most students can recite a few theories, it is more useful for future HR professionals to be able to apply theoretical concepts to actual practice. This can be facilitated by the reinforcement of theoretical knowledge through experiential learning *(experiential learning is discussed in Chapter 9)*, which is why the seminar elements of courses can be so helpful. The exercise below has been designed to give business students insights into the interpersonal interactions of cooperating teams in achieving agreed goals (see Axelrod, 1984, 1997; Argyle, 1995; Arnold et al., 1998).

The aim of the game is simple. Your team should achieve a positive score. At least two teams are required and a chairperson to collate the scores. There are ten rounds to the game and time is provided for the teams to consider their actions and responses. Teams can consist of two or more people.

Scoring

If both teams deploy a red or green, they will achieve two points each, but if one deploys a red and the other a green then neither team score any points. The team which uses a blue causes the other team to lose two points, but does not score any points.

During the final three stages (8, 9, 10) of the game, the teams can deploy a yellow, which can gain both teams ten points, providing both teams deploy a yellow at the same time. If one team deploys a yellow and the other deploys any other colour, then the team which deployed the yellow loses five points.

Scores

Red, Red = 2 points each team

Green, Green = 2 points each team

Green, Red = 0 points each team

Blue, Blue = –10 points each team

Blue, Red = Red –2 points

Blue, Green = Green –2 points

Yellow, Yellow = 10 points each team (yellow can only be deployed in rounds 8, 9, 10)

Yellow, Green = Yellow –5 points

Yellow, Red = Yellow –5 points

Yellow, Blue = Yellow –5 points

Meetings

Either team can request a meeting with a representative or all members of the other team after stages 3, 6 and 8. Teams may accept or decline an invitation to discussions.

Scorecard

Green Team	Red Team
1 _____	_____
2 _____	_____
3 _____	_____

Possible team meetings

1 _____	_____
2 _____	_____
3 _____	_____

Possible team meetings

1 _____	_____
2 _____	_____
3 _____	_____

Possible team meetings

1 _____	_____
2 _____	_____

Results discussion: please refer to the notes below **after** the exercise has been completed.

Discussion plan

Win–win

In a win–win relationship, both teams have achieved a positive score. The members have successfully worked with both their own colleagues and gained the trust and cooperation of the other team. This can be likened to an organization where different groups of people are able to cooperate for the common success of all. Given that resources can be limited, competing ambitions and human nature, this is by no means a foregone conclusion. The teams should discuss what led them to make the decisions at each stage and how and why they felt able to trust each other.

Win–lose

In this outcome, one team has gained more points than the other. The two groups should therefore discuss why they think this came about, including matters such as trust, cooperation and the issues which might arise when members are involved in future projects. Although one team has achieved the objective of a positive score, the other team has failed. To place this in an organizational context, it would be rather like the finance section meeting its targets by cutting the training and development budget: the organization's short-term outgoings have been reduced but future performance has been put in jeopardy. Hence win–lose.

Lose–lose

In this scenario, both teams have not been able to attain a positive score. It is therefore worth reflecting on what happened during team discussions and how a successful outcome might have been achieved. Placed into an organizational context, this would be true of situations where problems in employee relations hinder performance, for example arguments between management and employee representatives or team members.

Did you and your team work on the basis of you, we, I, or did you and the team place self before others?

PRACTISING HRM

PREPARE A PRESENTATION

You and your team are invited to design a 20-minute presentation, including a short question and answer session. The topics can be selected from the following questions, which are based on the chapters in this book. Select a topic you and your team are interested in and reread the relevant chapter for guidance.

1 Can integrated HR be described as a paradigm shift in HR, or is it more an evolution of previous models?

2 Why is the organizational context important to HR planning?

3 Why do teams work? How do teams fail?

4 Why do psychological contracts matter?

5 Can life and work be balanced in modern organizations? Discuss.

6 Does the right person always get the job? Discuss linking selection to AKS.

7 Evaluate how appraisals can be made more motivational.

8 Can investing in employee development make a difference to organizational performance? Discuss.

9 Different people have different requirements. How can HR help to address the opportunities and challenges of a diversified workforce?

10 Are rewards just about money? Discuss.

11 Evaluate the value of doing HR research before attempting to offer changes in policies and practices in either a for-profit or not-for-profit organization.

12 Why is the ability to market the HR function particularly relevant to modern integrated HR approaches?

13 Should organizational ethics be part of the HR portfolio? Discuss.

14 If HR is situation-specific, how does this influence the design of policy for international organizations?

Exercise 12.1

ASSESSING PRESENTATIONS: GRADING FRAMEWORK

Evaluate your own team or seminar group's presentation using the table below. Give each section a mark out of 100 then divide by 3.

GROUP NAMES	0%	20%	30%	40%	50%	60%	70%	80%	100%	Total
PRESENTATIONAL QUALITY Appropriate professional delivery. Management of allocated time available. Verbal and visual effectiveness. Effective use of video, voice or music recording, exhibition and display or supporting materials.										
STRUCTURE/CONTENT Clarity of objectives and structure, quality, sourcing, accuracy. Content. Appropriate methodological rigour.										
INTERACTIVE QUALITY Role plays. Dramatized performances. Leading question and answer sessions.										
Totals:										

EXAMINER OBSERVATIONS

_____
_____
_____
_____
_____
_____
_____
_____
_____

● CHAPTER SUMMARY

The modern HR professional should be able to present the HR function effectively in both written HR reports and presentations. Within a competitive resources environment, HR people need to be able to communicate proposed strategies to management colleagues. You should now also be able to organize and manage more productive meetings. Remember, it is more helpful to your personal development to practise newly acquired knowledge and skills within the safety of the seminar room, rather than the boardroom where your reputation and that of the HR team could be at stake. It is therefore helpful to be more effective in management meetings by practising the REACT model and placing the needs of other people high on your planning aims.

By designing and presenting a response to an HR question, you should also have gained confidence, knowledge and skills in presenting HR issues to other people. The activities in this chapter are designed to encourage team participation and also provide you with an opportunity to reflect on your interpersonal skills in managing and working with others. Try to enjoy presenting, it can relax you and the people you are working with.

● REFERENCES

Alberg, R. (2002) Counting with Numbers. *People Management*, 10 January.

Aragón-Sánchez, A., Barba-Aragón, I. and Sanz-Valle, R. (2003) Effects of Training on Business Results. *International Journal of Human Resource Management*, **14**(6): 25.

Argyle, M. (1995) *The Psychology of Interpersonal Behaviour*. Harmondsworth: Penguin.

Arnold, J., Cooper, C. L. and Roberson, I. T. (1998) *Work Psychology* (3rd edn). Harlow: Prentice Hall.

Axelrod, R. (1984) *The Evolution of Cooperation*. New York: Basic Books.

Axelrod, R. (1997) T*he Complexity of Cooperation: Agent-based Models of Competition and Collaboration*. Princeton, NJ: Princeton University Press.

Bedward, D., Rexworthy, C., Blackman, C., Rothwell, A. and Weaver, M. (1997) *First Line Management: A Practical Approach*. Oxford: Butterworth Heinemann.

Broadhurst, A. I. (2000) Corporate Ethics and the Ethics of Social Responsibility: An Emerging Regime of Expansion and Compliance. *A European Review,* 9(2).

Covey, S. (1999) *The Seven Habits of Highly Successful People.* London: Simon & Schuster.

Egan, G. (1994) *The Skilled Helper* (5th edn). California: Brooks Cole.

Garrett, E. M. (1992) Branson the Bold. *Success,* **39**(9).

Goffee, R. and Jones, G. (2000) Why Should Anyone be Led by You? *Harvard Business Review,* September/October.

Hayes, J. (1991) *Interpersonal Skills: Goal Directed Behaviour At Work*. London: Routledge.

Hunt, J. W. and Baruch, Y. (2003) Developing Top Managers: The Impact of Interpersonal Skills Training. *Journal of Management Development*, **22**(8): 729–52.

Morrell, M. and Capparell, S. (2001) *Shackleton's Way*. London: Nicholas Brearley.

Morris, D. (1978) *Manwatching*. London: HarperCollins.

Morris, D. (1994) *Bodytalk. A World Guide To Gestures*. London: Jonathan Cape.

Nieto, M. L. (2002) *Marketing: The HR Function* (2nd edn). London: Spiro Press.

Palmer, P. and Hoe, E. (eds) (1997) *Voluntary Matters. Management and Good Practice in the Voluntary Sector*. London: The Media Trust and The Directory of Social Change.

Stanton, N. (1996) *Mastering Communications* (3rd edn). Basingstoke: Macmillan – now Palgrave Macmillan.

Storey, J. and Sisson, K. (1993) *Managing Human Resources and Industrial Relations*. Buckingham: Open University.

Torrington, D., Hall, L. and Taylor, S. (2002) *Human Resource Management*. Harlow: Prentice Hall.

PERSONAL NOTES ON CHAPTER 12

Notes for seminars

_____

_____

_____

_____

_____

_____

_____

_____

_____

_____

_____

Notes for revision/reminders

_____

_____

_____

_____

_____

_____

_____

_____

_____

_____

_____

_____

_____

_____

_____

_____

Chapter 13

Human Resources: Corporate Social Responsibility and Business Ethics

Learning outcomes

After reading and completing the activities in this chapter, you should be able to:

1 Appreciate the growing importance of business ethics and corporate social responsibility (CSR) in twenty-first century organizational life.

2 Critically evaluate the role of business ethics and CSR in human resources policies and management.

3 Conduct an ethical audit.

4 Critically reflect on business situations in which ethical conflicts and issues can arise.

5 Appreciate the relationship between business ethics and CSR and organizational reputation.

6 Develop awareness of the ethical implications arising from corporate governance.

7 Reflect on the challenges of implementing ethical policies in organizations.

8 Critically evaluate the difference between espoused intents, publicity and actual organizational behaviour.

9 Reflect on matters of trust and organizational accountability.

10 Recognize the application and importance of business ethics to every discipline of organizational management.

● INTRODUCTION

This chapter provides business students with the opportunity to study materials and reflect on sometimes complex ethical business issues to form a personal and informed viewpoint. In areas such as business ethics and corporate social responsibility, it is important to recognize that each person has to make choices about how they behave, so this chapter aims to encourage self-reflection regarding organizational decision-making processes. These objectives can only be achieved with your proactive engagement with the materials – by discussing and reflecting on what you might do and how you could behave in a number of scenarios. The aim is to encourage reflection and evaluation and thereby nurture proactive engagement, rather than promote any particular philosophical or management approach. By reading and applying the materials presented in this chapter, HR and other management students should be able to develop the attitudes, knowledge and skills to critically evaluate organizations in areas such as HRM, marketing, advertising, customer services, finance and cooperate global responsibility.

Exercise 13.1

BUSINESS ETHICS: DOES IT MATTER?

Here are some questions to begin thinking about. What your answers may disclose is something of your own feelings and thoughts on business ethics.

- Does business ethics really matter?
- Should HR concentrate on local employment matters instead of pan-organizational matters like ethics?
- Isn't the way organizations behave controlled by laws anyway, so why bother with ethical issues?
- Ethics, that's nothing to do with my job in HR, marketing, sales, finance, production, IT, design, or is it?

TO BE HUMAN IS TO MAKE CHOICES

Each of us makes hundreds of choices everyday that have some influence on the lives and wellbeing of other people. Some of those people are close to us, while others work and live in distant places.

Bill Clinton, the former US president, speaking at the Dimbleby lecture (2001), highlighted some uncomfortable facts:

> In the twenty-first century, half the people on earth live on less than two dollars a day.

> A billion people live on less than a dollar a day. While a billion people go to bed hungry every night and a billion and a half people – one quarter of the people on earth – never get a clean glass of water.

Shocking, isn't it? But …

> Do or should organizations have a social responsibility, or do they exist just to make profit alone?

In organizations, does it matter how managers treat their 'workers'? According to research into modern slavery by Bales (1999, p. 4), unless organizations are very careful about their sources of raw materials, cheap products may come at a high human cost. Modern slavery is actually on the increase. The suppliers of raw materials or even finished goods are not directly employed by the high street brand names, so their corporate codes of ethics can appear untarnished, even though the organizations must know what is happening in their outsourced suppliers' workplaces because they have to inspect them to ensure the quality control of their brand. The brand image is very important to companies because it enables them to sell their product for much higher profits than a similar unbranded product. However, where do our responsibilities begin, as consumers, employees, managers, shareholders?

Modern organizations are recognizing that what they do and how they do it can move into the public domain faster than ever before. So, it is not entirely surprising that the subject of business ethics has been moving up the organizational agenda in recent years. Bad publicity can adversely impact on sales and profits. The improvements in global communication have enabled consumers to be more aware of how organizations behave. Furthermore, with access to a wider range of goods and services, consumers are more likely to express a preference, where all other factors are similar, towards an organization they can feel comfortable about. Perhaps the reality is not that we are all becoming more ethical than previous generations, but rather that when there is more choice, matters of corporate behaviour rise further into the consumer's calculations. The modern developments in global communications means that whatever an organization does in one part of the world is likely to become known in other parts within a short space of time. Corporate behaviour is therefore more in the public domain in the twenty-first century than in times past. A mission statement of a code of practice will no longer be able to conceal corporate indifference to matters of social responsibility.

Many aspects of HR and organizational conduct are dictated by legislation. Organizations have to comply with laws in areas such as discrimination, working conditions and minimum rates of pay as required. However, it would be unrealistic to suggest that because a law exists all organizational misbehaviour has disappeared. The application of business ethics not only accepts the minimum standards set out by national and international law, but goes further in caring for the interests of the organization's stakeholders. This requires the implementation of policies and interventions that include and accept the importance for organizations to behave in a more ethical manner.

Another aspect of organizational and stakeholder relations is often described as 'corporate social responsibility' (CSR). In common with business ethics, this concept argues for acceptance that organizations have responsibilities regarding their behaviour to a range of stakeholders, internal and external, that are directly or indirectly affected by what they do and how they conduct their business. This includes organizations in private, public, not-for-profits and non-governmental organizations. Business ethics and CSR are the responsibility of every employee and so it is important to emphasize the value of constructive engagement rather than prescription. In moral, ethical issues there are no simple prescriptions, competencies or models where one size fits all. Instead, each of us has to reflect on what we believe to be the most appropriate action in each situation we meet. This may mean learning through experience, although much can be achieved through seminar activities, case study evaluation and studying organizations as part of a degree course or managerial development plan. Our actions have consequences for other people so in business ethics and CSR the HR student is encouraged to reflect on the links between HR initiatives and organizational behaviour. Furthermore, organizations are not inanimate objects, instead, they may be likened organisms formed by people who are therefore responsible for the decisions and actions taken in the name of the organization *(see Chapter 2 for organic organizational structures)*.

The history of management has, regrettably, recorded many high-profile debacles of organizations where integrity, both individual and collective, has been called into question. It is not surprising if some modern stakeholders may have become disillusioned with the rhetoric of organizational 'spin'. It is therefore important for managers to address the key issues of business ethics and corporate responsibility. This proposition has resonance with many papers in the current academic debate, including Langlois and Schlegelmilch (1990), Brakel (2000), Broadhurst (2000), Goffee and Jones (2000), Hinman (2000), Argandona (2001), Brinkmann (2001), Lozano (2001) and Davidson (2002). The modern manager should be aware of the higher levels of scrutiny their actions are exposed to by a more proactive media and informed public. Watson (2003, pp. 167–85) has asserted that more attention should be given to business ethics. Furthermore, managers are subject to pressures from a broad range of stakeholders whereby the manager can elect to be either 'ethically assertive' or 'ethically reactive' to the situations they meet in the workplace. Consequently, matters of business ethics and corporate social responsibility are and should be an increasingly important element in managerial decision making.

The research by Trevino et al. (2003, pp. 5–37) found that senior executives have a significant role in establishing their organization's ethical tone. The research findings further indicated that ethical leadership requires more than personal integrity, it involves using the communication and the reward systems to guide ethical behaviour *(see rewards in Chapter 10)*. While I was conducting research on senior management and ethical behaviour, I found an interesting example of how a senior executive 'communicated ethical values'. The appointment we had agreed had been postponed so when I arrived to meet the executive we had a few minutes of introductory conversation. His answer as to why our earlier meeting had been cancelled was illuminating. The executive had personally travelled abroad to dismiss a regional manager who had been regularly and deliberately misleading clients in order to secure more business. Although the region was profitable and no specific complaints were registered, the senior executive wanted to communicate the message that deliberately misleading clients was unacceptable.

GROUP ACTIVITY

BUSINESS ETHICS PERSONAL BEHAVIOURAL QUESTIONNAIRE

Lets begin by stimulating some self-reflection and group discussion about the kinds of ethical decisions you might make in a number of organizational scenarios.

The questionnaire below provides a set of scenarios where you are required to make ethical choices. In reality, people make ethical choices frequently, on both personal and organizational issues. An organization's behaviour only reflects the prevailing culture, values and beliefs of the people responsible for defining and implementing policies. Yet organizations often have competing pressures such as profitability and customer service, while the public sector may be under pressure to meet targets and improve service levels to larger numbers of clients.

It would be unrealistic and arguably counterethical for any educationalist to attempt to offer a menu of ethical answers. Instead, it is more appropriate to encourage discussion and personal reflection on issues so that each person can then reflect on the choices they have made. The questions below may be used for both personal reflection or group activities. Reviewing our actions can also help us to move from unconscious reactive behaviours towards more measured assessments of personal and organizational practice.

Discussion questions

1 You find a £20 note on the floor of the reception where you work. Do you keep it or hand it into the receptionist in case someone claims it?

2 The £20 note was in a wallet with the name of the owner who you happen to know is one of the best-paid employees in the sales team. Do you keep it or return it to the owner? Would your decision be different or the same if the owner was one of the least well-paid staff?

3 A salesperson undercharges you for goods you have purchased. Do you tell them about the error or keep quiet?

4 Is it ethical to use your employer's stationary for private use?

5 What is your view on employers who regularly require employees to work longer hours than specified in their contracts without additional payments, rewards or time off?

6 If your organization imposed performance indicators, would you spend more time meeting them to impress management and external assessors or continue doing whatever work was in the overall best interest of your clients, customers, patients or students?

7 The company you work for uses low-cost producers in a developing country who pay very low wages and sometimes illegally employ child

labour to reduce costs. An important customer asks you about your company's ethical employment policies, as this will influence their decision whether to place a large order with your company. Do you tell them about what you know or deny that such abuses occur?

8 A university, to which your organization has provided sponsorship funds, conducts research highlighting failures in your HR policies and practice that require immediate attention. Do you consider following the recommendations or withdraw the sponsorship?

● TRUST AND ACCOUNTABILITY (CORPORATE SOCIAL RESPONSIBILITY)

To what extent are or should organizations be accountable to the wider society? Organizations cannot distance themselves from their commercial activities and the values these betray (Albrow, 1996), so improvements in communication also increase stakeholder awareness of organizational behaviours.

According to a report by the CIPD, it is the role of HR departments or HR-trained professionals to push the CSR agenda through their organizations (Watkins, 2003, p. 10). Each organization has a responsibility to its internal and external stakeholders with regard to its conduct. Clearly some stakeholders may carry more immediate influence than others, but it is a mistake to disregard sections of the stakeholder community. So, for example, a stock market quoted corporation that mistakenly focuses on the interests of shareholders, but ignores its employees or the quality of customer services delivery will soon place its profits and share price in jeopardy. In the case of a charity, the focus might be placed in placating the trustees and retaining volunteers, but the organization may lose public support unless it is seen to deliver its services and aid effectively.

CSR is more than just a mission statement, or an HR policy document. Stakeholders are unlikely to be fooled for very long by PR that has little substance in practice. CSR should therefore be both espoused and acted on lest critically evaluative stakeholders uncover the gaps between what an organization claims to do and its actual practice. Colloquially, organizations have to walk the walk as well as talk the talk. CSR is consequently about gaining the hearts and minds of employees and therefore presupposes significant progress in HR is already in place. It would be difficult to envisage an organization with indifferent attitudes towards rewards, diversity, life–work balance and career development encouraging its people to respect its reputation, values and standards. Delivering effective CSR underlines the value of recognizing that HR should be an integrated service that touches every aspect of an organization's operation from the boardroom to customers. HR can lead the way, but it requires organizational commitment to achieve results. An ethical audit can be used to research employee attitudes whereby a plan of HR initiatives can be designed to address issues uncovered by the audit *(see the HR auditing and planning techniques outlined in Chapter 11)*.

The implementation of CSR therefore begins with the development of effective HR implementations. According to Mike Emmott, CSR specialist with the CIPD, the largest influence on employee attitudes still comes from managing people well, by giving them interesting jobs and helping them to achieve a satisfactory work–life balance (Emmott cited in Peasaud, 2003, p. 37). Effective CSR therefore begins in the hearts and minds of employees, volunteers, workers (depending on the type of organization) *(see employee relations in Chapter 4 and work life balance in Chapter 5)*.

Figure 13.1 depicts the intersections of personal morality with that of the organization, professional standards and the law (both national and international). The balance of these will vary from one individual to another, so it is the role of HR professionals to encourage their organizations to collectively meet the appropriate standards for their particular environment. Even so, the levels of CSR may vary considerably. Some organizations might not always comply with the law, whether this is by deliberate commission or more usually through omissions such as poor awareness of HR legislation. More responsible organizations may ensure that they comply with the law by employing specialist legal HR advisers, and SMEs may call on the advice of an external legal expert or consult the CIPD website or other legal advice webpages. However, the more ethically oriented organizations may extend their policies and practices beyond minimum compliance.

Figure 13.1 The intersections of personal, corporate and legal accountability

Members of an organization may experience some conflict from to time between their responsibilities to management, colleagues, clients and the wider society. It is also quite possible that some of these constituencies may have different requirements. Hence, stereotypically, an employer may seek profit maximization, the professional body may require that quality standards be upheld and clients may want the best services or products at the least cost. These do not have to be mutually exclusive and the aspiration of professionals should be to serve the various stakeholders to the best standards that the organization's abilities and resources allow. For individuals, accountability is therefore about being able to justify intentions, actions and omissions to other stakeholders.

Figure 13.2 Conflicting demands on employee accountability

The meaning of trust and accountability was discussed by O' Neill (2002b) for the Reith Lectures. The particular lecture from which this following extract was drawn was provocatively entitled: Licence To Deceive. For O'Neill, organizations have a duty of care not to deceive which, she asserts, is based on a long tradition of philosophical and intellectual heritage. Our duty not to deceive ensures that we do not treat others as lesser mortals, indeed victims.

The reality of corporate business ethics exposed in the scandals relating to accounting inconsistencies where global names have been found to have misled and deceived authorities to enhance share values is a reminder of the temptations facing organizations that are measured by financial performance. The victims of such white-collar crimes are the many small investors who lose their savings and, of course, employees who are made redundant when the corporations collapse. The onus of integrity is, ultimately on the individual, although, self-evidently, organizations are composed of the interactions of many individual minds conforming to, or sometimes resisting, the norms and values of the majority.

HRM IN ACTION

BUSINESS ETHICS FOR THE TWENTY-FIRST CENTURY

The following extracts from are from a paper I delivered to the Business Ethics Conference at the University of Surrey, 6 March 2002, entitled, Business Ethics For The Twenty-first Century. After reading the extracts, discuss the questions that follow.

ACADEMICS LEADING THE WAY

A group of academics from several leading universities were invited to an international management consultancy. The group were invited to form what could be described as a think tank on business ethics and ethical auditing.

Why? My impression was that business ethics and organizational values is an area of increasing interest to organizations and more enlightened consultancies are keen to build their expertise and knowledge in this area. There is also research evidence to indicate that ethical issues in organizations have been steadily moving up the managerial agenda. The work of Kitson and Campbell (1996, p. 118) and Chryssides and Kaler (1996, p. 193) noted that more organizations are interested in establishing codes of ethics. Indeed, as early as 1990 a study by Langlois and Schlegelmilch found that just over 50 per cent of organizations in their study had a written code of ethics (pp. 519–39).

Hence, it would appear that both academics and management consultancies have recognized a growing interest for 'honest and independent professionals' to provide organizations with audits and benchmarking of their ethical standards. There are arguably exciting opportunities for research activity and, yes, practical consultancy for a university, which decided to take an active interest in working with organizations in the area of business ethics and organizational values.

PUBLIC AWARENESS

The modern organization can ill afford to ignore an increasingly informed public, which has become more proactive in vocalizing displeasure regarding organizations that fail to perform in an ethical manner. Indeed, it is likely that consumer boycotts and political lobbying have played a part in making senior managers much more sensitive to their internal and external stakeholders. Thus, organizations, which might have regarded business ethics as a matter of second order strategic importance, have recognized the need to rethink their outlook.

IS GREED GOOD?

The later part of the twentieth century was influenced by the famous 1980s Thatcherite assertion that there is no such thing as society. If there is no society, then organizations are also merely collections of individuals and as such have no identity beyond that which is promoted by the senior management. Thus managers might focus on particular incidents, or difficulties, and safely ignore the deeper issues of values. However, for Albrow (2000, p. 1), society is back in the frame, although it is not so clear that sociology has illuminated the development, or advanced a counterweight to excessive emphasis on the economy. At an organizational level it is even easier to remain fixated with the economic and the statistically measurable because profits have traditionally been used as the key measure of business performance. The assertions made by Oliver Stone's fictitious character Gordon Gecko in the 1987 archetypal film *Wall Street* that *'greed is good'*. presupposed that the only way to produce corporate economic health is by concentrating on creating more profit, at any human cost.

REPUTATIONS AND STAKEHOLDERS

If the image of an organization and its brands can influence profitability, it is all the more important for organizations to consider how their stakeholders see them. A paper presented by Walsh (2001), Building a Sustainable Business Brand, at Kingston University argued that in both global corporations or local enterprises, brand is probably what gets new business while reputation is what probably keeps the business. Organizations that actually invest in maintaining a positive reputation are more capable of withstanding setbacks and surviving in a competitive market. Work by Nieto (2001, pp. 73–80) with the Virgin group found evidence that successful commercial performance was achievable when profits were placed third in importance, below staff and customers. By contrast, it could also be argued that 'maintaining a reputation' might be a cosmetic marketing ploy in itself, but such activities would eventually be betrayed by the organization's behaviour and should be uncovered in an ethical audit.

DISCUSSION QUESTIONS

● Why do you think an international management consultancy asked academics to help to design an ethical auditing model?

● What are the benefits to organizations of becoming more sensitive to issues of social responsibility?

● The modern organization can ill afford to ignore an increasingly informed public. What can stakeholders do (within the law) to influence corporate social responsibility?

● What is the difference between legal compliance and ethical business behaviour?

● How would you differentiate between business ethics and corporate social responsibility?

● If there is such a thing as society, what responsibilities do organizations have as 'corporate citizens'?

● Why is brand image not sufficient in itself to maintain organizational reputation?

TOO MUCH COMPLIANCE: NOT ENOUGH ETHICS?

If some organizations cannot be trusted to present their products, services and performance levels honestly, it might be argued that what is required is still tighter regulatory legislation and more externally controlled performance indicators. Modern organizations operate in a complex legal frame of external and internally regulated corporate governance. Indeed, in recent years the culture of central control of organizations has proliferated in both the US and Europe. The interesting question is whether much progress has been made in the way organizations behave through compulsion to conform to a set of performance indicators? O'Neill (2002a) argues that, on the contrary, a climate of control can be counterproductive to encouraging trust and improved performance. O'Neil asserted that the new accountability culture aims at ever more perfect administrative control of institutional and professional life, including the requirement for detailed conformity to procedures and protocols, detailed record keeping and the provision of information in specified formats and compliance to imposed targets. Furthermore, the regulatory culture applies to the work and performance of health trusts and schools, universities and research councils, the police force and social workers. Beyond the public sector, increasingly detailed legislative and regulatory requirements have also been imposed on businesses, the voluntary sector, self-employed professionals and tradesmen.

Institutions face new standards of recommended accounting practice, more detailed health and safety requirements, increasingly complex employment and pensions legislation, more exacting provisions for ensuring non-discrimination and, of course, proliferating complaint procedures of accreditation by external quality assurance organizations. However, does all the documentation generated encourage or discourage staff to be committed to the espoused standard or just comply? It may be surmised that external ethical controls alone are unlikely to deliver high standards of integrity in the way organizations operate. Arguably, the sum of an organization's integrity may exceed the individual standards of its employees, or not, depending on the extent to which core values are integrated into operational transactions and rewards, both intrinsic and extrinsic *(rewards are discussed in Chapter 10)*. Furthermore, the strength of commitment by management has to value all employees and thereby encourage trust and commitment.

During my years of conducting academic research, consultancy and lecturing, I have found it fascinating to listen to the diversity of beliefs expressed by people in organizations and during seminars. The range of acceptable versus non-acceptable behaviours can vary considerably, thereby stimulating some interesting discussions. By doing the exercise below, 'My Ten Commandments', you can experience some of the issues which organizations face in designing codes of ethics. If, as can be the case, a small group of people find it challenging to agree a list of agreed 'commandments', it is likely to be harder for large organizations to agree and then apply national and transnational codes of ethics.

For a code of ethics to have any real validity, it should proactively influence the way an organization operates day to day. Alternatively, an ethical code may become no more than a piece of public relations material. In such cases, the code of ethics and other documents such as mission statements may pronounce admirable, attractive virtues to be aspired to, but actually have little impact on daily organizational life.

This is not, however, an argument for excessive compulsion or organizational regulation, whether internally or externally imposed. Indeed, organizational life is so complex that it would be difficult to attempt to codify a specified behaviour for every eventuality. In the classic science fiction novel *Brave New World*, Aldous Huxley (1975) presented the reader with a world in which everything was controlled and individual choice had been replaced by complete social conformity. However, humans with free will are likely to be less compliant. Although codification of behaviour may be imposed, employees who are required (by company regulations) to comply, but without any personal sense of ownership, are unlikely to work with any commitment to management's objectives.

GROUP ACTIVITY

'MY TEN COMMANDMENTS'

Form a small group of between two and ten people. Each member prepares a list of ten personal rules, which they believe are the most important ones governing their behaviour. Once completed, the group can discuss the individual lists and try to create one collective set of ten rules, which everyone can agree to. The group discussion should also assess the extent to which the agreed set of rules could be applied to an organization.

Individual list:

1 ....
2 ....
3 ....
4 ....
5 ....
6 ....
7 ....
8 ....
9 ....
10 ....

Group agreed list:

1 ....
2 ....
3 ....

4 ....

5 ....

6 ....

7 ....

8 ....

9 ....

10 ....

One of the learning outcomes of the exercise may be for group members to recognize the personal commitment they have to make in order that, collectively, organizational behaviour can reflect whatever codes of ethics they agree to.

● REPUTATIONS: THE VALUE OF A GOOD NAME

The role of reputation is arguably an important factor in the long-term success of an organization. The passing of time and fashions may dictate changes in products and services, yet a sound reputation can serve as a valuable constant factor in maintaining stakeholder loyalty. One current example where the brand reputation appears to lead, rather than follow the product lines is Virgin. The research conducted (Nieto, 2001) on the Virgin group indicated that senior managers felt a high degree of brand value awareness and that products with the Virgin brand label could achieve greater success by association with the values espoused by the company. Aaker and Joachimsthaler (2000, p. 37) also found that Virgin is a remarkable example of how a brand can be successfully stretched far beyond what would be considered reasonable. The brand identity of Virgin is created by design and is defined by a set of brand statements: service quality, innovation, fun and entertainment, value for money, the underdog, the Virgin personality, and Virgin symbols. Brand values such as service quality, innovation, value for money and symbols (the images and logos associated with the product) are likely to be found in competing organizations. However, fun and entertainment, the underdog, and Virgin personality arguably differentiate Virgin products from their competitors. Virgin uses its good reputation to add value to products not directly produced by Virgin, for example Virgin Cola. It follows that if the values associated with the company are helping to promote products, reputation is a distinct factor, which can influence the success of a product or service. This strategy evidently places more importance on corporate values that individually branded products.

A good reputation is a valuable asset in its own right and endows credibility on an organization's products and services. Organizations therefore invest large amounts of money enhancing their image with consumers, precisely because consumer perception of an organization can influence profitability. It follows that organizations should consider how their stakeholders see them and act in ways that add to that reputation. In a global economy where there is more choice, consumers can elect to buy similar products or services elsewhere. Although it could also be argued that 'maintaining a reputation' might be a cosmetic marketing ploy in itself, such activities would eventually be betrayed by the organization's behaviour. It appears that some organizations are aware of the need to actively take steps in communicating positive messages, not just about their services or products, but about who they are. However, unlike a product or service, which can be replaced, reputations are entwined within the network of interpersonal messages, transmitted by employees and their interaction with both each other and the organization's stakeholders.

● HOPE DECEIVED AND POSTMODERN ILLUSIONS

The extent to which organizations accept and practice ethical policies can vary according to what fits into the organizational plans and policies. Although, to use the American colloquialism, organizations recognize the PR benefits of talking the talk on ethics, there is some evidence to suggest that not all organizations walk the walk. For example, a report by the think tank Demos, reported by Tomlinson (2002), found that despite the rhetoric of social responsibility, FTSE 100 companies gave only 0.4 per cent of their pretax profits to charity and community projects. Stakeholders are quite able to recognize the differences between corporate PR and operational reality and it is ultimately on their interactions with the consumer where the organization's reputation will rest. Organizations are rightly expected to convey information about their products and services in an honest and transparent manner. If information is deliberately conveyed in a manner which may mislead, it is a deception. To deceive is defined by the Collins Dictionary as: to mislead by deliberate misrepresentation. Interestingly, the archaic meaning is given as: to disappoint, his hopes were deceived. It would be interesting to consider how organizational communications policies might change if they sought to ensure that their products and services were not hyped to the point where the consumers might be disappointed by the gap between advertisements and reality.

Today many organizations invest large amounts of money promoting their brand image. There are many advantages to promoting brands because an organization can add value to a product or service according to how they are perceived by the consumer. Hence, the value that customers attach to a product or service can be influenced by the image created by the producer. It is therefore quite possible for the actual cost of manufacture or service delivery to have little or no bearing on how much the consumer is charged.

The first impression of brands might be that it is something of an illusion. Yet to understand the influence of brand values it is necessary to reflect on the context. In the postmodern affluent nations, many people already have most of their needs and wants satisfied. For example, in wealthy nations, it is taken for granted that owning a pair of shoes is attainable, so the issue then becomes which brand of shoe conveys the 'right image' about the wearer. The product itself and any utilitarian purpose it has become less important than the image it conveys about the user.

According to Legge (1995, p. 85), from a postmodernist perspective, it is inappropriate to regard rhetoric, the brand illusions, as less important than reality. In a brand-driven environment, the rhetoric is the real world. Products are differentiated more by image than substance. However, can an organization sustain a good reputation on little more than product brand image? The values ascribed to the organization, how it interacts with the community, local and global, the environment and its employees and clients and consumers may provide a more sustainable basis for reputations. If hopes are deceived, postmodern illusions of brand values may seem truly vacuous.

Exercise 13.2

THE ETHICAL CONSUMER

Consider the following two questions:

● As a consumer, are you willing to pay more to guarantee fair working conditions for workers in developing countries?

● Should organizations be prepared to share more of their profits with the workers who produce the goods and services?

● CONDUCTING AN ETHICAL AUDIT

As organizations become more aware of how their behaviour can impact public perception, there is a growing need for independent audits. Audits can also provide benchmarking of what other organizations are doing in a similar environment. However, the act of comparing an organization's behaviour within their market does not, in itself, validate its actions and operating policies. After all, just because others behave in a similar manner does not absolve an organization from its own misdemeanours, where they occur. More usefully, research that is conducted by students with academic supervision can provide a catalyst for organizational reflection and re-evaluation of behaviour. Indeed, having conducted research into organizational values for several years, I have found that most organizations appreciate the opportunity to learn about themselves through the research work, providing it is conducted in a sensitive and professional manner. Alternatively, organizations may employ the services of a consultancy firm to audit their ethical policies and practices.

It is perfectly possible, with appropriate tutorial support, for a team of HR students to conduct an ethical research audit and gain valuable insights into an organization's ethical life. In most cases, it is usually possible to gain some access to organizations for this type of research work, although confidentiality is crucial. If necessary, materials can be presented either with the names removed or as a case study with fictitious job titles to protect the innocent (or guilty) within organizations. This is necessarily so because it is ultimately the organization that decides whether or not to grant researchers access. The anonymity of respondents should be respected, which sometimes enables researchers to gain a richer source of material than people might otherwise care to divulge *(details of how to conduct HR research studies can be found in Chapter 11).*

PRACTISING HRM

PRIMARY RESEARCH: HRM AND BUSINESS ETHICS

With this kind of research project, it may be helpful to work as part of a research set rather than individually.

Approach an organization and arrange to conduct a research project into:

either

Their ethical policies and practices

or

The organization's practices in corporate social responsibility

Deliver a report or presentation to your seminar group.

EVALUATING PRESENTATIONS

Apply the marking criteria below to evaluate your seminar group's presentations. Give each section a mark out of 100 then divide by 30.

	0%	20%	30%	40%	50%	60%	70%	80%	100%	Total
PRESENTATIONAL QUALITY Appropriate professional delivery. Management of allocated time available. Verbal and visual effectiveness. Effective use of video, voice and music recording, exhibition and display and supporting materials										
SHARED LEARNING Clarity of objectives and structure, quality, sourcing, accuracy. Appropriate methodological rigour. Participative role play. Dramatized performance. Leading question and answer sessions.										

	0%	20%	30%	40%	50%	60%	70%	80%	100%	Total
CONTENT Evidence of critical examination of ethical dilemmas and social issues. Explores the relationship between organizational performance and the impact on stakeholders. Identifies a range of managerial practices relevant to the chosen area of study.										

NOTES:

_____

_____

_____

_____

_____

_____

_____

_____

⬤ CHAPTER SUMMARY

This chapter has provided materials to engage discussion and thought on the place of business ethics and corporate social responsibility in organizations. Thereby promoting a critical evaluation of the role of business ethics and CSR in HR policies and management. The key purpose has been to stimulate further personal reflection and application of the learning outcomes to organizational situations. You should also be able to prepare an ethical audit as a learning activity.

⬤ REFERENCES

Aaker, D. A. and Joachimsthaler, E. (2000) *Brand Leadership*. London: Free Press.

Albrow, M. (2000) Sociology after the Third Way in the UK and USA. Lecture at City University, London, 13 October.

Argandona, A. (2001) Managing and Acting 'Beyond the Call of Duty'. *Business Ethics: A European Review*, October.

Bales, K. (1999) *Disposable People. New Slavery in the Global Economy*. London: University of California Press.

Brakel, A. (2000) Professionalism and Values. *Business Ethics: A European Review*, April.

Brinkmann, J. (2001) On Business Ethics and Moralism. *Business Ethics: A European Review*, October.

Broadhurst, A. I. (2000) Corporate Ethics and the Ethics of Social Responsibility: An Emerging Regime of Expansion and Compliance. *Business Ethics: A European Review*, April.

Chryssides, G. and Kaler, J. (1996) *Essentials of Business Ethics.* London: McGraw Hill.

Clinton, B. (2001) *The Struggle for the Soul of the 21st Century*. The Dimbleby Lecture: 14 December.

Davidson, H. (2002) How to Make Vision and Values Work. *People Management*, 26 September.

Goffee, R. and Jones, G. (2000) Why Should Anyone be Led by You? *Harvard Business Review,* September/October.

Hinman, L. (2000) *Integrity*. Paper from Department of Philosophy, University of San Diego.

Huxley, A. (1975) *Brave New World*. London: Penguin Modern Classics.

Kitson, A. and Campbell, R. (1996) *The Ethical Organisation. Ethical Theory and Corporate Behaviour.* Basingstoke: Macmillan – now Palgrave Macmillan.

Langlois, C. C. and Schlegelmilch, B. B. (1990) Do Corporate Codes of Ethics Reflect National Characteristics? Evidence From Europe and the United States? *Journal of International Business Studies.*

Legge, K. (1995) *Human Resource Management. Rhetoric's and Realities.* Basingstoke: Macmillan – now Palgrave Macmillan.

Lozano, J. F. (2001) Proposal for the Elaboration of Ethical Codes Based on Discourse Ethics. *Business Ethics: A European Review*, April.

Nieto, M. L. (2001) *Marketing The Human Resource Function.* Oxford: Chandos Press.

Nieto, M. L. (2002) Business Ethics For The Twenty-first Century. Paper delivered to Business Ethics Conference at the University of Surrey, 6 March.

O'Neill, O. (2002a) Is Trust Failing? *Reith Lecture.* BBC Radio 4, April.

O'Neill, O. (2002b) Licence To Deceive. *Reith Lecture.* BBC Radio 4, April.

Peasaud, J. (2003) In Good Company. How Can Organisations Encourage their Employees to Absorb and Adopt the Message of Corporate Social Responsibility? *People Management*, July.

Tomlinson, H. (2002) Ethics Treated 'As PR Exercise', *Independent on Sunday,* 21 July.

Trevino L. K., Brown, M. and Hartman, L. P. A. (2003) Qualitative Investigation of Perceived Executive Ethical Leadership: Perceptions from Inside and Outside the Executive Suite. *Human Relations*, 1 January.

Walsh. J. (2001) *Building A Sustainable Business Brand: Effective Communication to Stakeholders on Environmental and Social Performance*. Conference paper presented at Kingston University, 6 December.

Watkins, J. (2003) HR Must 'Deliver On CSR'. *People Management*, August.

Watson T. J. (2003) Ethical Choice in Managerial Work: The Scope for Moral Choices in an Ethically Irrational World. *Human Relations*, 1 February.

PERSONAL NOTES ON CHAPTER 13

Notes for seminars

_____
_____
_____
_____
_____
_____
_____
_____
_____
_____
_____
_____

Notes for revision/reminders

_____
_____
_____
_____
_____
_____
_____
_____
_____
_____
_____
_____
_____
_____
_____
_____

NOTES ON CHAPTER 13 CONTINUED

Notes for revision/reminders

_____

_____

_____

_____

_____

_____

_____

_____

_____

_____

_____

_____

_____

_____

_____

_____

_____

_____

_____

_____

_____

_____

_____

_____

_____

_____

_____

_____

_____

_____

Chapter 14

International Human Resources: Locally Sensitive, Globally Aware

Learning outcomes

After reading and completing the activities in this chapter, you should be able to:

1 Appreciate the opportunities and limitations of HR initiatives across national and cultural boundaries.

2 Evaluate the influence of cultural diversity in international relations.

3 Recognize the value of HR initiatives within the context of a changing international environment.

4 Critically evaluate the contemporary debate on the influence of globalization on organizational behaviour and reputations.

5 Develop international cultural sensitivity. Understand and apply the attitudes, knowledge and skills needed for success in global organizational management.

6 Appreciate the place of HR in influencing strategic organizational global policy.

7 Design a HR training programme for employees sent on international assignments, for both exit and re-entry to their home organization.

● INTRODUCTION

This chapter focuses on the role of HR in an increasingly global employment environment. In the preceding chapters, you have learnt about the place and value of integrated HR in organizational success and those attitudes, knowledge and skills are equally relevant to international HR. However, there are some additional HR initiatives that are particularly valuable to improving international organizational performance, and it is those areas that you will study in this chapter.

In a globalized environment, where customers have many more choices of supplier, it is becoming more important for organizations to recognize that their behaviour towards stakeholders, both local and global, can hold the key to long-term success. HR professionals can assist organizations in designing their international strategic plans, training and managing people to work more successfully across the diversity of global cultures. These kinds of initiatives are just as relevant to a university or a charity, a car or computer manufacturer. Investing in people's international attitudes, knowledge and skills can make a valuable contribution to organizational performance.

The HR professional should be aware that there are national sensitivities towards HR, particularly in preferences for management approaches and styles. It is more prudent for HR and other senior managers to avoid imposing global practices on groups of workers without providing the opportunity for diversity. This approach to international HR follows the underpinning philosophy of this text that HR delivery should be situation-specific and tailored to local needs and aspirations.

● TOWARDS CULTURAL SENSITIVITY

The term 'globalization' is a relatively new definition for the movement of trade and people around the globe (Albrow, 1996). During the twentieth century, there was a tendency to recommend the development of local expertise. Hence expatriates stayed in one region and thereby gained localized in-depth knowledge, or possibly not, if the expatriates clustered around their own expatriate social groups. This perception of global relationships followed the traditions going back to the European empires. One of the disadvantages of this approach was that many expatriates found it difficult, if not impossible, to readjust upon returning to their 'home nation'. This was sometimes described as a person who had 'gone native', in as much as they were perceived to have more in common with their adopted area than their country of origin *(re-entry culture shock is discussed later in this chapter)*.

The traditional approach to international management also informed many of the late twentieth-century commentators' work with the proposition that there are some stereotypical characteristics that can define each nation or region. However, the increasing movement of people and work around the globe, combined with faster communication of information, means that the twenty-first-century manager needs to be the cultural equivalent of multilingual. Rather than becoming a local expert, it is more useful to develop cultural sensitivity. This approach includes tolerance of diversity and flexibility in working with teams of people who may come from a varied mix of international cultural influences. It is therefore more useful to develop attitudes, knowledge and skills that accept and respond to diversity non-judgementally, than to attempt to memorize any given set of international stereotypes that may not inform us about the individuals we meet in the workplace. Indeed, the evidence of HR work, as we have discussed in earlier chapters *(see Chapter 2 for different organizational structures and cultures)*, indicates that what is expected from employees, priorities and working practices can differ considerably between organizations, so this would be even more the case across continents. It is therefore reasonable to anticipate additional differences in working patterns across national boundaries. This can be challenging and controversial. For example, it would be difficult for an organization to implement an equal opportunities policy in a country where women do not have the same legal rights as the EU or the US. Cultural diversity can be a challenging issue. Instead, the nature and form of corporate management policies and HR should be designed to fit the local situation. (For examples, see Donnelly 1999, 2001; Donnelly and Dunn, 2001 for work on South Africa.) Each nation, with its individual cultures and traditions, requires a situation-sensitive approach (Figure 14.1). Furthermore, multinationals should avoid cultural arrogance; the implied belief that there is a best practice and that it should therefore be imposed on everyone else.

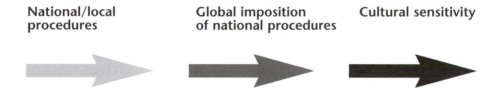

National/local procedures   **Global imposition of national procedures**   **Cultural sensitivity**

Figure 14.1 Global sensitivity

The breadth and speed of cultural globalization is also being advanced by access to faster intercontinental communications. For example, the former US President Bill Clinton (2001) described the expansion of the internet during his address for a BBC lecture. 'The information technology revolution: when I became president in 1993, there were only 50 sites on the worldwide web – unbelievable – 50. When I left office, the number was three hundred and fifty million and rising.' It is not surprising that by the late twentieth century, academic research had also identified a trend towards the globalization of cultures. So, for example, Domaine (1990, pp. 50–4) has argued that one of the outcomes of the global exchange of ideas and organizational activity is that our cultural differences are diminishing. This view is also supported by the vast expansion of international communication through the internet, conveying information and cultural values across the globe.

From the perspective of writing in this century, our outlook toward the trends towards globalization may be tempered by some of the counter-reactions, even hostility exposed in the tragic 9/11 terrorist attack on New York. So, it is also important for us to be sensitive towards counter-reactions, actual or perceived, of 'westernization', sometimes referred to as 'McDonaldization'. These terms describe popular movements in cultural values and ideas where segments of a culture are exported globally, although this process has been in motion for many years. For example, in the 1960s when the late John Lennon, of the Beatles pop group, commented that the Beatles were as well known around the world as Jesus Christ, there was public outrage and some people in the USA were sufficiently offended to burn Beatles' records. Today's commentators would probably concur that 'globalized brands' such as the Beatles are very well known, yet the more culturally sensitive would perhaps avoid making controversial comparisons.

Our growing global interdependence is a significant factor in determining organizational success or failure, so it is all the more important for local managers to appreciate international influences. For example, financial recessions are usually more global than local, so the early twenty-first-century international dot-com crash unsettled the confidence of many young entrepreneurial workers in their 'unsinkable' faith in businesses led by new technology. In one company whose fortunes I followed, they fell from maximum share value of around £50 million, at the height of the dot-com boom, to an actual sale value of just £100,000 in 2004. Furthermore, the shift to developing states of many info-technical jobs through the use of the internet has also changed the way organizations are structured, and increased the value of people who have knowledge and skills of team working with culturally diverse groupings rather than just technical knowledge *(how to be successful with teams is discussed in Chapter 3)*. Modern organizations therefore operate within complex global environments. Consequently, HR has to be able to provide support and development plans so that people are globally and locally sensitive *(see PEST analysis, Chapter 10 and REACT and SMARTA in Chapter 11)*.

Although some of the more prescriptive national stereotypes of the twentieth century may have become outdated, cultural sensitivity should critically evaluate elements of research work where some culturally common forms may be indicated. The research work of Hofstede (1984, 1994) emphasized the importance of organizational culture in employee behaviour. It also indicated that if people are insecure, their tendency will be towards less risk taking and the prevailing organizational culture will move towards uncertainty avoidance. Hofstede (1994, p. 116) highlighted the point that even more than reducing risk, uncertainty avoidance leads to a reduction of ambiguity. Uncertainty avoiding cultures shun ambiguous situations and people in such cultures look for structure in their organizations where relationships and events are predictable. One of the benefits that expatriate workers can therefore contribute to their newly assigned organization is a fresh perspective on the accepted practices and behaviours of the organization, providing they feel sufficiently secure and confident to comment. This can be particularly true in organizations where anyone who is critical of the status quo tends to be ignored, discouraging discussion or new approaches to work situations. It also cautions managers not to overbureaucratize procedures and thereby build in inflexibility to change *(groupthink is discussed in Chapter 3)*. Conversely, this does not represent an advocacy for change for change's sake, but instead a willingness to preserve the best of the past while embracing the possibility of new innovations.

● THINK INTERNATIONAL, WORK LOCAL

The HR message can be difficult to communicate when managers are preoccupied with their busy schedules. This applies all the more when the team may be both multinational and distributed around different parts of the globe. Management researchers and writers, for example Tuckman (1965), Janis (1982),

Belbin (1993) and Perkins (1999), recognized the value of developing effective team working *(team working is discussed in Chapter 3)*. The challenges of creating effective teams are all present in transnational corporations, with the addition of diverse national cultures to be included into the team dynamic. It is therefore all the more valuable for organizations to invest time in developing the interpersonal aspects of teams through group exercises and training, so that individual members can get to know and understand each other before embarking on their assigned work task. Inadequate investment in helping people to work harmoniously can have high costs in employee dissatisfaction and even legal disputes (Kopp, 1994). The efficacy of developing sound interpersonal human relations *(the human relations approach is discussed in Chapter 1)* is also part of any healthy workplace environment and requires particular attention when larger numbers of people are brought together. The isolation that an expatriate may feel initially can take longer to overcome in a large, anonymous organizational structure. By definition, organizations that have offices all around the globe are large, but that does not mean they have to be impersonal. By encouraging effective local management initiatives, where people are closest to the working situation, the problems stemming from centrally imposed HR methods of working can be avoided. It is relevant to note that the type of organizational structure selected influences working relations for local employees too *(organizational structures are discussed in Chapter 2)*. This reinterprets the term 'best practice' to represent the most effective local solution, accepting the requirement for diversity, rather than the notion that there is only one way to do things nationally and internationally.

● OFFSHORE OUTSOURCING

Another trend in twenty-first century globalization is offshore outsourcing, although, in reality, this kind to movement of work has happened throughout the world's industrialized history. The key difference is that whereas before the tendency was to build industrial plant in low-cost areas of the globe, now the use of internet technology means that many additional administrative roles can be outsourced abroad. One of the common growth areas is the call centre where customer calls regarding a wide range of services from airline ticketing to credit card enquiries can be outsourced offshore to a lower cost employment area of the world. In India, the development of software technology parks has produced growth from a small niche sector in the 1990s to a significant part India's economy by the twenty-first century (see Elmuti and Kathawala, 2000; Crabb, 2003).

The developed nations' jobs can be completed more cost effectively in lower pay areas in the developing and least developed nations of the world. The services and products are then returned to the higher profit areas of the developed world. The new work opportunities then provide the developing and least developed nations of the world with more potential to purchase products and services.

**Developed
countries jobs** **Developing and
least developed
countries centres** **Developed countries
markets**

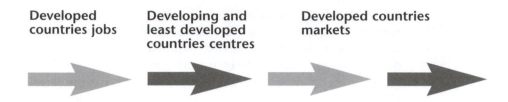

Figure 14.2 Globalization of work distribution

The distribution of new jobs in, hopefully, clean, air-conditioned workplaces around the globe is good for developing economies (Figure 14.2). According to predictions by the technology research company Gartner, up to 25 per cent of traditional IT jobs in the West today will be outsourced to the emerging markets such as India by 2010 (see Webb and Watts, 2004). If this prediction is even half right, the patterns of employment around the globe are about to change radically. The economic argument adds even greater weight to the prediction. In 2004, major international banks were paying employees in Indian call centres around £2500 per year, compared with almost £20,000 in the UK. Well-qualified Indian business graduates were being paid as little as £7000, a fraction of the salary that a graduate usually expects in the West. Furthermore, whilst some of the more conservative Western organizations still tend to select non-business graduates, the more modern international approach of the emerging economies focuses on attending business degrees. It is not that someone with a degree or three in ancient academic studies or sciences is not intelligent, but rather whether they know anything useful about managing organizations. The role of HR should therefore be to encourage specific management development and more relevant recruitment criteria *(recruitment is discussed in Chapter 7)*, so that the knowledge and skills of their people become and remain at the leading edge in a competitive global employment market. There should also be HR input into strategic decisions so that any plan for staff cost reduction does not lead to a waste of the organization's most valuable assets, people and the 'corporate memory' *(corporate memory and the value of employee experience are discussed in Chapter 4)*.

If an organization decides to outsource, then HR has an important role to play in ensuring that service quality is not sacrificed to cost expediency. It will be the organizations 'local' managers and administrators who are best placed to advise on the kinds of issues and areas of knowledge and skills that new offshore employees will require. For example, knowledge that may be generic to the citizens of one country will have to be included in a general familiarization training programme. So, while the seaside university town of Bournemouth is well known to most British citizens, this may not necessarily be common knowledge to a call centre person in Delhi. However, this kind of local knowledge matters when someone is trying to tell their credit card provider that they have lost their credit card on the beach. Therefore cultural training is central to the performance of any offshore, outsourced enterprise's success. This creates new opportunities and challenges in international HR where whole departments may be moved to new locations where extensive training and development programmes will be necessary (see Sisodia, 2004). It can be difficult to condense British culture into a short training course. However, the international students who study for business degrees, undergraduate and postgraduate, can return to their home countries with an expectation of a successful career because they will have been taught in a UK or USA university and had an opportunity to learn about Western culture. The kudos of an international education, together with immersion into a Western culture, has commercial and career advantages. Conversely, the emerging markets also offer opportunities for organizations that take the trouble to understand the world outside their local frontiers.

As with other HR initiatives, used appropriately, offshore outsourcing can have a valuable role to play in an organization's overall management strategy, providing it is corrected planned and organized. The introduction of appropriate HR training and development initiatives and the continued use of experienced employees to oversee the outsourced are more likely to ensure connectivity with the head office and consistent quality. The development of offshore outsourcing also underlines the value of cultural sensitivity, where managers in the head office are in communication with support and services from colleagues from a diversity of nations and cultures.

HRM IN ACTION

WHEN THE JOB GOES ABROAD

This HRM in Action case is based on primary research *(see Chapter 11 for research methods)* on employment practice within an international company. The names have been altered to protect the identity of the organization and current and former employees.

Peter, a London-based IT specialist, regarded his job as secure. Information technology is a skilled job and professionals like Peter with several years' industry experience can usually command a high salary. He worked for an international communications organization as an IT specialist and had been with the company for several years.

Peter began to hear rumours of an efficiency improvements programme where there might be some staff reductions. However, as a well-qualified professional working with leading-edge technology, Peter felt little concern for his own position. After all, if there were going to be staff cuts, then the organization would be even more dependent on technology to manage the business. Peter was therefore surprised when he learnt that one of the casualties of the new efficiency plan was the IT department. Peter's team was earmarked for redundancy. The IT operation was to be moved abroad where willing and well-qualified IT employees would work for much lower rates of pay than UK-based employees. In fact the new IT department would be based in Kuala Lumpur.

Although the efficiency planners had identified a potential wages saving, it soon became apparent that the new employees needed more training and development to deliver the company's IT requirements than they originally anticipated. The senior management therefore belatedly approached Peter and offered him a generous financial package, if he agreed to go to Kuala Lumpur to assist in training the new IT team. The assignment seemed intriguing and a useful addition to his CV, so Peter agreed to do the work. In fact he enjoyed the new, if temporary role, as an IT trainer. He found the new team pleasant to work with and kept in contact with them after he returned to the UK. Peter did, however, have reservations about the extent to which it was possible to teach the new team all the intricacies of the company's systems, which he had learnt over years, in such a short space of time. However, the new IT team were keen to learn, and with a well-designed longer term training programme they could become proficient. This would mean that a continuing development programme would need to be put in place. However, it was unclear how such ongoing support might be delivered, given that the company's UK expertise in IT, the organization's 'corporate memory', had all been made redundant.

The initial promise of the new team, who had successfully completed their initial training with Peter, encouraged the company that even greater cost reductions were possible. So before the team could begin to demand more remuneration commensurate with their improving performance, the company began looking for their replacements in another, lower cost area of the world. Peter's concerns regarding quality standards were disregarded.

DISCUSSION QUESTIONS

- Discuss the advantages and disadvantages of relocating departments to low-wage areas of the globe.

- 'Corporate memory' describes employees' long-term knowledge of their organization. This includes interpersonal contacts with internal and external stakeholders and knowledge of processes and practices. Why is corporate memory difficult to replace and costly to lose?

- Why is cross-cultural team-working attitudes, knowledge and skills likely to enhance employability in the twenty-first century?

- Discuss the advantages and disadvantages of offshore outsourcing.

- Why do you think the lack of ongoing training for a new offshore team could be a false economy?

In an age of fast communications, what an organization does in one part of the world can be communicated very quickly around the globe. This means that an organization's reputation can be influenced not only by how it treats employees in its home country, but also around the world. Reputation is a key element of brand image and reputation can be influenced as much if not more by employee attitudes as expensive marketing campaigns.

On the 5 May 2000, a BBC Radio 4 news broadcast reported that the American multinational Nike had cancelled its sponsorship of three American universities whose research alleged that some of Nike's products were being manufactured in low-cost workshops. It was alleged that a number of factories in developing countries employed child workers for low pay. Nike disputed the veracity of the research but whether or not the detail of the research was entirely fair, the publicity was undoubtedly negative. It is also interesting to note that there are many other manufacturers using low-cost production facilities, selling lower profile products at more modest prices that do not attract the same curiosity as global brand names such as Nike. Indeed, if their sales propositions are extrinsically utilitarian statements of fitness for purpose, then it is difficult to criticize them on the grounds of being disingenuous (products sold on the basis of low price rather than other marketing claims and brand images). This would, of course, make no difference to an emerging country's employee's wages and it can be argued that the existence of brands and established reputations provides the consumer with leverage that they do not have over unbranded product lines. For example, if a person buys a burger from McDonald's, they have the opportunity to complain to the company if the burger was of poor quality. The same could not be said if the burger was purchased from a travelling street trader who has no brand or reputation to protect and no customer services department to complain to.

The examples simply illustrate that the way employees are treated has a bearing on organizational reputations across the globe, so HR should be proactive in ensuring the quality of employee conditions throughout global operations, including franchisees and suppliers whose actions can reflect on their organization's reputation. The results of research by Park et al. (2003) supported the proposition that employee attitudes, knowledge and skills are a key factor in producing successful HR outcomes within multinational corporations. The HR initiatives are therefore central to success and are more likely to be consistently managed by an in-house HR team, although external auditors could be utilized to conduct surveys and research into the delivery of policy and practices.

There are clear advantages for an organization's international reputation in investing in HR initiatives that improve working conditions. Organizations who want to improve their public image need to inspire and engage with their employees. Thomson et al.'s (1999, p. 821) research found that by using internal communication to inform, then remind staff about their brand values, staff became more attuned to recognizing that they are contributors to the brands' image with customers. Hence, the attitudes, commitment and values of employees are a potential conduit to greater organizational success. According to

Free (1996, cited in De Chernatony and McDonald, 2000, p. 209), a key factor in successful brand strategy was to encourage employees to understand and be committed to the brand vision.

The development of HR in an international setting can be challenging because many of our core values are established in childhood and so different national cultures and norms are likely to influence workplace behaviours. This is described as 'culture shock'. Furthermore, according to research by Professor Sparrow, professor of international HR at the Manchester Business School, the 'cultural pathways' people form in their development have a significant influence on how they respond to various types of HR initiatives. He argued that organizations should therefore avoid one best way solutions when they are designing global HR systems (Roberts, 2003, p. 11). His research echoes the central theme of this text in championing situation-specific HR solutions rather than prescriptive one-size-fits-all models. An inherent flaw in the simplistic pursuit of 'best practice' is that the sheer diversity of organizational life, even in the same sector and nation state cautions HR professionals to listen to local needs and respond with situation-specific initiatives.

The international dimension therefore introduces additional issues for HR professionals to those which are likely to be present in the home-based organization. One of the factors influencing the success or failure of employees sent on international assignments is the expatriate's ability to manage culture shock (Shilling, 1993; Nguyen et al., 1999). There are specific challenges related to the relocation of employees and the recruitment of new employees. A well-organized situation- and person-specific induction programme can provide a valuable contribution to the international performance of employees.

It is also worthwhile noting that although the programme presented in this chapter is designed for international assignments, employees moving to a different part of their own country would also benefit from many elements of the support outlined in this chapter. While 'local relocations' will not encounter language issues, many of the practical matters relating to housing, medical, schooling for children and workplace interpersonal relations are still relevant. For example, someone moving from a small regional town to a major city and vice versa will need to make adjustments in their lifestyles. So, in practice, an effective relocation induction procedure is helpful to someone relocating from a northern British town to London or from California to New York as well as across continents.

The disruption to someone's life of moving location is potentially considerable and also has implications for their immediate family and social network (Forester, 1990; Munton and Forester, 1990; Lawson and Angle, 1994). HR professionals, particularly those involved in international organizations, should prioritize interventions to support people who are relocating to other parts of the organization. The research by Black et al. (1991) found that up to 40 per cent of American employees who relocated to foreign assignments elected to return sooner than originally planned. The work performance of as many as one in two expatriates was also found to be a disappointment. Even when other related factors such as differences in organizational structure *(for structure see Chapter 2)* are taken into consideration, this kind of poor performance is an indicator that more could and should be done to assist relocating employees.

INTERNATIONAL TRAINING PROGRAMMES

In the preceding part of this chapter we have evaluated those issues and challenges which are of particular relevance to the international sector. It is also relevant to acknowledge that international HR should be underpinned by the same professional research and evaluation as local HR management *(see Chapter 11 for auditing and planning HR)*. Before a new programme is developed, it is helpful to ascertain what the key issues are by conducting a local study of HR provision, its successes and areas for development.

Employees are more likely to settle into a new location and job role if they receive training and support. Research by Bennett (1986) postulated a progression in intercultural sensitivity from low competence towards international sensitivity. As with other areas of personal development, the progression towards improved performance is likely to be improved by investment in a suitable training programme. Even within the same country, HR professionals usually design training and induction programmes for people starting a new job (Trompenaars and Woolliams, 2003). This is because we anticipate that people are likely to go through a period of adjustment, and this is even more likely to be the case if they have relocated to a different part of the world where they also need to change their home and social arrangements. However, in addition to the factors HR could expect to be relevant to local relocations, there are the particular aspects of moving to a job into a country with a different culture and different ways of working. HR initiatives can therefore improve the personal comfort and professional effectiveness of expatriate employees by preparing them for their new assignment and location.

Pre-departure training should include developing intercultural sensitivity so that s/he can more easily adapt to a different cultural environment. This kind of HR initiative reduces potential problems for the expatriate and the organization they are joining. For example, developing awareness of the potential impact of cultural shock, when an otherwise capable professional may find the many new situations and different procedures and expectations difficult to cope with. The expatriate is encouraged to develop cultural attitudes, knowledge and skills, thereby improving their awareness of the situation they are about to enter.

INTERNATIONAL ATTITUDES, KNOWLEDGE AND SKILLS

Attitudes

The attitudes include preconceptions and personal prejudices, both positive and negative, regarding the country or region they are being posted to and the assignment they will be required to complete. These attitudes predispose a person to certain perceptions of other cultures and the situations they will be entering.

The cultural attitudes awareness programme can include:

● An *evaluation* of the applicant's ability to adapt to the new environment as part of the selection procedure.
● *Discussion and support* regarding any concerns and apprehensions about the new opportunities and challenges that they may meet in their new assignment.
● *Development* of improved self-awareness through discussions and self-assessment questionnaires to assist in the preparation to depart to a new national assignment.
● The *initial assessment programme* should be used to tailor the subsequent training in knowledge and skills, which can provide positive reinforcement for attitudinal development.

Knowledge

Prior to departure to a new assignment, HR can provide a tailored programme designed to meet both the personal and professional training needs required for success in the location they are going to. In practice this requires supported research and planning by the employee to prepare her/him for their new assignment. The research can include:

● *Discussion and support:* Regarding any concerns and apprehensions about family relocation and personal matters, such as accommodation, health-care provision, schooling and social networks.
● *Agreed plans:* Practical matters such as short-term accommodation should be agreed so that they have a suitable place to live on arrival.
● *School places:* if required, should be organized prior to departure. It is important to acknowledge that the expatriate is more likely to succeed if their immediate family also feels comfortable in their new environment.
● *Accommodation:* Where would be a good longer term place to live? If the expatriate were taking family with them, s/he would probably like information on local property market.
● *Partner employment:* Are there good job opportunities for his/her partner? Can the necessary visas and work permits be provided?
● *Living conditions:* Appropriate information for factors such as climate and the kind of working and living conditions the expatriate can expect to experience. Will the new location be cold, hot, wet? Can they expect to work in an air-conditioned office or not?
● *Transport:* How reliable is the local public transportation?
● *Cultural values:* Learn about local customs and traditions. Encourage tolerance in areas such as religious faiths, work routines and dress codes.
● *Communication:* What is the main language used for business purposes? Are local people likely to speak the expatriate's language or is a short

language course necessary? Are there any specific matters regarding business etiquette and protocol? For example, in some European countries such as Switzerland and Germany, precise punctuality is regarded as important, whereas areas such as South America are generally more relaxed about precise time keeping. Is the host's organizational management culture formal or informal in terms of address?

Skills

There are considerable differences between knowledge and skills. For example, a theoretical understanding of cultural diversity is quite different from moving to and working in a different country. The development of cultural skills therefore empowers a person to put what they know into practical action. To facilitate cultural skills improvement HR can provide a scheme of training. The skills training programme can include:

- *Learning materials:* Using learning exercises, video and interactive on-line materials and relevant textbook learning materials. This programme may be designed within the in-house HR group or sourced via an external provider, such as a consultant or a university business school.
- *Role playing:* This can be a very useful source of interactive learning, especially if there are several people being posted to an overseas assignment together.
- *Interactive seminars:* If a group of people are to be sent on assignment together, then interactive seminars, including regional research activities and team building, can be a useful experiential learning tool.
- *Orientation trips:* If it is practical, a short orientation visit to the area of placement can provide useful first-hand experiences for employees who are relocating for an extended period of time. It will also provide them with the opportunity to personally experience what living in their new country might be like, prior to taking on their full job role responsibilities.

POST-ARRIVAL INDUCTION ACTIVITY PROGRAMME

It is helpful to smooth the new expatriate's arrival to their new assignment by providing an orientation programme for his/her work and personal life, preferably in the first week of arrival. This could include:

- *Orientation activities:* Including a tour of the local area. Information on accommodation, local facilities, banking, medical, social, sports clubs, transportation.
- *Working practices:* Local working hours, rest breaks. Information of organizational structure and culture (the way we do things here).
- *Introductions:* It is helpful to have a local manager arrange meetings with new colleagues and key people.
- *Mentoring:* It is useful to provide the new expatriates with a mentor who

they can turn to for ongoing support and advice. The mentoring schedule may be organized to the convenience of both although regular monthly or bimonthly meetings are likely to be appropriate.

COMING HOME: THE RE-ENTRY PROGRAMME

Although HR provision is more likely to be given to expatriates, it is less common for people returning home from overseas assignments. Yet employees returning from overseas assignments may experience reverse cultural shock and require a support programme (Gregersen, 1992; Stroh et al., 1998). This may be all the more poignant because they are unlikely to be expecting assimilation difficulties on returning to their home country. Nevertheless, it is sensible to recognize that someone who has adapted to a whole new environment may find the return home initially disorientating.

Furthermore, the world that the employee departed from is also likely to have moved on during the time they have been abroad. For example, old and trusted colleagues may have changed roles or left the organization. Conversely, new people may have joined the organization, bringing changes in management style and practice. The home organization is likely to have put in place alternative arrangements regarding the expatriate's former job role, so this may have either changed or no longer exist in its former configuration. Consequently, the old familiar working environment might have been reorganized or replaced altogether. Indeed, their department or work group could have moved location so that the expatriate's old office might not even still exist. It is, on reflection, not at all surprising that people can experience a reverse culture shock when so much of what they thought they were returning to may have changed.

Reorientation Plan

A reorientation plan might include the following:

- *Pre-return:* Arrange for meetings with home company representatives a few months before returning home from the assignment. Update the returning employee on current and new developments.
- *Re-orientation:* Provide a re-entry pack to include relevant news and information, such as the current housing market and economic environment.
- *Working practices:* Compile a briefing paper on any relevant changes to working practices. This is particularly relevant to senior managers who may find that their junior home-based colleagues are now more up to date on current policies than they are.
- *Introductions:* On return, introduce the returnee to new colleagues and encourage people to include them in the usual social and information interactions.
- *Mentoring:* Organize a home mentor for the returnee.

DESIGNING AN INTERNATIONAL INDUCTION PROGRAMME AND PRESENTATIONS

The activity encourages interactive research including academic literature, the internet and the preparation of a training programme supported by a presentation. The activity can be competed by either an individual student or a team. There are advantages to designing the activity as a team exercise as this more closely replicates real working situations. There are also benefits in selecting team members from a range of nationalities so the experience of completing the assignment also provides experiential learning, working with international diversity. I am grateful to Rupert Leathes, retired senior lecturer in HRM of Bournemouth University, who designed the original model for this activity. It has since been adapted and modified (continuous development is also good pedagogical practice). However, the main learning outcomes for students have continued to be particularly useful in heightening cultural awareness and team working.

The activity may be delivered as either a group or individual presentation and group or individual briefing paper. I have been involved in team teaching and examining this kind of exercise with colleagues at Bournemouth University where our postgraduate international business students have enjoyed working in teams, thinking about foreign assignments and presentations.

Design an international induction programme for a manager (who is or will be working in **one** of the following areas:

- Sales or marketing, finance, general administration or production management.
- You may select their assignment to be with any *one* of the following:
    - A multinational company
    - A voluntary organization
    - A governmental department.
- The organization selected *must* be real. This creates a realistic HR scenario.
- The organization selected may not, necessarily, currently have a presence in the country to which the employee is relocating.
- Remember to include information on the country to which the employee is being placed, including main language spoken, local customs, working conditions, practices, religion and climatic environment.

Recommended programme scheme

It is helpful to include the following headings:

Pre-departure planning; Arrival induction; Continuing support; Returning to home country; Pre-return; Post-return

CHAPTER SUMMARY

In this final chapter of the book we have studied those principals of HR which provide an underpinning of support to international organizational activities. There are both opportunities and limitations to what HR initiatives can achieve across national and cultural boundaries and so the development of employee intercultural sensitivity through the recognition of cultural diversity can contribute to successful international performance.

By reading this chapter you should have become more aware of how globalization can influence the behaviour and reputation of organizations. Furthermore, you should be able to understand and apply the attitudes, knowledge and skills which enhance success in global organizational management. I also trust that the exercises and particularly the HR training programme for employees sent on international assignments has stimulated further research and discussion into the practicalities of international HR management.

REFERENCES

Albrow, M. (1996) *The Global Age*. Cambridge: Polity Press.

BBC Radio 4 (2000) *Nike*. 5 May.

Belbin, R. M. (1993) *Team Roles At Work*. London: Butterworth-Heinemann.

Black, J. S., Mendenhall, M. and Oddou, G. (1991) Toward a Comprehensive Model of International Adjustment: An Integration of Multiple Theoretical Perspectives. *Academy of Management*, **16**.

Bennett, M. (1986) A Developmental Approach to Training for Intercultural Sensitivity. *International Journal of Intercultural Relations*, **10**(2).

Clinton, B. (2001) The Struggle for the Soul of the 21st Century. *The Dimbleby Lecture*. 14 December, BBC.

Crabb, S. (2003) East India Companies. *People Management*, 20 February.

De Chernatony, L. and McDonald, M. (2000) *Creating Powerful Brands in Consumer, Service and Industrial Markets*. Oxford: Butterworth Heinemann.

Domaine, B., (1990) Corporate Citizenship. *Fortune*, 29 January.

Donnelly, E. (1999) Democratic Corporatism in the New South Africa: Advance or Retreat? In M. Upchurch (ed.) *Globalization, the State and Capitalism*. London: Mansell.

Donnelly, E. (2001). Borrowing From Europe? Employers' Views on Associability and Collective Bargaining Reform in the New South Africa. *International Journal of Human Resource Management*, **12**(4).

Donnelly, E. and Dunn, S. (2001) *Policy Discretion for Transforming States? The Case of Labour Relations Reform in the New South Africa*. Cardiff University: Employment Research Unit Conference, September.

Elmuti, D. and Kathawala, Y. (2000) The Effects of Global Outsourcing Strategies on Participants' Attitudes and Organisational Effectiveness. *International Journal of Manpower*, **21**(2).

Forster, N. (1990) A Practical Guide to the Management of Job Changes and Relocations. *Personnel Review*, **19**.

Gregersen, H. B. (1992) Commitments to a Parent Company and a Local Work Unit during Repatriation. *Personnel Psychology*, Spring.

Janis, I. L. (1982) *GroupThink*. Boston: Houghton Mifflin.

Hofstede, G. (1984) *Culture's Consequences. International Differences in Work-Related Values*. London: Sage.

Hofstede, G. (1994) *Cultures and Organisations. Software of the Mind*. London: HarperCollins.

Kopp, R. (1994) International Human Resource Policies and Practices in Japanese, European and United States Multinationals. *Human Resource Management*, Winter.

Lawson, M. B. and Angle, H. (1994) When Organisational Relocation Means Family Relocation: An Emerging Issue for Strategic Human Resource Management. *Human Resource Management*, **33**.

Munton, A. G. and Forster, N. (1990) Job Relocation: Stress and the Role of the Family. *Work and Stress*, **4**.

Nguyen, H. H., Messe, L. A. and Stollak, G. E. (1999) Toward a More Complex Understanding of Acculturation and Adjustment. *Journal of Cross-Cultural Psychology*, January.

Park, H. J., Mitsuhashi, H., Fey, C. F. and Björkman, I. (2003) The Effect of Human Resource Management Practices on Japanese MNC Subsidiary Performance: A Partial Mediating Model. *International Journal of Human Resource Management*, December.

Perkins, S. J. (1999) *Globalization: The People Dimension: Human Resource Strategies For Global Expansion*. London: Kogan Page.

Roberts, Z. (2003) Culture Key to Global HRM. *People Management*, December.

Shilling, M. (1993) Avoid Expatriate Culture Shock. *HR Magazine*, July.

Sisodia, R. (2004) India's John Smiths Speak Perfect English. Now They Have a Month to Become British. *Independent On Sunday*, 12 May.

Stroh, L. K., Gregersen, H. B. and Black, J. S. (1998) Closing the Gap: Expectations Versus Reality among Repatriates. *Journal of World Business*, Summer.

Thomson, K., de Chernatony, L., Argannbright, L. and Kahan, S. (1999) The Buy in Benchmark: How Staff Understanding and Commitment Impact Brand and Business Performance. *Journal of Marketing Management*, **15**, pp. 819–35.

Trompenaars, F. and Woolliams, P. (2003) *Business across Cultures*. Chichester: Capstone.

Tuckman, B. W. (1965) Development Sequences in Small Groups. *Psychological Bulletin*, **63**.

Webb, T. and Watts, J. (2004) We Can't Argue Liberalisation Abroad and Protectionism at Home. *Independent On Sunday*, 12 May.

PERSONAL NOTES ON CHAPTER 14

Notes for seminars

NOTES ON CHAPTER 14 CONTINUED

Notes for revision/reminders

And Finally ...

Integrated HR is about working within all the rich diversity of organizational life. This book is designed to address real-life HR management situations. The reality is that sometimes you are going to find work situations difficult, frustrating and even personally upsetting.

Designing HR initiatives that can help to bring out the best from the people you work with requires a range of attitudes, knowledge and skills that encourage people to develop to their full potential. Notwithstanding your best efforts, you are also going to meet people who are selfish, self-centred and difficult to work with. Sometimes colleagues will obstruct you and even your best efforts will not prevail. Even so, HR can help us to understand situations and, in many cases, improve the workplace. Try to learn what you can from each situation.

Use what you have learnt in this book as a guide to help you in your studies and work situations. Integrated HR focuses on the implementation of strategic plans and direction, which is useful to for-profit, not-for-profit, voluntary or public sector organizations.

Enjoy your studies and look forward to a career in management. Remember: to learn is to change.

Michael L. Nieto

PERSONAL NOTES

My key development areas:

_____

_____

_____

_____

_____

_____

_____

_____

_____

_____

_____

Learning and revision

_____

_____

_____

_____

_____

_____

_____

_____

_____

_____

_____

_____

_____

_____

Authors, Organizations and Place Names Index

Subject Index

If you find indexes really boring …
here's one with a user-friendly system designed around the student reader's needs.
If a subject is a core theme it is labelled as such in italic since it is likely to appear on the majority of pages!
If a subject is a core chapter theme it is labelled in bold.